THE CAVENDISH Q & A SERIES

SUCCESSION

Cavendish
Publishing
Limited

TITLES IN THE Q&A SERIES

BUSINESS LAW

CIVIL LIBERTIES

COMMERCIAL LAW

COMPANY LAW

CONFLICT OF LAWS

CONSTITUTIONAL & ADMINISTRATIVE LAW

CONTRACT LAW

CRIMINAL LAW

EMPLOYMENT LAW

ENGLISH LEGAL SYSTEM

EQUITY & TRUSTS

EUROPEAN COMMUNITY LAW

EVIDENCE

INTERNATIONAL TRADE LAW

JURISPRUDENCE

LAND LAW

PUBLIC INTERNATIONAL LAW

REVENUE LAW

SUCCESSION, WILLS & PROBATE

TORTS LAW

'A' LEVEL LAW

THE CAVENDISH Q & A SERIES

SUCCESSION

Ian Jones, LLB, Solicitor
School of Law
The Manchester Metropolitan University

Cavendish
Publishing
Limited

First published in Great Britain 1996 by Cavendish Publishing Limited,
The Glass House, Wharton Street, London WC1X 9PX.
Telephone: 0171-278 8000 Facsimile: 0171-278 8080

© Jones, I 1996
First edition   1995
Second edition   1996
   Reprinted   1997

All rights reserved. No part of this publication may be reproduced, stored in a retrieval system, or transmitted in any form or by any means, electronic, mechanical, photocopying, recording or otherwise, without the prior permission of the publisher and copyright owner.

The right of the author of this work has been asserted in accordance with the Copyright, Designs and Patents Act 1988.

Any person who infringes the above in relation to this publication may be liable to criminal prosecution and civil claims for damages.

British Library Cataloguing in Publication Data

Jones, I
Succession, Wills and Probate - (Q & A Series)
I Title II Series
344.2'0652

ISBN 1-85941-273-4

Printed and bound in India

Acknowledgment

Some of the questions used in this book have been taken from past University of London LLB (External) Degree examination papers (some of which I have set myself) and kind acknowledgment is made to the University of London.

Ian Jones
Manchester
March 1996

Preface

I owe particular thanks to Kerry Whitty (nee Young) and Marie Cotgrave at the Manchester Metropolitan University for their assistance in the production of the first edition. The second edition takes account of the Law Reform (Succession) Act 1995 and recent case law. Continuing thanks go to Kate Nicol and the editorial team at Cavendish for their encouragement and electrifying faxes.

Ian Jones
Manchester
March 1996

Contents

Acknowledgment   *v*
Preface   *vii*
Table of Cases   *xi*
Table of Statutes   *xix*

1   The Will Making Process   1

2   Formal Validity   23

3   Family Provision   69

4   Construction   99

5   The Administration of the Estate   127

Index   193

Table of Cases

A

Adams *In the Goods of* (1872) LR P & D 367 100
Adams, *Re* (1900) LR 13 Eq 381 ....41, 42
Agnew v Belfast Banking [1896] 2 IR 204 ....119, 120
Alexander's WT, *Re* [1948] WN 220 19
Allan v Morrison [1900] AC 604 42
Allen v McPherson (1847) 1 HLC 191 15
Allsop (dec'd), *Re* [1968] 1 Ch 39 114
Anderson v Anderson (1872) LR 13 Eq 381 21
Anstead, *Re* [1943] Ch 161; [1943] 1 All ER 522 ....166, 167
Ashburner v McGuire (1786) 2 Bro CC 108 123
Attenborough and Son v Solomon [1913] AC 76, HL................... 128, 129, 131, 174

B

Bacharach's WT, *Re* [1959] Ch 245 19
Bahin v Hughes (1886) 31 ChD 390 171
Bailey, *Re* [1951] Ch 407..108
Banks v Goodfellow (1870) LR 5 QB 549 ....1, 6, 11, 12, 13, 14, 28, 46, 47, 48
Barry v Butlin (1838) 2 Moo PC 480 ....11, 49
Basham, *Re* [1987] 1 All ER 405 ....79, 97
Beaney, *Re* [1978] 2 All ER 595 95
Beaumont's WT, *Re* [1950] Ch 462 ....166, 168
Beaumont, *Re* [1902] 1 Ch 889 117
Benjamin, *Re* [1902] 1 Ch 723 133
Berger (dec'd), *Re* [1989] 1 All ER 591 ....1, 3, 4, 5, 21, 25, 27
Besterman, *Re* [1984] Ch 458; [1984] 2 All ER 656 ....69, 73, 75, 76, 79, 86, 91, 92
Betts v Doughty (1879) 5 PD 26 16
Bigg's Estate (1966) P 118 140
Bingham, *Re* [1959]..156
Birmingham, *Re* [1959] Cg 523; [1958] 2 All ER 397 ....149, 150
Bishop v Plumley [1990] 1 All ER 236, CA 72, 94
Bohrmann, *Re* [1938] 1 All ER 271 ....1, 12
Booth, *Re* (1926) P 118 37
Bothamley v Sherson (1875) LR 20 Eq 304 ....102, 125
Bowlby, *Re* [1904] 2 Ch 685 178
Boyes v Cook (1880) 14 ChD 53 110
Brassington (1902) P 1 41
Bravda, *Re* [1968] 2 All ER 217; [1968] 1 WLR 479 27
Brunt v Brunt (1873) 3 P&D 37 41
Bunning, *Re* [1984] Ch 480; [1984] 3 All ER 1 ....41, 69, 73, 75, 79, 86, 92
Butterfield v Scawen (1775) (cited in Allen v McPherson) 15

C

Caine v Moon [1896] 2 QB 283 ....118, 120
Callaghan, *Re* [1984] 3 All ER 790 83
Casson v Dade (1781) 1 Bro CC 99; [1781] 28 ER 1010 ....21, 29
Chalcraft, *In the Goods of* (1948) P 222..44
Charter v Charter (1874) LR 7 364, HL...103, 106, 110

Cheese v Lovejoy (1877) LR 2 P&D 78 ....37, 39, 40, 41
Chelsea Waterworks v Cowper (1795) 1 Esp 275 145
Cherrington, Re [1984] 2 All ER 285; [1984] 1 WLR 772 2
Christian, In the Goods of [1849] 163 ER 1260 ....33, 50
Christie, Re [1979] Ch 168 ....80, 82, 83
Clark (dec'd), Re (1991) Fam Law 564 76
Clayton v Lord Nugent [1844] 153 ER 83 ....111, 112, 115
Clore, Charles (dec'd), Re [1982] Ch 456; [1982] 3 All ER 419, CA;
  see also, IRC v Stype 134, 140, 189
Cockburn's, Re [1957] Ch 438 130
Coleman, Re [1976] Ch 1; [1975] 1 All ER 675 ....2, 36, 37, 39
Colling, Re [1948] 44, 45
Colling, Re [1972] 3 All ER 729: [1972] 1 WLR 1440 ....29, 30
Collins v Elstone (1893) P 1 ....18, 49
Commissioners of Stamp Duty v Livingstone [1965] AC 694;
  [1964] 3 All ER 629 ....179, 180, 181
Cook, Re [1948] Ch 212 ....110, 115
Cook, Re [1960] 1 All ER 689 ....25, 26, 27
Cope, Re (1880 16 ChD 49 189
Corbett v Newey [1995] 1 All ER 570 5
Coventry, Re [1979] 3 All ER 815 ....71, 77, 80, 81, 82, 83,
                                                                                                                          84, 86, 89
Craig v Lamoureux [1920] AC 349 15
Craven's Estate (No 1), Re [1937] 3 All ER 323 ....117, 118
Crippen, Re (1911) P 108 126
Crispin's Will Trusts, Re [1975] Ch 245; [1974] 3 All ER 772, CA 57, 62, 63
Crowden v Aldridge [1993] 3 All ER 603 ....180, 181
Crowther, Re [1895] 2 Ch 56 187

D

Davey, Re [1980] 3 All ER 342; [1981] 1 WLR 164 1
Davidson, Re [1949] Ch 670 ....109, 115
Davis v Lush (1991) (unreported) 76
Davis, Re (1952) P 279; [1952] 2 All ER 509 33
De Renville v de Renville (1948) P 100 39
Dennis, Re [1981] 2 All ER 140 81
Dew v Clark (1826) 3 Add 79 ....1, 12
Dillon v Public Trustee ex New Zealand [1941] AC 491;
  [1941] 2 All ER 7, 8
Diplock, Re [1948] Ch 465; [1948] 2 All ER 318 184
Doe d Gord v Needs (1936) 2 MW 129 100
Douglas-Menzies v Umphelby [1908] AC 224 4
Drakes WT, Re [1970] 3 All ER 32 110
Dudman, Re [1925] 1 Ch 553 120
Duffield v Elwes (1827) 1 Bli NS 497 119
Dunstan, Re [1882] 26

E

Elliott v Davenport (1708) 2 Vern 521 126
Elliott v Dearsley (1881) 16 ChD 322 165

F

Fenwick, *Re* (1972) LR 1 PD 319 11
Finn, *In the Estate of* [1935] All ER Rep 419 50
Finnemore (dec'd), *Re* [1992] 1 All ER 800 38
Fish, *Re* [1894] 2 Ch 413 .... 112, 115
Flemming, *Re* [1974] 3 All ER 323 126
Fluyder, *Re* (1889) 2 ChD 562 145
French's Estate, *Re* (1910) P 169 190
Fullard, *Re* [1982] Fam 42 89
Fulton v Andrew (1875) LR 7 HL 448 .... 49, 50

G

Gage, *Re* [1934] Ch 536 99
Gardner v Parker (1818) 3 Mudd 184 .... 117, 119, 121
Gill v Gill (1909) P 157 41
Gill, *Re* (1873) 3 PD 113 142
Gillett's WT, *Re* [1950] Ch 102 165
Godfrey, *Re* (1893) 69 LT 22 .... 41, 42
Goodchild, *Re* [1996] 1 All ER 670 87
Goodwin, *Re* [1968] 3 All ER 12 90
Gordon, *Re* [1940] Ch 769; [1940] 3 All ER 405 .... 151, 153, 154
Gray v IRE [1950] 181
Greville v Browne (1859) 7 HLC 689 .... 164, 166
Groffman, *Re* [1969] 2 All ER 108; [1969] 1 WLR 733 29
Grosvenor, *Re* [1916] 2 Ch 375 175
Guardhouse v Blackburn (1866) LR 1 PD 109 .... 12, 14, 15, 49
Gunstan, *Re* [1882] 80 WR 505 .... 29, 33, 34

H

Hall v Hall (1868) LR 1 P&D 481 .... 14, 15
Hammersley v De Biel [1845] 8 ER 1312 8
Hardy v Shaw [1976] Ch 82 ; [1975] 2 All ER 1052 .... 58, 59
Harland-Peck, *Re* [1941] Ch 182 .... 153, 154, 156, 157, 167
Harlow v National Westminster Bank,*Re*
  (1994) *The Times*, 31 January 77
Hart v Tulk (1852) 3 De GM & G 300 19
Harvell v Foster [1954] 2 QB 367 .... 128, 130, 190
Hedges v Hedges (1708) Prec Ch 269 116
Hickman v Peacey [1945] AC 304 .... 64, 65
Hobbs v Knight [1838] T Curt 768; [1838] 163 ER 2667, PC 41
Horner, *Re* [1965] VR 177 5
Horrocks, *Re* [1939] 1 All ER 579; (1939) P 198 .... 17, 19
Hutchinson, *Re* [1955] 1 All ER 689 61

I

Inns, *Re* [1947] Ch 576 .... 79, 81
IRC v Stype Investments (Jersey) Ltd [1982] *see* Clore dec'd, *Re*

J

Jackson, *Re* [1933] Ch 237 .... 101, 104, 112, 113, 116
James, *Re* [1947] Ch 256; [1947] 1 All ER 402 .... 151, 152, 153, 154
Jelly v Iliffe [1981] 2 All ER 29, CA 72, 78, 94
Jessop v Jessop (1992) 1 Fam Law 591 90
Job v Job (1877) 6 ChD 562 146
Jones, *Re* [1976] Ch 200; [1976] 1 All ER 593 .... 38, 39, 42, 43
Jones, *Re* [1981] 1 All ER 1 183

K

K (dec'd), *Re* [1985] Ch 85; [1985] 2 All ER 833, CA 126, 180, 181
Kell v Charmer (1856) 23 Beav 195 .... 111, 112
Kempthorne, *Re* [1930] 1 Ch 268 .... 152, 154
King's Will Trust, *Re* [1964] Ch 268 .... 128, 130, 131, 176
Kourgey v Lusher (1982) 12 Fl 86 FD 78, 85
Kuyper's Trusts, *Re* [1925] Ch 244 .... 102, 105, 124

L

Lamb v The Lord Advocate [1976] SLT 151 65
Lamb, *Re* [1929] 1 Ch 723 .... 157, 165
Lambell v Lambell [1831] 162 ER 1266 42
Langston, *Re* (1953) P 100 36
Leach, *Re* [1985] 2 All ER 754 .... 77, 83
Leigh's Will Trusts, *Re* [1970] Ch 277 180
Lewis v Madocks [1803] 32 ER 310 9
Lillingstone, *Re* [1952] 2 All ER 184 .... 117, 118, 119
Loveday, *In the Goods of* (1900) P 154 .... 133, 190

M

Malone v Harrison [1959] 1 WLR 1353 .... 79, 82, 87
Marsland, *Re* [1939] 3 All ER 148 9
Martin, *Re* [1955] Ch 698 .... 167, 168, 169
McKee, *Re* [1931] 2 Ch 145 166
McPhail v Torrance (1909) 25 TLR 810 8
Meldrum, *Re* [1952] Ch 208 .... 151, 152, 154
Midgley, *Re* [1955] Ch 576 .... 166, 168
Miller, *Re* (1961) 105 SJ 207 .... 96, 117
Mills v Millward (1889) 15 PD 20 41
Mills v Shields (1948) IR 367 .... 118, 120
Millward v Shenton [1972] 2 All ER 1025, CA 84
Ministry of Health v Simpson [1951] AC 251;
 [1950] 2 All ER 1137, HL 184
Moody v Stevenson [1992] 2 All ER 524 92
Morley's Estate, *Re* [1937] Ch 491 178

Table of Cases

Morris, dec'd, *Re* (1971) P 62; [1970] 1 All ER 1057 ....18, 49, 111, 112
Morton, *Re* (1887) 12 PD 141 37
Mountford v Gibson (1804) 4 East 441 ....141, 142

N

National Society for the Prevention of Cruelty to Children v
 Scottish National Society for the Prevention of Cruelty to Children
 [1915] AC 207 ....105, 109, 113
Needham v Kirkham [1820] 106 ER 755 9
Needham v Smith [1828] 38 ER 825 9
Neeld, *Re* [1962] Ch 643; [1962] 2 All ER 335 181
New York Breweries v Attorney General [1899] AC 62 ....133, 138, 140, 142
Nunn (1936) 154 LT 498 ....37, 43

O

Oxley, *Re* [1914] 1 Ch 604 186

P

Palmer (dec'd) (a debtor), *Re* [1993] 3 All ER 835 161
Parfitt v Lawless (1872) LR 2 P&D 462 15
Parker v Clark [1960] 1 All ER 93 7
Parker v Felgate (1883) 8 P&D 171 46
Parkinson, *Re* (1975) *The Times*, 4 October 90
Pepper v Pepper (1870) 5 IR Eq 85 37
Perrin v Morgan, *Re* [1943] AC 399 ....103, 104, 106, 107,
                                                                                                              109, 110, 115
Perry v Hicknell [1982] 151
Phelan, *Re* (1972) Fam 33 17
Phelps, *Re* [1980] 1 Ch 275; [1979] 3 All ER 373 68
Pilot v Gainfort (1931) P 103 37
Pollock, *Re* (1943) 2 ARL SR 443 178
Ponder, *Re* [1921] 2 Ch 59 ....128, 130

R

Raine, *Re* [1929] 1 Ch 716 179
Rattenbury, *Re* [1906] 1 Ch 667 178
Redell v Dobree (1839) 10 Sim 244 118
Reynolds, *Re* [1966] 1 WLR 19 ....61, 62
Ricketts v Turquand [1848] 9 ER 842 116
Rigden v Vallier (1751) 2 Ves Sen 252 117
Roberts v Walker (1830) 1 R & My 752 ....164, 167
Roberts, *Re* [1978] 3 All ER 225; [1978] 1 WLR 653 ....9, 32, 39
Robertson v Broadbent (1883) 8 AC 812 164
Robinson v Ommanney (1883) 2 ChD 285 9
Rose, *Re* [1949] Ch 78 102
Ross v Caunters [1980] Ch 297; [1979] 3 All ER 580 ....18, 112
Rowlands, *Re* [1962] 2 All ER 837 ....103, 104, 109, 114
Rowley v Adams [1839] 41 ER 379 46

S

Sabatini, *Re* (1969) 114 SJ 35 42
Salmon, *Re* [1981] Ch 167; [1980] 3 All ER 532 86
Sanger, *Re* [1939] Ch 238 152
Scale v Rawlins [1892] AC 342; (1892) 66 LT 542 .... 109, 114
Schaefer v Schuhman [1972] 1 All ER 621 8
Scott v Scott (1859) 1 Sw & Tr 258 42
Selby-Walker, *Re* [1949] 2 All ER 178 179
Sen v Headley [1991] 2 All ER 636 .... 95, 118, 120, 136
Sharland v Mildon [1845] 67 ER 997 140
Shore v Wilson [1842] 8 ER 450 111
Sigsworth, *Re* [1935] Ch 89 126
Sinclair, *Re* [1985] Ch 446 .... 2, 39
Sivewright, *Re* (1922) 128 LT 416 175
Skinner, *In the Estate of, Re* [1958] 3 All ER 273 158
Slater, *Re* [1907] 1 Ch 665, CA 99, 102, 105, 124
Smalley, *Re* [1929] 2 Ch 112 109
Solicitor, A, *Re* [1975] QB 475; [1974] 3 All ER 853 .... 1, 15
Southerden (1925) P 177 38
Sperling, *In the Goods of, Re* (1863) 3 Sw & Tr 272 27
Stalman, *Re* (1931) 145 LT 339 .... 25, 29, 50
Stephens v Taprell [1840] 163 ER 473 41
Stevens, *Re* [1897] 1 Ch 422 185
Stevenson, *Re* [1897] 140, 146
Stirrup's Contract, *Re* [1961] 1 All ER 805; [1961] 1 WLR 447 175
Sugden v Lord St Leonards (1876) 1 PD 154, CA 38, 42, 43
Swords, *In the Goods of* [1952] 3 All ER 281 17
Syer v Gladstone (1885) 30 ChD 6141 49
Sykes, *Re* [1870] 18 WR 551 .... 125, 126
Synge v Synge (1901) P 317 .... 7, 8

T

Tankard, *Re* [1942] 1 Ch 69; [1941] 3 All ER 458 .... 147, 155
Taylor v Taylor [1875] 20 Eq 155 .... 58, 59
Taylor, *Re* (1890) 63 LT 230 42
Thompson v Mechan (Ontario CA) [1958] OR 357 96
Thompson v Thompson [1821] 147 ER 152 146
Thompson, *Re* [1936] 1 Ch 203 .... 163, 165, 166, 168, 169
Thorn v Dickens [1906] WN 54 .... 108, 110
Ticehurst, *Re* (1973) *The Times*, 6 March 1, 12, 13, 50
Trimmer v Danby (1856) 25 LJ Ch 424 118
Turner v Buck (1874) 43 LJ Ch 677 178

U

UCNW v Taylor (1908) P 140 21
Underwood v Wing (1855) 4 De GM WLR G 633 64

Table of Cases

V

Valpy, *Re* [1906] 1 Ch 531	153
Vynior's Case (1609) 8 Co Rep 816	40

W

W, *Re* (1975) LS 9	89
Weatherhill v Pearce (1994) *The Times*, 7 November	2, 23, 30, 50
Webb, *Re* [1964] 2 All ER 91; [1964] 1 WLR 509	38
West, *Re* [1913] 2 Ch 345	174, 175
Whitby, *Re* [1944] Ch 210; [1944] 1 All ER 299	61
White, *Re* [1990] 2 All ER 1	26, 27, 30, 34
White, *Re* [1993] 3 All ER 481	2, 21
Whitrick, *Re* [1957] 1 WLR 884	19, 20, 111, 112
Whyte v Ticehurst [1986] 2 All ER 158	89, 98
Wigram Rules	112, 116
Wilcocks, *Re* [1921] 2 Ch 327	125
Wilkes v Allington [1931] 2 Ch 104	117, 121
Wilkinson, *Re* [1978] 1 All ER 221	78, 94
Wilson v Joughlin [1866]	15
Wilson, *Re* [1966] 2 All ER 867	163, 167
Winfield v Billington (1990) (unreported)	80, 91
Wingrove v Wingrove (1885) 11 PD 81	14
Wintle v Nye [1959] 1 WLR 284	12, 15, 50
Wood v Smith [1992] 3 All ER 556	2, 11, 23, 24, 26, 28, 30, 32, 34, 50
Woodard, *Re* [1994]	95, 136
Woodward v Woodward (1992) RTR 35	118
Wordingham v Royal Exchange Trust Co Ltd [1992] 3 All ER 204	18, 19, 112
Worthington, *Re* [1933] Ch 771	163, 165, 166, 167
Wright v Netherwood (1793) 2 Salk 593n	64

Table of Statutes

Administration of Estates Act 1925	156, 163, 165, 168

s 7 .... 129, 143, 160, 190, 191
s 281 41
s 335 .... 2, 165, 166
  (1) 165
  (2) 165, 166, 167
s 34 152
  (iii) 150, 151, 163
  (3) 148, 149, 155–157, 163–167
s 351 .... 48, 149, 155
  (1) 156, 157
s 361 .... 75, 176
  (4) 130, 176
  (5), (7) 176
s 41 .... 176, 177
  (1)(ii), (3) 177
s 43(2) 176
s 465 .... 2, 57, 60
  (1) 93
  (3) 65
s 47 .... 53, 55, 59
  (1) 24, 59
  (a) 53
  (i) 24, 68
  (iii) 53, 58
s 47A 67
s 49 .... 55, 59
  (1) 58, 60
s 55 .... 53, 56, 57, 67
  (1)(vii) 167
  (x) 53, 55, 57, 60, 61, 63, 67, 94
Sched 1, Pt II 155, 163, 164

Administration of Estates Act 1971—
s 9 140

Administration of Estates (Small Payments) Act 1965	137, 138

Administration of Justice Act 1982	28, 36, 99, 111

s 9 .... 25, 26, 28, 29, 30, 31
  (a), (b) 26
s 17 .... 23, 24, 25, 28, 29, 33, 45, 50
s 183 .... 3, 36
  (2) 35

Administration of Justice Act 1982 (contd)—
s 19 .... 124, 126
s 20 .... 1, 18, 99, 107, 109, 112, 113
(1)(a) 19
s 21 .... 8, 99, 100, 107, 112, 113
(1)(a) 112
(b) 100, 112, 113
(c) 101, 112, 113, 114, 122

Administration of Justice Act 1985—
s 48 184

Building Societies Act 1986 — 138

Children Act 1989—
ss 2, 4, 5 189

Civil Evidence Act 1968 — 84

Family Law Reform Act 1987 — 173
s 1(3)(c) 126
s 18 68
s 20 173

Forfeiture Act 1982 — 125
s 2(1) — 126

Inheritance (Provision for Family and Dependants) Act 1975
10, 35, 44, 66, 69, 70, 71, 74, 80,
81, 83, 84, 85, 88, 89, 90, 91, 94, 96, 97

s 1 86
(1)(a) 72, 80, 85, 88, 91
(b) 69, 80, 89
(c) 71, 76, 80, 83, 85, 89
(d) 69, 77, 80
(e) 69, 78, 80, 85, 94
(2), (b) 80
(3) 85, 94
s 2 86
(1) 87
(a) 75
s 3 .... 76, 77, 89
(2) 75, 91
(a)–(f) 71, 87
(a) 87

```
    (5) .................................................... 84
    s 4 .................................................... 76
    s 9 .................................................... 90
    s 10 ........................................... 69, 79, 96
    s 11 ............................................... 69, 90
```

Inheritance Tax Act 1984—
```
    s 199 ................................................. 141
    s 200 ................................................. 141
    (1)(c) ................................................ 119
```

Insolvency Act 1985   161
```
    s 228 ................................................. 161
```

Intestate Estate Act 1952—
```
    Sched 2 ................................................ 67
```

Law of Property Act 1925—
```
    s 177 .................................................. 36
    s 184 ............................... 63, 64, 65, 100, 103, 135
```

Law of Property (Miscellaneous Provisions) Act 1989—
```
    s 2 .................................................. 7, 8
```

Law Reform (Miscellaneous Provisions) Act 1934   89

Law Reform (Succession) Act 1995   23
```
    s 1 ............................................... 97, 135
    (1), (2) ............................................... 55
    (3) .................................................... 59
    s 2 .................................................... 78
    (1) ............................................ 71, 78, 87
```

Limitation Act 1980   183, 184
```
    ss 5, 24 .............................................. 183
```

Married Woman's Property Act 1882—
```
    s 11 .................................................. 136
```

Matrimonial Causes Act 1973—
```
    s 18(2) ................................................ 54
```

Powers of Attorney Act 1971   170
```
    s 9 ................................................... 171
```

Social Security Act 1975   162

Statute of Frauds 1677   28, 39, 40

Supreme Court Act 1981—
s 61......182
s 114 54
s 117 182
s 118 189

Trustee Act 1925   170
s 6 183
s 23 .... 134, 147, 170
s 27 .... 133, 145, 172, 173, 183
(2) 173
s 30 170
s 36 129
s 61 .... 147, 171, 183

Wills Act 1837   4, 6, 23, 25,
                                               28, 29, 40, 41, 46
s 9 .... 2, 3, 11, 14, 20, 21, 23,
.... 24, 25, 28, 29, 32, 33, 34, 35,
.... 39, 44, 45, 47, 48, 50, 56, 101
(a) 28, 33
(b) 33, 50
(c), (d) 33
s 11 25
s 15 .... 7, 21, 27, 38
s 18 .... 2, 6, 32, 37, 40
(1) 36
(a) 32, 33, 36
(1) 35
(4) 37, 39
s 18A 2, 23
s 20 .... 2, 6, 32, 37, 39, 40, 44, 46, 51
s 21 .... 27, 34, 41, 101
s 22 33
s 24 .... 8, 102, 125, 126
s 33 .... 13, 122, 124–126, 129, 175
s 34 99

Wills Act (Amendment Act) 1852   25, 29

Wills Act 1968—
s 1 .... 7, 27
s 18 9

Chapter 1

The Will Making Process

Introduction

The questions in this chapter deal with the broad topic known as the will making process. Careful study should be made of the nature of the will. Contrast, for example, a testamentary instrument, that is, a will or codicil, with a deed, a gift *inter vivos* and a *donatio mortis causa*.

A will has two key characteristics:
- A will is revocable by the testator until death;
- A will is only effective on the death of the testator.

These two key characteristics run like a thread through the law of succession. The nature of a testamentary instrument was considered by the court in *Re Berger* (1989).

Study of the area of mental capacity to make a will should be broken down into the general test of capacity set out by Cockburn CB in his lengthy judgment in *Banks v Goodfellow* (1870). There are specific defects which can render the whole will invalid or an individual gift inadmissible as in the case of delusions, see, for example, *Dew v Clark* (1826) and *Re Bohrmann* (1938). In addition there are the problems which arise where the testator is still alive but lacks the requisite mental capacity and the effect this has on powers of attorney and the usefulness of the enduring power of attorney. Related to this is the possibility of making a statutory will on behalf of a testator lacking requisite mental capacity. A useful study here of the kind of practical problems that can arise is in relation to the background and case of *Re Davey* (1980).

Issues of capacity broaden into the general test of knowledge and approval which includes suspicion, including the duties of a solicitor to his or her client. Useful studies here include the cases of *Re Ticehurst* (1973) and *Re A Solicitor* (1975) together with the Law Society Guidelines on Professional Conduct. There can be a tendency to blur the distinction between suspicion on the one hand and undue influence on the other. In order to establish undue influence there must be some evidence of coercion. In order to establish fraud there must be proof of deceit. Finally with regard to capacity there are the cases on mistake and the limited statutory powers of rectification contained in s 20 of the Administration of Justice Act 1982.

The next stage in this broad chapter deals with the important area of the requirements as to formal validity contained in the amended s 9 of the Wills Act 1837. This requires careful study, in particular to understand the reason for the changes and the subsequent important decisions in *Wood v Smith* at both first instance and in the Court of Appeal, together with the intervening report of *Re White* (1993) and the subsequent case of *Weatherhill v Pearce* (1994). Study of the formal requirements should include a broader study of the nature of private property holding and alternative methods of transfer. For a detailed analysis of alternative methods see the article by Professor Langbein in the *Harvard Law Review* (1981). In addition, one should consider the alternative, adopted in some countries, of the doctrine of substantial compliance. There are a number of useful references in *Cases and Materials in the Law of Succession* (1986) by CE Wright (Butterworths).

There can be some tricky part questions regarding alterations and obliterations as to wills, and the extent of evidence admissible to establish what had been written prior to an inadmissible alteration.

The law concerning the revocation of wills can throw up some difficult issues. One needs to carefully analyse ss 20, 18 and 18A of the Wills Act. In the case of the first part of s 20, merely describing a will as 'the last will' does not effect an express revocation but can effect an implied revocation of earlier wills. In the second part of s 20, revocation by destruction, the key is to match the extent of the destruction with the contemporaneous intention.

To understand the changes made by the revised s 18 of the Wills Act one should study the judgment of Vice Chancellor Megarry in *Re Coleman* (1976). Introduction of revocation by divorce in s 18A has presented some practical problems in the light of the interpretation given by the court in *Re Sinclair* (1985). The Law Commission (Law Comm 219) have recommended a modification to the rule to adopt the interpretation of the court in *Re Cherrington* (1984) rather than *Re Sinclair*.

Question 1

On a visit to the local community centre you overhear part of a talk by Ernest who describes himself as a local historian. Ernest is talking about 'the language of the law' and you overhear him say '... for example, *animus testandi* means the capacity to make a will ...'.

Rather than interrupt you decide to write to Ernest querying the accuracy of his statement. What would you say?

Answer plan

The statement is inaccurate. The question is inviting consideration of the nature of a will and the clear intention required to make a will, that is, intention unaffected by lack of mental capacity.

Answer

The statement is inaccurate. *Animus testandi* refers to the intention to make a will. An essential requirement of a valid will is an intention by the testator *at the time of its execution* that it shall take effect as a testamentary document. *Animus testandi* means an intention to make a 'revocable ambulatory disposition of the maker's property which is to take effect on death' *per* Lord Mustill in *Re Berger dec'd* (1989).

Re Berger was concerned with the status of a *zavah*, that is, a document written in Hebrew, which is a mixture of religious exhortations and dispositions of movable property. A *zavah* is intended to be binding in Jewish law but it was not clear what the relationship was to English wills. The problem arose because the last will of the testator, dated 9 August 1977, was signed with only one witness. Therefore this will was inadmissible under s 9 of the Wills Act 1837. However, on the previous 6 August the testator had executed a *zavah* which did comply with the formalities required by s 9. Probate was sought of this *zavah* incorporating the 9 August will. (The testator had been in possession of the will subsequently dated 9 August at the time he executed the *zavah*.)

A testator has only one will but this can be made up of several dispositions provided they are testamentary in nature. Admission of a number of documents was considered in *Douglas-Menzies v Umphelby* (1908): 'It is the aggregate or the net result that constitutes his will, or, in other words, the expression of his testamentary wishes. The law ... on a man's death, finds out what are the instruments which express his last will ... In this sense it is inaccurate to speak of a man leaving two wills; he does leave, and can leave, but one will.'

The problem in *Berger* was, did the testator intend the *zavah* to operate as a will and be granted probate? Did he have the necessary *animus*? There was no clear evidence. The facts established that the testator had made a document which he intended to have dispositive effect, and this document was executed in the manner required by the Wills Act. Despite there being no evidence as to the testator's *animus* concerning the *zavah* operating as an English will the court admitted the *zavah* with the August will incorporated, a decision affirmed by the Court of Appeal. Mustill LJ concluded that the various *zavah* were intended to operate in the shadow of the English wills. Even though Mustill LJ added that the testator may have been startled to learn that the *zavah* was being admitted by an English court of probate rather than a rabbinical tribunal.

Sir Dennis Buckley stated the law on *animus testandi* as follows:

'English law does not require a document which is intended to have testamentary effect to assume any particular form or to be couched in language technically appropriate to its testamentary character. It is, says Jarman (*On Wills*, 8th edn, 1951) sufficient that the instrument, however irregular in form or artificial in expression, discloses the intention of the maker respecting the posthumous destination of his property. It may be made in any language. If it is made in a foreign language, the court must be furnished with an authenticated translation made by a qualified translator. It is that translation, not the text in the foreign language, which is admitted to probate. It is from the document so admitted to probate together with any other relevant testamentary instruments that an English court will ascertain the testator's testamentary intentions and determine their effect and validity.'

In order to admit a testamentary instrument there must be the necessary *animus*. The absence of *animus* may be proved by parol evidence in relation to an instrument which on the face of it appears to be a valid and properly executed will – *Re Horner* (1965). In the Australian case of *Re Horner* the testator executed two documents on the same day, not having made up his mind at that time which document was to be his will. The court held that *at the time of execution* the testator did not intend either document to be the depository of his testamentary wishes; therefore he did not have the necessary *animus testandi*. Accordingly the remaining document could not be admitted to probate.

At first instance in *Corbett v Newey* (1995) Eben Hamilton QC distinguished *Re Horner* on the basis that at the time of execution the testator in *Horner* had not made up his mind which of the two documents was to be his will. In *Corbett v Newey* there was no doubt as to the testatrix's wishes, although she may have been misguided as to whether they would become effective. The decision has been overturned on appeal.

In *Corbett* the testatrix, by an earlier will, bequeathed two farms to a nephew and niece respectively and left the bulk of the residue between them. She then decided to transfer the farms to the beneficiaries *inter vivos* but, in view of this, to change the destination of the residue to benefit her great nephews. It became clear the deeds of gift would not be available for execution at the same time as the new will. The testatrix made arrangements to execute the will in September 1989 but to leave the date blank, requesting the solicitor to date the new will contemporaneously with the date of the deeds of gift. The testatrix mistakenly believed that the dating of the will was essential to its operation. She had no *animus* to execute an unconditional will. Reference was made to the *dicta* in *Re Berger* on the meaning of *animus testandi*.

The Court of Appeal (Waite LJ) said that since the will operated from the moment of its execution it necessarily followed that to possess the necessary *animus testandi* the testator had to intend that that dispositive, although revocable and ambulatory, regime would be called into play immediately and not postponed to, or made dependent upon, some future event or condition. The only conclusion open on the evidence was that at the moment of execution the testatrix, because of the misapprehension under which she was acting, lacked the *animus* to make any valid will, in the sense of a will intended to be immediately dispositive, at all. Even if the testatrix had had an immediate *animus testandi* to make a conditional will, it was not an *animus* to which she ever succeeded in giving effect for the will she executed was unconditional. Waite LJ said that it would be against the weight of authority and contrary to the express terms of the Wills Act 1837 to allow extrinsic evidence as to her intention to be used to write into her will, for probate purposes, a condition which she had neither stated in writing or signed.

The *animus testandi* must be freely formed and not tainted by lack of mental capacity. The classic test was that laid down by Cockburn CJ in *Banks v Goodfellow* (1870) when he said the testator must possess sound mind, memory and understanding. That is to say the testator must understand he is making a testamentary disposition; he must be aware of the property at his disposal, not in detail but sufficiently to know the value of the major items and give consideration to those close to him to whom one would expect him to have regard. This is not to say that the testator has to leave property to those apparently close to him but to ignore them may indicate a lack of mental capacity to form the necessary *animus*.

Question 2

James makes a will leaving all his property to his niece, Kay. He then asks Kay to live in his house and act as his housekeeper and promises he will not alter his will. When James dies Kay discovers he has made a later will leaving all his property to a named charity. Kay alleges James was bound by the promise not to alter his will.

Would it make any difference if instead of making a later will James had married with the result that the will in favour of Kay had been revoked by the subsequent marriage?

Answer plan

The problem is addressing the relationship between the key characteristic that a will is revocable until death and the effect of a contract to make a will. Has the promisee a right of action against the estate if the will is not made or subsequently altered? Further, what is the effect if the will is revoked by the subsequent marriage of the testator, s 18 Wills Act 1837, rather than by revocation by the testator (*animus revocandi*) in accordance with s 20?

Answer

Kay may be able to take action against the estate of James for breach of contract in respect of the personal estate. A will is always revocable. However in *Synge v Synge* (1894) the court held that a contract to make a will leaving property in a certain way was valid. The court ordered the beneficiaries under the will to convey the property to the promisee. *Parker v Clark* (1960) said that a contract where the testator would leave his house to a woman if she acted as his housekeeper could be valid. This is unlikely to apply today in respect of dispositions of land in view of s 2 Law of Property (Miscellaneous Provisions) Act 1989. Section 2 provides that the contract must be in writing and incorporate all the terms agreed in one document, either by setting them out in the document or by reference to some other document; and be signed by each party to the contract. In the case of a will this is signed by the testator alone; therefore the will alone could no longer form the contract. If, by chance, the promisee had been a witness to the will which incorporated the terms of the contract in respect of realty one would have to consider the relationship between s 15 Wills Act 1837, the denial of gift to the witness beneficiary and the beneficiary/promisee as signatory to the purported contract. A further complication is where the witness could avoid s 15 by invoking s 1 Wills Act 1968.

The decision in *Synge v Synge* shows that the rules as to freedom of testamentary disposition do not make such contracts invalid. The contracts fall into two broad categories. One is the contract merely to make a will, the other, the contract which ensures that specified property will pass to the promisee in any event. The first type of contract is completely discharged by performance when the will is made. If the will is not made the promisee is entitled to be placed only in the same position as if the contract had been made. In *Dillon v Public Trustee ex New Zealand* (1941) Henry Dillon was involved in litigation with his sons. The dispute was settled on the basis that Henry would make a will leaving certain land to them. Henry executed a will leaving the land as agreed with the residue of the estate to his wife. On his death his widow applied for reasonable provision from the estate. The issue was whether the widow could go against the land specifically devised in seeking an order. The court said yes; by making the will Henry had discharged his obligation to the sons; therefore they were in the same position as any other devisee. It follows that a contract merely to make a will does not protect the promisee because the contract, once made, does not imply the will will not be revoked. Compare the decision in *Dillon* with *Schaefer v Schuhman* (1972) 1 All ER 621 (PC) where the promisee established the contract was founded on part performance and claimed the house as a creditor and not as devisee.

Where the contract is construed as one where the promisor intends the property to pass to the promisee in any event the contractual obligation is only discharged by performance when the property actually passes to the promisee (*Synge v Synge*). If the property does not effectively pass under the will the promisee, Kay in this problem, will have a right of action against the estate – *Hammersley v De Biel* (1845).

The court will not restrain the revocation of a will, however, where a contract can be proved. The court will recognise the contract by restraining dispersal of the property in contravention of the contract, as in *Synge v Synge*, or award damages for breach as in *Hammersley v De Biel*. In order to establish the existence of a contract the basic elements of contract must be present. Kay would have to prove there was an intention to create legal relations. This should not be difficult given the relationship of employer and employee. There must be offer and acceptance, here the request to stay in the house combined with the promise not to alter the will. Such promises would provide the requisite consideration. However, the effect of s 2 of the 1989 Act would make it unlikely Kay could enforce a contract in respect of the house itself. But the promise is to leave all James's property. The house apart this would be construed as a general residuary gift, that is, providing sufficient certainty of subject matter. Compare this with a provision to leave 'ample provision'. Such a vague description could fail (see *McPhail v Torrance* (1909)) unless s 21 Adminstration of Justice Act 1982 could allow the admission of extrinsic evidence.

There may be difficulty in fixing the moment in time to identify the property, for, in this case James, has left all his property. Does this mean all the property he owns at the date of the will or at the date of his death? In the absence of a clear intention to the contrary the court will invoke s 24 Wills Act 1837 and construe the words as an intention to leave all the property at the date of death. How does this equate with the contract made at the date of the will not to revoke? There is no implied promise the testator will not reduce his estate prior to death (*Needham v Smith* (1828)). It follows that the testator is free to dispose of property in his lifetime which was acquired after the contract was made (*Needham v Kirkham* (1820)). What is uncertain is where the promise relates to only a part of the testator's property and how far this property is protected by the promise. While the testator can make a genuine outright disposal of the whole or part of the property, if he converts the property into other property which he retains, the conversion will not be allowed to operate to the disadvantage of the promisee. So in *Lewis v Madocks* (1803) the contract was to leave the testator's personalty to the promisee. The testator sold some personalty and purchased land. The court held the land stood charged with a sum to the purchase money to be held in favour of the promisee. Although, as stated above, Kay would have difficulty in enforcing a contract in respect of realty she could argue this latter point if James sold, say, shares and acquired more land prior to his death.

If James had entered into a valid or voidable (*Re Roberts* (1978)) marriage after the date of the will the marriage would revoke the will (s 18 Wills Act 1837) unless the will was made in expectation of the marriage (s 18). There is no evidence James had made the will in expectation of his marriage. If Kay has established a contract in respect of at least a part of the property in the estate what is the effect of the revocation?

Whether Kay can take action depends upon the nature of the contract. Has James merely contracted not to revoke his will or has he contracted to the effect that the property is to pass to Kay in any event? If James had revoked the will under his own volition, as above, the estate would be liable under either head. However, where the will is revoked by operation of law, as in this case, by s 18, this is not a deliberate revocation on the part of the testator. If the contract as proved is construed as a contract not to revoke the will there is no breach of contract where the revocation occurs as a result of operation of law, see *Re Marsland* (1939). However, if the intention in entering into the contract is to leave the property to the promisee in any event then the contractual obligation remains outstanding until the death (*Robinson v Ommanney* (1883)).

Whether Kay could take action in this latter case will therefore depend upon the construction of the contract.

Question 3

Helen died in March this year, a spinster aged 84. She had lived as a recluse for the last 20 years in a large house set in 30 acres of remote countryside. Her only companions were the housekeeper, Laura, and Eric, the estate manager, who also took care of all her financial matters. Helen had inherited the house together with its valuable paintings from her father.

Two weeks before Helen's death Eric had written to Cyrus, the family solicitor, asking him to draw up a will for Helen leaving the house and land to Laura, her collection of paintings to Eric and the rest of the estate to Ben, John and Simon, her brothers, in equal shares. Cyrus prepared a draft will and sent it to Eric.

When Eric read the draft he telephoned Cyrus and said 'I take it that if any of Helen's brothers die before her, the survivors will get all her residuary estate'. Cyrus replied 'yes'. Ben, survived by his children, Vicky and Elizabeth, died a week before Helen.

While Helen was executing the document as her will, she said to Sally, her good friend and one of her witnesses, that her brothers were persecuting her and that her father had spoken through one of the portraits hanging in the gallery, telling her not to leave them any substantial part of the estate.

The house is valued at death at £1.4 million, the paintings at £650,000 and the residuary estate at £40,000. Eric is named executor and is anxious to file for probate as soon as possible.

Advise John and Simon as to the validity and effect of the dispositions contained in the will and the initial steps they should consider should they challenge the will.

Ignore any possible claims under the Inheritance (Provision for Family and Dependants) Act 1975.

Answer plan

This question concerns the general test as to capacity to make a valid will, the effect of the apparent delusions, knowledge and approval and undue influence. In addition, there are the effects of the pre-deceased, Helen's brother. Finally, there is the administrative point where one is asked to advise on the initial steps to be taken in a challenge to the will.

Answer

In order to be admissible to probate, a will must express the clear intention of the testator (*animus testandi*) and satisfy the requirements as to form contained in s 9 Wills Act 1837 as amended. There is nothing to suggest any defect in form. The challenge to the admissibility of the will is based upon the likely lack of mental capacity of the testatrix at the time of execution.

There is no statutory definition of the mental capacity required to make a valid will. The class test to apply is the one enunciated by Cockburn CJ in *Banks v Goodfellow* (1870). Cockburn CJ said that the testator must have sound mind, memory and understanding. That is to say, one must prove that the testator understood at the time of execution that he was making a will; was aware of the extent of the property at his disposal and could appreciate the claims which would normally be made against his estate. The testator must be free from any disorder of the mind, such as a delusion, that could bring about a disposal which he would not have contemplated had he been able to form a clear *animus*.

Given the discrepancies in Helen's estate between the value of the house and the paintings as against the residuary estate, the initial challenge by John and Simon could be on the basis of the second limb of the Cockburn test, that is, that Helen did not have sound memory. In *Wood v Smith* (1992) the Court of Appeal rejected the last will, executed days before the death, on the basis that the courts were not satisfied that, at the time of execution of the will, the testator was fully aware of the true value of her estate. The burden of proving the will rests with the person applying for the grant (*Barry v Butlin* (1838)). Where the will is rational on the face of it there is a presumption as to full capacity (*Re Fenwick* (1972)). The effect of *Re Fenwick* is to throw the burden upon those who allege lack of capacity. However, given the discrepancy in values, John and Simon should be able to switch the burden back to Laura and Eric to prove that Helen had the intention to make substantial provision for Laura and Eric.

The court must be satisfied that the testator had knowledge of the contents of the will and approved the form of the will at the time of execution (see the dictum of Lord Penzance in *Guardhouse v Blackburn* (1866)). *Prima facie*, execution by the testator indicates knowledge and approval. However, the fact that the will was prepared as a result of instructions given by Eric, a principal beneficiary, provides evidence of suspicion, and on that basis the court is more likely to reject the will because of a lack of knowledge and approval (*Wintle v Nye* (1959); *Re Ticehurst* (1973)).

Strong challenges can therefore be made to the validity of the will on the basis of the general test in *Banks v Goodfellow* and a lack of knowledge and approval based upon suspicion. There is a third possibility. There is evidence that at the time of execution it would appear that Helen was suffering from a delusion.

Where the delusion affects the whole of the form of the will, the will is inadmissible for want of capacity (*Dew v Clark* (1826)). If the delusion affects only a part the remainder could be admissible (*Re Bohrmann* (1938)). However, in this case it is likely, given the discrepancy between the value of the residuary gift and the devises, that the whole will would be inadmissible.

John and Simon should lodge a caveat against Helen's estate. The effect of the caveat would be to prevent a grant being issued until John and Simon were notified when they could then bring *prima facie* evidence of lack of capacity.

Whether Eric could use the reference to query to the solicitor the effect of a brother predeceasing as evidence that he has shown the will to Helen and she approves of the terms is debatable. The courts take a strong line where there are suspicious circumstances. In any event there is still the evidence of delusion. The effect of Ben's predeceasing Helen is that his share of the residue will lapse. There is no evidence of a gift over and the residue has been given to the three brothers as tenants in common. Ben's share would therefore be property undisposed of by the will and devolve on intestacy to the surviving blood relatives, namely John and Simon. In any event, given the strength of evidence to mount a challenge on the grounds of lack of mental capacity, it is likely that the will would be inadmissible and the whole of Helen's estate would devolve on intestacy. The estate would then be divided three ways:

one-third to John, one-third to Simon and one-third divided between Vicky and Elizabeth, the issue of the deceased brother Ben.

Notes
1. In *Banks v Goodfellow* the court had to consider the admissibility of a will where the testator had suffered from a long history of delusions that he was being molested by evil spirits. However, the court concluded that the delusions did not have any bearing upon the gifts in the will and therefore the will was admitted to probate.
2. *Re Ticehurst* is a good example of a clear change of direction in the last will which had been effected as a result of an intermediary, the wife of one of the main beneficiaries. Although the evidence was given that the testatrix was an alert person for her age (82) the court concluded that the circumstances were too suspicious.
3. A person is said to be suffering from a delusion when he persists in believing something which no rational person would sustain.
4. For the rules as to procedures on caveats see r 44 of the Non-Contentious Probate Rules 1987.
5. Section 33 Wills Act 1837 as amended is irrelevant here as s 33 applies to gifts to children and remoter issue and not, for example, brothers.

Question 4

Distinguish between fraud and undue influence as factors affecting testamentary capacity.

Answer plan

This is a straightforward essay contrasting two vitiating factors concerning the intention to make a valid will. Undue influence and fraud should both be defined and both illustrated by reference to the case law.

Answer

In order to make a valid will the testator must comply with the formal requirements in s 9 of the Wills Act 1837. In addition, the testator must have the capacity to form a clear intention to make the will, the *animus testandi*. The testator must not only be mentally capable of forming the intention (*Banks v Goodfellow* (1870)) but must also demonstrate that he knew and approved of the contents of the will (*Guardhouse v Blackburn* (1866)).

The testator must be able to exercise a free choice in determining the objects of his bounty, that is to say, the testator must be free from undue influence or fraud in the making of the will. What is undue influence? In *Wingrove v Wingrove* (1885) Sir James Hannen P said that:

'To be undue influence in the eyes of the law there must be – to sum it up in a word – coercion. The coercion may of course be of different kinds, it may be in the grossest form, such as actual confinement or violence; or a person in the last days or hours of life may have become so weak and feeble that a very little pressure may be sufficient to bring about the desired result; it may even be, that the mere fact of talking to him at that stage of an illness and pressing something upon him, may so fatigue the brain that the sick person may be induced for quietness' sake to do anything. This would equally be coercion, though not actual violence.'

In other words the testator must be made to do that which he does not desire to do. The law will allow any amount of importuning in order to encourage receipt of a gift under the will. However, where importuning or persuasion turns into coercion or threat then the gift or the whole will can be set aside on the grounds of undue influence.

In *Hall v Hall* (1868) Lord Penzance said that a testator may be led but not driven. The will must be the offspring of the testator's own volition.

In *Hall v Hall* the will was set aside on the basis that the testator had been subject to a threat and, for the sake of peace and quiet, had agreed to the terms of the will in favour of his wife, a will which he did not approve.

The key element therefore is evidence of coercion. So an immoral influence exercised over the testator by another person would not constitute undue influence in the absence of evidence of coercion.

There is no relationship between undue influence in the law of wills and the equitable doctrine of undue influence. Therefore, a person seeking to disapprove a will on the basis of a particular relationship will be rejected as for example, the relationship of priest and parishioner in *Parfitt v Lawless* (1872). The relationship of solicitor and client, where the solicitor receives a benefit under the will, may give rise to rejection by the courts on the grounds of suspicion, that is, lack of knowledge and approval, in addition to possible breach of the professional guidelines laid down by the Law Society. Examples such as *Wintle v Nye* (1959) and *Re A Solicitor* (1975) are authorities on lack of knowledge and approval, not undue influence. The burden of proving undue influence rests with the person making the allegation (*Craig v Lamoureux* (1920)).

Fraud arises where the testator has been misrepresented or deceived by the beneficiary. There must be evidence that in some way the testator was misled. In *Butterfield v Scawen* the testator had revoked a request in favour of a principal beneficiary owing to a false representation that the beneficiary had attempted to poison the testator. It would be fraud, for example, where a clause is inserted in a will before the will is signed but without the testator's knowledge. Fraud can also arise where there is a deliberate misreading of the will so as to deliberately omit a reference to a gift in favour of the person reading the will to the testator as in *Wilson v Joughlin* (1866). Although in *Guardhouse v Blackburn* Lord Penzance said that reading over the will to the testator can amount to proof of knowledge and approval, where the reading deliberately omits passages this can amount to fraud.

A will made as a result of undue influence or fraud is inadmissible to probate. Where the evidence of undue influence or fraud only affects a part of the will then the remainder may be admitted (*Allen v McPherson* (1847)) (4).

Notes
1 Lord Penzance in *Hall v Hall* said: 'Persuasion, appeals to the affections or ties of kindred, to a sentiment of gratitude for past

services, or pity for future destitution, or the like – these are all legitimate, and may be fairly pressed on a testator. On the other hand, pressure of whatever character, whether acting on the fears or the hopes, if so exerted as to overpower the volition without convincing the judgments, is a species of restraint under which no valid will can be made ... In a word, the testator may be led but not driven; and his will must be the offspring of his own volition, and not the record of someone else's.' This last sentence is often quoted to form an essay question on this topic.

2 Parry & Clark (9th edn) at p 57 gives a good example of influence falling short of coercion, therefore influence which would not be considered undue. For example, a man's mistress may make use of her unbounded influence to induce him to make a will in her favour to the exclusion of his wife and children, but in the absence of coercion this does not constitute undue influence.

3 A solicitor must not act where his own interests conflict with the interests of a client or a potential client. The Law Society's Guide as to professional conduct states that 'where a client intends to make a gift *inter vivos* or by will to his solicitor or to the solicitor's partner, or a member of staff or to the families of any of them and the gift is of a significant amount, either in itself, or having regard to the size of the client's estate, and the reasonable expectations of prospective beneficiaries, the solicitor must advise the clients to be independently advised as to that gift, and if the client declines, must refuse to act.'

4 Parry & Clark cites *Betts v Doughty* (1879) on the principle that where a beneficiary under the will of a testator prevents him by undue influence or fraud from altering the will, or making a new will, in favour of other persons, the court will probably impose a trust on the beneficiary for those other persons. In that situation an equitable remedy is needed because no remedy is available in a court of probate. See 9th ed p 58.

# The Will Making Process

Question 5

To what extent could a court alter the words of a will?

Answer plan

This question addresses the effectiveness of the court where it is alleged that the will does not reflect the wishes of the testator. There are three areas to consider:

- omission of words on the basis of lack of knowledge and approval;
- the power of the court to rectify the will; and
- the court acting as a court of construction.

Answer

Courts are reluctant to interfere with the wording of a will on the basis that the will, having been signed by the testator and attested, reflects the last wishes of the testator. However, if words in the will can be challenged successfully on the basis of lack of knowledge and approval, the court can omit words and, to a limited extent, can order rectification of the will.

In *Swords* (1952) a codicil was challenged on the ground of lack of knowledge and approval where the testator had confused the numbering of the clauses in the will. The courts ordered the omission of words revoking particular clauses in view of the inaccuracy between the clauses as stated in the codicil and the reference in the will. In *Re Phelan* (1972) the court admitted a series of codicils in the form of will-forms with the omission of the printed revocation clauses in the will-forms on the basis that the testator never applied his mind to those clauses.

A more difficult situation arises where the testator is deemed to know and approve of technical language used by drafters. Such technical language will be admitted to probate even though the drafters were mistaken as to the legal effect. For example, in *Re Horrocks* (1939) the use of the word 'or', instead of 'and' in a gift of residue to 'charitable or benevolent' objects, was the solicitor's deliberate choice under a mistake as to the legal effect rather than the result of a typist's error. Even where the testator queried the inclusion of a clause and was wrongly advised, the court has said that the testator is bound by the clause as in *Collins v Elstone* (1893). The inclusion of a clause on the basis of wrongful legal advice would give rise today to an action in negligence under the principle in *Ross v Caunters* (1980).

If the testator died before 1983 the court could only order omission of words. There was no power to rectify the will. For deaths after 31 December 1982 s 20 of the Administration of Justice Act 1982 enables the court, in limited circumstances, to order rectification. The power to rectify is limited to where the will does not reflect the intention of the testator as a consequence of a clerical error or a failure to understand the testator's instructions. A good example of a clerical error occurred in *Re Morris* (1971) where there was a typing error in the numbering of clauses in a subsequent codicil which had the intention of revoking one particular legacy. The court at that time could only omit the reference to the number and then seek to construe the testator's intention on the basis of lack of knowledge and approval. Today, if the same facts occurred, the court could order rectification of the codicil on the basis of a clerical error. The statutory power to rectify has been considered by the court in *Wordingham v Royal Exchange Trust Co Ltd* (1992). Here the court considered the meaning of 'clerical error' and held that such an error should be construed as an inadvertent error made in the process of recording the intended words of the testator in the drafting or transcription of his will. Here the facts clearly showed that the testatrix intended to include a power of appointment, which had appeared in earlier wills, in her last will. The solicitor who drafted the new will failed to include the power of appointment and the evidence pointed to omission by way of a clerical error.

The statutory power is limited, so, for example, if the drafter understood the instructions from the client but consciously omitted an intended legacy s 20 would not apply and the court could only omit words on the basis of lack of knowledge and approval and would not be in a position to order rectification.

A Court of Construction can construe the will as if certain words had been inserted, omitted or changed, if it is clear from the will itself both that an error has been made in the wording and what the substance of the intending wording was. The substance of the intention must come from the will itself 'from the four corners of the document' (*Re Whitrick* (1957)). It must be clear therefore from the instrument what has been omitted from the will. This does not mean a knowledge of the precise words but the essence of the intention of the testator.

So in *Hart v Tulk* (1852) 'fourth' schedule was read as fifth schedule in accordance with the general intention from the will. In *Re Bacharach's WT* (1959) the words of the will were rearranged in accordance with the general intention. Gifts in a will may be irreconcilable. In this situation the court has to glean the intention of the testator by looking at the will as a whole. In *Re Alexander's WT* (1948) the will bequeathed a bracelet to A and later in the same will bequeathed the same bracelet to B. The court concluded that each legatee was entitled to half the value of the bracelet.

Parry & Clarke emphasises that the power of the court to supply, omit or change words as part of the process of construction is very limited. The substance of the intended wording must come from the will itself.

The problems that can arise in relation to the limited power to alter the will emphasise the importance of sound legal advice and professionally drawn wills, provided care is taken in the office when the will or codicil is transcribed to its final form ready for execution.

Notes

1. Parry & Clarke (9th edn) points out that it has been held the court does not order the omission of words, of which the testator did not know and approve, if this would alter the sense of the rest of the will (see *Re Horrocks* (1939)) and an article by WA Lee (1969) 33 *Conveyancer New Series* pp 329–34.
2. In *Wordingham* the Deputy Judge concluded by saying that if he was wrong in the interpretation of s 20(1)(a) then he would have been minded to strike down the whole of the will as not being made with knowledge and approval.
3. Parry & Clarke points out at p 56 that the power to rectify or power to omit do not provide any remedy in three situations:
    - the testator's failure to appreciate the legal effect of the words used in his will; or
    - uncertainty as to the meaning of his intended wording; or

- a lacuna in the will, because he never had any intention relevant to the event which actually occurred.

4 In *Re Whitrick* (1957) the testatrix by her will left her entire estate to her husband and provided that 'In the event of my husband ... and myself both dying at the same time' her estate should be held upon trust for X, Y and Z equally. The testatrix's husband pre-deceased her and consequently, according to the literal meaning of the words used, the gift to X, Y and Z failed and the testatrix's entire estate passed on intestacy. The Court of Appeal held that it was clear from the will as a whole that the testatrix intended, by means of the gift to X, Y and Z, to provide for the contingency of her husband not surviving her. The will was therefore read as if it had directed that X, Y and Z were to take in the event of the husband pre-deceasing the testatrix, as well as in the event of them both dying at the same time.

Question 6

In 1983, William, who was blind, executed a will which was principally typed but had certain parts of it written in ink. There was no attestation clause, although at the bottom of the first page William had signed and beneath his signature were the signatures of Charles and Angela, who at the time, was engaged to be married to Robert. The will left realty to Robert and provided that the personalty should be shared between certain friends of William whose names would be found in the back of his diary for 1982.

Two years later a codicil was executed with an attestation clause, which appointed fresh executors and left Blackacre to Charles, but otherwise confirmed the earlier will. This was witnessed by Angela, who is now married to Robert, and another person. It now transpires that at the time the codicil was witnessed the signatures of the witnesses may have been affixed to the codicil whilst William was out of the room.

Advise Robert upon the admissibility of the will and codicil to probate.

Answer plan

This question requires application of s 9 of the Wills Act 1837 and the affidavit evidence required by the court given that the testator is blind. The rules concerning incorporation by reference should be applied and consideration given to the effect of the codicil.

Answer

Given that the testator is blind and there is no attestation clause, the court will call for affidavit evidence, primarily from the witnesses, in order to establish that the testator knew and approved of the contents and that the will was validly executed in accordance with s 9 Wills Act 1837. The affidavit evidence should show that the will was read over to William prior to his signing. The position of the signatures would appear to be in accordance with s 9. It must be satisfied that the signature of the testator was giving effect to the whole will (see *Re White* (1993)), and, by signing, the witnesses were attesting to the signing by William. The fact that Angela is engaged to Robert will not preclude Robert from taking under the will as Angela has not yet married Robert. Section 15 Wills Act 1837 refers to signing by a beneficiary. Further, the court would have to be satisfied that the parts written in ink were written prior to execution and not inserted afterwards.

With regard to the gift to the friends of William, the court must be satisfied that the list in the diary is clearly identifiable by the reference to it in the will and that the complete list was in existence at the date of the execution of the will (see *UCNW v Taylor* (1908)). (For a re-statement of the law on incorporation of documents see *Re Berger (dec'd)* (1989).)

Is the codicil validly executed? If the witnesses, when they attested, were within sight and earshot of William, there could still be a valid execution with s 9. However, to establish 'presence' something must have been said at the time of the signing by the witnesses in order to establish that William was aware that the attestation was taking place. 'Presence' denotes a mental and a physical presence (see *Casson v Dade* (1781)). Assuming the codicil is validly executed, the witnessing by Angela will not affect the validity nor deny Robert taking his gift for Robert will take his gift by reference to the will and not the codicil. Similarly, Charles will be able to take his gift for he did not witness the signing of the codicil (*Anderson v Anderson* (1872)).

Chapter 2

Formal Validity

Introduction

A will is admissible to probate if there is a clearly formed *animus testandi* and the document complies with the requirements as to form as stated by the Wills Act 1837. The amendments to s 9 of the Wills Act by s 17 of the Administration of Justice Act 1982 have resulted in a greater flexibility in interpretation (see, for example, *dicta* in *Wood v Smith* (1992) as applied in *Weatherhill v Pearce* (1995)). However, the key requirements as to form, that the will should be signed or acknowledged by the testator in the presence of two witnesses and the witnesses sign or acknowledge in the presence of the testator remain. There is no doctrine of substantial compliance in English law although the court was prepared to apply the presumption *omnia praesumuntur rite et solenniter esse acta* in *Weatherhill v Pearce*.

This chapter continues with questions on intestate distribution. The topic must be studied carefully. The rules of intestacy apply not only where the will is for some reason inadmissible to probate but in situations where the will fails to dispose of all the property of the deceased. The law on intestate distribution, in particular how it affects the surviving spouse, was reviewed by the Law Commission in 1989 (Law Com 187 of 1989). Some recommendations arising from the report together with a review of the interpretation of s 18A Wills Act 1837 have been implemented by the Law Reform (Succession) Act 1995.

Intestate distribution problems can appear daunting. A useful approach is to set on one side of a column those persons who survive the intestate deceased and who are potentially entitled to share in the estate and on the other side the actual entitlement of the beneficiaries. Care should be taken, for example, when one is considering issue that the list is confined to issue of the intestate deceased and not issue of the marriage. The stepchild, for example, is outside the rules on intestate distribution unless the stepchild has been lawfully adopted by the deceased. Listing all those who are potentially entitled will give you the order of persons who would be entitled to a grant of administration to the estate of the deceased (with the addition of creditors) under Rule 22 Non-Contentious

Probate Rules 1987. In questions on intestate distribution expect some reference to a critique. Study should be made of the changes in society including the political and economic influences which led to the review of the law in the later 1980s.

Question 7

In 1992 Tim wrote a letter addressed to his son John saying that he wished to put his affairs in order. The letter contained various good wishes to friends, together with a series of gifts of money to friends and a request that the rest of this property should be divided in three equal parts between Tim's daughter Susan, his sister Betty and John.

The letter headed 'from Tim Wood' is unsigned. Tim shows the letter to John who says, 'I think this should be witnessed'. Tim then calls in his neighbours Bill and Cath saying, 'I would like you to authenticate this letter'. Bill replies, 'Should you sign?'. Tim says, 'There is my name at the top.' Bill, Cath and John then sign their names on the back of the paper.

Tim has died and Susan is claiming that her father's estate should be distributed on intestacy. Betty consults you as to the validity of the letter.

Advise Betty.

Answer plan

The question deals with the preliminary point as to the nature of a testamentary document. Thereafter, the question is concerned with the formal requirements for a valid will: in particular, an examination of the position of signature in the light of the revised s 9 of the Wills Act 1837 as amended by s 17 Administration of Justice Act 1982 and the interpretation in *Wood v Smith* (1992).

Answer

If Tim has died intestate then the only people entitled are his children John and Susan who would take the whole of the estate in equal shares on the statutory trusts (s 47(1)(i) Administration of Estates Act 1925). The only way in which Betty could share is by establishing that the letter is admissible as a will. In order to do this Betty would have to establish that the letter complied with the formal requirements as laid down by s 9 Wills Act 1837 as amended by s 17 the Administration of Justice Act 1982.

In order to be admissible a will must be in writing (the only exception is the dispensing with formalities where the circumstances fall within s 11 of the Wills Act 1837 relating to privilege wills which are not relevant here). The document must also convey testamentary intention. The document need not be described as a will so long as it contains disposition intended to take effect on death and is executed in the manner laid down by the Wills Act. In *Re Berger* (1989) the court admitted a document written in Hebrew known as a *zavah* where the document, apart from containing a series of religious exhortations also contained dispositions and was signed and attested in accordance with s 9. On this basis the court admitted the document as a valid will (1).

A will can be expressed in the form of a letter (*Re Cook* (1960)). Here Tim has expressed that he wished to put his affairs in order and the letter contains various dispositions. On the authority of *Re Berger* (1989) the letter would be accepted as a will. The problem of admissibility then turned upon whether the letter is correctly executed and attested in accordance with the formal requirements in s 9.

A will must be signed by the testator in such a way that the testator intended his signature to give effect to the will and that signature must be made or acknowledged by the testator in the presence of two or more witnesses who either attest and sign or acknowledge their signatures in the presence of the testator (s 9). Has Tim correctly signed the will? Under the terms of the original s 9 Wills Act 1837 the will had to be signed at the foot or end thereof. Problems arose as to the literal interpretation of these words and the 1852 Amendment Act referred to the signature being placed, *inter alia*, at or after, under or beside, or opposite the end of the will so that it should be apparent on the face of the will that the testator intended to give effect to his signature. The court would not accept a signature placed at the top of the will (*Re Stalman* (1931)) as the 1852 Act said that nothing following or under the signature shall be admissible. The aim of the reform of formal validity expressed in the revised s 9 in the 1982 Administration of

Justice Act is to achieve greater flexibility but at the same time protecting against possible fraud.

In order to establish admissibility Betty would be relying upon the Court of Appeal decision in *Wood v Smith* (1992). The facts here are similar to the question in *Wood v Smith* where the testator wrote out a document starting, 'I Percy Winterborne ...'. When the testator asked the witnesses to sign, one witness pointed out that the testator had not signed and he replied 'Yes I have' pointing to his name at the top. At first instance the court refused to accept that the will complied with s 9. Although a signature can comprise any form *Re Cook* (1960) (2) it need not necessarily be the name of the testator (3). The court in *Wood v Smith* said that at the time the testator signed, namely at the top, the document did not contain any dispositions, therefore one could not describe it as a will. On appeal Scott LJ did not agree. In between the first instance decision and the hearing by the Court of Appeal *Re White* (1990) had been reported and here the court (Andrew Park QC sitting as a Deputy Judge) accepted that one could have a signing at the top and thereafter the dispositions and a statement by the witnesses provided the exercise was all in one operation. Scott LJ in *Wood v Smith* said that the object of Parliament was to simplify execution and the requirements in s 9(a) and (b) that the will should be in writing, signed by the testator and that it appears that the testator intended by his signature to give effect of the will, are complementary. He said that the object of the signature of the testator is to authenticate the written document in question and that if the writing of the will and the appending of the signature are all in one operation it does not matter whereabouts on the document or when in the course of writing the signature is appended.

On the authority of *Wood v Smith*, provided Tim had the clear intention to make the will, then his heading at the top would be accepted as a signature to give effect to the will. There is, however, a further problem that the signature must be attested by the witnesses in the presence of the testator. It is clear that all the parties are present and there is no specific requirement as to where on the will the witnesses should sign provided there is evidence that they are attesting to assigning or there is an acknowledgement by the testator. Here, the comment by Bill followed by Tim's reply indicates that Tim has acknowledged his name on the will and provided the witnesses can see the name this would be accepted as a valid acknowledgement (*Re Dunstan* (1882)). However, one of the witnesses is Tim's son John, a beneficiary under the alleged will. By s 15 Wills Act 1837 the validity of the will is unaffected by a witness beneficiary but that beneficiary cannot claim the gift under the will. However, following the decision of the Court of Appeal in *Re Bravda* (1968) s 1 of the Wills Act 1968 says that where there are at least two independent witnesses, that is, witnesses who do not take a benefit under the document, any additional signing can be disregarded as being superfluous. Therefore, should Betty be successful in her claim to admit the document as a will the residuary estate would be split in three ways and John would receive his share.

Notes

1 In *Re Berger* the court relied upon the propositions of fact and ignored the issue as to whether the testator had the requisite *animus testandi*. Mustill LJ referred to a presumption of *animus* if the document has the necessary dispose of effect and is duly executed. However, he added that Mr Berger would have been startled to discover that the document was enforceable in the probate court. This appears to negate the presumption of *animus* rather than support it.

2 In *Re Cook* the letter was addressed to the testatrix's children and commenced, 'I Emmie Cook ...' and was signed at the end 'your loving mother'. The court accepted 'your loving mother' as the signature which could be identified by reference to the commencement.

3 *Re Sperling* illustrates that a witness need not sign his or her own name. Here the witness signed 'servant to Mr Sperling'. The court accepted this as a valid attestation since the servant could be easily identified.

4 In *Re White* the testator made a will in 1981. In 1984, the year before he died, he asked a friend to make certain alterations to the percentages of residuary bequests which numbered 18 separate gifts in the original will. When the alterations had been made the testator then wrote on the original will 'alterations to will of 14 December 1981' and below that he wrote 'witnesses'. The witnesses signed but the testator did not sign again. The alterations were therefore inadmissible for they did not comply with s 21 Wills Act 1837 as not being executed and attested by both the testator and the witnesses. The alternative argument was that the exercise in 1984 amounted to the making of a new will. This raised the question as to whether the will had been

signed by the testator. The court concluded that the alleged 1984 will was conceptually a different will and the signature four years earlier did not meet the requirements in s 9(a). The court did say that if the exercise were all in one operation then the signature could have been accepted. This was the point that was taken up by Lord Justice Scott in *Wood v Smith*.

5 Although the Court of Appeal in *Wood v Smith* accepted the validity of the signing, the court still rejected the will for want of capacity holding that the testator failed the second limb of the test in *Banks v Goodfellow*, namely that he did not appreciate at the time of execution the extent of the property at his disposal.

Question 8

'The Administration of Justice Act 1982 made only minor and inconsequential amendments to the law of wills when a thorough modernisation of the law was required.'

Discuss, with references to the formalities required for the proper execution of wills.

Answer plan

This essay requires consideration of the key changes effected by the revision of s 9 contained in s 17 of the Administration of Justice Act 1982. The three points approach is required, firstly to identify the changes that were made to s 9; secondly to critically consider the impact of these changes, and thirdly to consider any other changes which the Act may have made.

Answer

The first requirements as to form in the execution of wills appeared in the Statute of Frauds of 1677. The provisions were replaced when the Wills Act of 1837 was passed and the requirements of form were contained in s 9. The gist of s 9 is that the will should be signed by the testator or by someone on his behalf and in his presence, in the presence of two or more witnesses present at the same time. The witnesses should then attest to the signing of the testator by adding their names as witnesses. The witnesses must sign in the presence of the testator but not necessarily in the presence of one another. The testator need not sign in the presence of the witnesses but can merely acknowledge his signature in their presence. For this to be effective the witnesses must be in a position to see the signature (see *Re Groffman* (1969) and *Re Gunstan* (1882)). 'Presence' has been interpreted to mean both physical and mental presence so that the witnesses must be physically present with the testator when he signs or acknowledges and aware of what is going on. The testator must similarly be present when the witnesses sign, although this has been widely interpreted (see for example *Casson v Dade* (1781)). The underpinning of the requirements as to form contained in s 9 are a protection against fraud.

Section 9 goes on to require that the will be signed at the 'foot or end thereof'. Following the passing of the Wills Act in 1837 many wills failed because the courts construed strictly the words 'foot or end thereof'. As a result the Wills Act (Amendment Act) of 1852 was passed which indicated that the signature will be admissible so long as it is placed in such a way, under or following the words, as to indicate that the testator is giving effect to the will but, the section added, nothing following or under the signature shall be admissible. The result of this is seen in, for example, *Re Stalman* (1931) where the testator signed the will in the top right hand corner and the will was ruled to be inadmissible.

The Law Reform Committee considered the whole question concerning the formalities in the making and revoking of wills in a report in 1974. Earlier, the case of *Re Colling* (1972) had illustrated the problems that can arise where one has a 'mechanical failure'. Here the testator had started to sign his will in the presence of two witnesses and one was called away from the presence. The testator continued to sign and the first witness added his name. The second witness then returned and added his name. The will was ruled to be inadmissible, albeit there was no suggestion of any fraud. The Law Reform Committee took note of this case and sought in their recommendations to strike a balance between protection against fraud and avoidance of such mechanical failure.

The result of their deliberations materialised in s 17 of the Administration of Justice Act 1982 which replaced the former s 9 but is still cited as s 9 of the Wills Act 1837. The new section repealed the 1852 Amendment Act and says that the testator can sign the will in such a way that it appears that the testator intended by his signature to give effect to the will. This has been widely interpreted and can include where the testator has, for example, written his name at the top of the will prior to commencing the dispositions (see *Wood v Smith* (1992) and where the testator's name appears handwritten in an attestation clause as in *Weatherhill v Pearce* (1994)). The new s 9 goes on to provide that the witnesses may either attest to the testator's execution of the will by signing or acknowledging their signatures. This was included in an attempt to overcome the example of mechanical failure in *Re Colling*.

The combined effect of these changes could result in the testator and the witnesses adding their names to a blank sheet of paper and the testator subsequently writing in the dispositions. This point was considered but rejected at first instance by the courts in *Wood v Smith*. The court said, 'how can one give effect to 'a will' if the piece of paper does not contain any dispositions?' However, in the intervening period between the first instance decision and the Court of Appeal consideration in *Wood v Smith*, *Re White* was reported. This case did recognise that one could have a document signed in blank provided the dispositions were then added 'as one operation'. The testator and the witnesses would then acknowledge their signatures on the document. Lord Justice Scott in the Court of Appeal in *Wood v Smith* agreed but emphasised that the writing would have to be in one operation. What constitutes one operation and how far the courts are prepared to go in interpreting this remains to be seen. The courts adopted a flexible approach in *Weatherhill v Pearce* where the testator's name only appeared in a handwritten form in the attestation clause; the will was not signed separately by the testator. The court referred to *Wood v Smith* saying that the testator can place his signature in any part of the will so long as there is evidence that he is intending to give effect to the will. The cases of *Wood v Smith*, *Re White* and the *Weatherhill* case do indicate that the courts are taking a much more flexible line with regard to s 9 so long as there is evidence that the will was signed by the testator or his signature acknowledged in the presence of the two witnesses. Again in *Weatherhill* the courts took a lenient view here where the testator and the two witnesses were present in a large kitchen diner and the court did place emphasis on the evidence that the witnesses were astute ladies with an eye for detail. Although indicating a more flexible approach, the courts are still tied down by the central requirements of s 9 that the will is to be signed by the testator or his signature acknowledged in the presence of the two witnesses. It would appear therefore that this flexible line is not moving towards a doctrine of substantial compliance that has been adopted in certain other jurisdictions.

Should the legislature have gone further in their reform of the formal requirements? To substantially change the formal requirements could undermine the protection afforded to the will which, of course, in dealing with the last wishes of the testator, is an important document. Against this one has to consider the extent of private property which now passes with formality. Examples include title to houses which are held as beneficial joint tenants where title passes to the surviving joint tenant. Also, the benefits of pension rights and life assurance policies can be assigned during life with the minimum of formality. These all represent major assets in the private estate of an individual. Why not then reduce the requirements in the making of a will? Why should there not be, for example, simply one witness or an acceptance of wills in other forms, for example, tapes or even videos? In formulating the new s 9, the aim was to strike a balance reflecting the protection against fraud but removing some of the rigidity. Certainly, the judiciary have entered into the spirit behind the section as evidenced in the recent case law. For a detailed consideration of property passing with minimal formality see the article by Professor Langbein 'The Non-Probate Revolution', *Harvard Law Review*, 1981.

Question 9

This question takes the form of three parts based upon the same set of facts. The purpose of the series of questions is to consider various aspects of revocation.

In 1984, Phil, prior to leaving to work in the US made a will leaving all his property to his parents. In 1986 whilst working in New York he met and married Annie. In 1987 they both returned to settle in England and, later that year, Phil wrote on the back of his will, 'My estate is now to be divided in equal shares between Annie and my parents Ben and Lucy Moon'. He initialled the end of this paragraph in the presence of his friend William and William then signed his name.

The next day he asked William and William's wife, Joan, to call in and, producing the will, pointed to what he had written and said to Joan, 'I think you had better witness this as well'. Phil turned to William who nodded in agreement. Joan then added her name.

In 1990 Phil and Annie were divorced. Phil erroneously blamed his father Ben for the break up of his marriage and crossed Ben's name out of the will.

In 1992 Phil and Annie were reconciled. Later that year Phil wrote out the following, 'I Phil Moon leave my estate in equal shares between Annie and my mother Lucy'. He then asked William and Joan to call in and, pointing to the paper, said, 'I want to do what is right, please witness this'. William and Joan then added their names. Joan then said that she thought Phil was being unfair to his father, and after some thought, Phil said 'You're right' and he wrote in the words, 'my father Ben', after the reference to Annie. He then turned to William and Joan and said, 'Do you think that's right?' William and Joan both said, 'Yes'.

Advise upon the distribution of the estate.

Answer plan

This question involves consideration of the effect of s 18 and 18(a) of the Wills Act, revocation by marriage and the effect of divorce. In addition, a consideration of revocation under s 20 of the Wills Act 1837 coupled with an examination of the formal requirements in the signing of a will by the testator, or his acknowledgement and the attestation by the witnesses. These provisions in s 9 of the Wills Act 1837, need to be considered in the light of the interpretation in *Wood v Smith* (1992).

Answer

One way to approach a long question like this is to take the order of events from the commencement, and comment on each stage of the moves made by the testator, Phil.

One can assume, since there is no other reference to the contrary, that the 1984 will is properly executed and on the basis of that will Phil's parents would take all the property. The effect of marriage to Annie, which would be recognised by the English courts (*Re Roberts* (1978)), would be to revoke the will of 1984 (s 18

Formal Validity

Wills Act 1837 as amended by s 18 of the Administration of Justice Act 1982).

One would then consider the situation later in 1987 concerning the writing on the back of the will. The writing cannot be a revival of the 1984 will for, although revival can be effected by re-execution of the instrument, s 22 Wills Act 1837 as applied in the estate of *Davis* (1952), the writing does not repeat the will of 1984 but revokes it in part by dividing the estate, now in three parts, between Annie and Phil's parents. In order to consider the paper as an admissible testamentary instrument, one would have to argue that the paragraph added in 1987 is a new will. One then has to consider the question, has this been correctly executed and attested? There is no doubt that the initialling by Phil at the end of the paragraph would amount to a signature within s 9(a) Wills Act 1837 (see, for example, in the goods of *Christian* (1849)). Further, one can say that by the initialling Phil intended to give effect to the will within s 9(b). However, the signing does not comply with s 9(c) in that there is only one witness present.

The only way in which one could argue that the 1987 will would be an administrable testamentary instrument would be to establish a valid acknowledgement by Phil the next day, the acknowledgement being followed by a valid attestation. Has this happened? One would have to argue that by pointing to what he had written, this could amount to a valid acknowledgement provided the two witnesses, William and Joan, were in a position to see Phil's initials, applying *Re Gunstan* (1882). Joan has added her name as a witness; therefore one can argue that she has attested to the acknowledgement by her signing thereby complying with s 9(d). The issue then would be whether William has, by nodding in response to Phil's comment, validly acknowledged his signature as a witness thereby complying with s 9 as amended by s 17 of the Administration of Justice Act 1982. If this is the case, then at that stage the paragraph would be admissible as a valid will.

One would then turn to the situation in 1990 following the divorce. The effect of a decree absolute would cause the gift of one-third of the residue to Annie to lapse (s 18(a) Wills Act 1837). The gift of the residue to the three parties in the will of 1987 is a gift to them as tenants in common; therefore, since there is no gift over in default, Annie's share would lapse and devolve on a partial intestacy. There is no mention in the question of any issue of Phil;

therefore the lapsed share would pass equally to Phil's surviving parents, Ben and Lucy. Ben and Lucy would therefore take two-thirds of the estate under the 1987 will and the remaining one-third as on a partial intestacy. The crossing out of Ben's name by Phil would not effect this distribution and this would amount to an unattested alteration within s 21 Wills Act 1837. The extent of the crossing out is not made clear and one would have to adduce what was 'apparent on the face of the instrument' to try to determine the reference to Ben's name.

Following the reconciliation in 1992 one would finally have to consider whether the writing by Phil amounts to a valid will. Clearly the words show evidence of testamentary intention. The question again arises as to whether this document is validly executed in accordance with s 9. There is no indication to say that Phil has signed the will. The only reference is to his name at the commencement. Since the will is a holograph will, that is to say, it is under Phil's own hand, the writing of 'I Phil Moon' could amount to a valid signature by Phil as interpreted in *Wood v Smith*. The facts suggest that he wrote the words out alone. When he does call in William and Joan his words could amount to a valid acknowledgement provided William and Joan could see his name at the top (*Re Gunstan*). On the authority of *Wood v Smith* one could argue that Phil's estate would then be divided equally between Annie and Lucy. The final problem is whether the estate could be divided three ways following the insertion of Ben's name. The issue here would be how far the court would be prepared to be flexible in interpreting the wording of s 21 of the Wills Act. Following Phil's death evidence could be adduced by William and Joan that the alteration was made at the time. The problem is that alterations have to be executed and attested. The difficulty here would be that the acknowledgement by Phil of his writing in the presence of William and Joan preceded his writing in of Ben's name and therefore can one say that the alteration has been executed. There is no doubt that it has been attested and it would depend upon the view of the court as to how liberal an interpretation the court is prepared to make in the spirit of the changes effected by the amendments to s 9 and given the interpretations and commentary in *Wood v Smith* and *Re White* (1990).

Formal Validity

Question 10

Paul married Helen in 1974. They have one son, Dan, born in 1977. In 1984 Paul made a will leaving everything to Helen. In 1988 Helen divorced Paul after he had left her to go and live with Susan. Paul has now died. Disregarding the possibility of any claims under the Inheritance (Provision for Family and Dependants) Act 1975, advise the disposition of Paul's estate on each of the following alternative hypotheses:

- Paul made a new will in April 1989 leaving Blackacre to Susan but containing no other provision.
- Paul made a new will in April 1989 leaving Blackacre to 'my wife Susan'. The will contained no other provision. He married Susan in the May of 1989.
- Paul made a new will in 1989. The new will expressly revoked the 1984 will and left all his property to Susan (in this case he did not marry Susan but remained living with her until his death). In 1992, after a discussion one evening with a friend, he tore up the 1989 will saying, 'I don't need a will; Susan will get all my property anyway'.

Answer plan

The purpose of this question is to consider various methods of revocation. In particular the effect of the divorce upon the 1984 will; the distribution of the property which would create a partial intestacy; the effect of the marriage upon the 1989 will; finally one would have to consider the doctrine of dependent relative revocation.

Answer

One would assume in a question of this nature that the wills referred to are all validly executed in accordance with s 9 Wills Act 1837. The will of 1984 is straightforward. The issue is the effect of the divorce in 1988. In the case of deaths on or after the 1 January 1983 s 18(a)(1) of the Wills Act 1837 created by s 18(2) of the Administration of Justice Act 1982 provides that where a testator has made a will and subsequently the marriage is dissolved any devise or bequest to the former spouse shall lapse (1).

In the case of part (a) there is no mention in the will of April 1989 that the will contained an expressed revocation clause. Assuming the will does not contain such a clause the 1989 will revokes the will of 1984 to the extent of the gift of Blackacre to Susan. The 1989 will does not contain any other provision; therefore, one would fall back to the earlier will of 1984. However, since that will gave all the property to Helen and, subsequent to the 1984 will, Helen and Paul have divorced, Helen would not be able to take the remainder of the property under the 1984 will (s 18(a)). The remainder of the property would therefore devolve on intestacy. Helen would not be entitled as she is no longer a spouse. Susan could not take on the intestacy as she is not married to Paul; therefore, Dan would take the remainder of the property as he is an issue of Paul. Dan would be able to take absolutely as he is now of age.

The effect of the will of April 1989 would partially revoke the will of 1984. The difference here is to consider the effect of the marriage of Paul and Susan subsequent to the will of April 1989. Section 18(1) of the Wills Act 1837 as amended by s 18 of the Administration of Justice Act 1982 provides that a will shall be revoked by the testator's marriage (2). If the will of 1989 is revoked by the subsequent marriage then, depending upon the value of Paul's estate this would be divided on intestacy between Susan as the surviving spouse and, if there are sufficient funds after dealing with the personal chattels and the statutory legacy of £125,000, both of which go to Susan, then Dan would be entitled to a share of half the remaining value of the estate.

Section 18 of the Wills Act goes on to provide that where it appears from the will that the testator was expecting to be married to a particular person then the will is not revoked by a subsequent marriage to that person. Susan would be arguing here for the will not to be revoked for she could then claim Blackacre under the will in addition to claiming her share of the remainder of the estate on intestacy as the surviving spouse. Is the will made in expectation of marriage? The Administration of Justice Act 1982 amended s 18 by repealing the original provision, s 177 Law of Property Act 1925, which referred to any will made in contemplation of marriage. The law was reviewed by Megarry VC in *Re Coleman* (1976) where he confirmed that a will is not revoked where the whole of the property is left to a named fiancée and the testator subsequently marries that person as in *Re Langston* (1953) (3). However, Megarry disapproved of the decision in *Pilot v Gainfort* (1931) where the beneficiary was described by the testator as 'his wife' when at the time of the will he was not married to the person but did marry her some time after the will. The court held that the will was made in contemplation of marriage however, Megarry said that contemplation denotes a future event whereas describing someone as 'my wife' refers to a past event namely the previous marriage. The issue here would be whether the court would accept that a reference to 'my wife' when the marriage takes place shortly afterwards would be sufficient to amount to an expectation that is to say an impending marriage. In *Re Coleman* Megarry said that the whole will must be made in contemplation of marriage. By s 18(4) of the amended s 18 one can now have individual gifts in a will expressed to be in expectation of marriage. Therefore, if the court accepts the reference to 'my wife' then the gift of Blackacre to Susan will not be revoked by the subsequent marriage.

Whether or not the 1989 will contains an express revocation clause, the fact that it is wholly inconsistent with the 1984 will will mean that the 1989 will revokes the 1984 will in total. See for example, *Pepper v Pepper* (1870). In any event the subsequent divorce will have caused the gift to Helen to lapse; therefore, if Paul had died prior to making the 1989 will, the whole of the property will have passed on intestacy to Dan. As it is, all the property would pass to Susan under the 1989 will provided Paul has not revoked the will of 1989 following the conversation in 1992.

Section 20 of the Wills Act 1837 provides, *inter alia*, that a will may be revoked by 'burning, tearing, or otherwise destroying the same with the intention to revoke'. The act of destruction and the intention, must be concurrent. We are told that Paul tore up the will of 1989. As a physical act this would amount to a total revocation, see, for example, in the goods of *Re Morton* (1887), in the estate of *Nunn* (1936) but compare the lack of destruction in *Cheese v Lovejoy* (1877) (4). However, apart from the act of destruction, one must prove that the testator formed a clear intention to revoke, the *animus revocandi*. So, for example, in *Brunt* (1873) the will was not revoked where the testator tore up the will in the course of suffering from delirium; or, *Re Booth* (1926) where the will was accidentally destroyed by fire.

It would appear at first glance that Paul does intend to revoke the will. However, in order to be valid the intention must be clear and without any qualification. Paul is mistaken in that since he has not married Susan, she would not be entitled to share on Paul's resulting intestacy (5). Susan could still take if she could successfully argue that the 1989 will is not revoked on the basis of the doctrine of dependent relative revocation. Susan could argue that Paul's intention to revoke is flawed in that it has been made on a mistaken belief as in the estate of *Southerden* (1925). In *Southerden*, Pollock MR said:

'... the two of you may be that a revocation grounded on the assumption of fact which is false takes effect unless, as a matter of construction, the truth of the fact is the condition of the revocation or, in other words, unless the revocation is contingent upon the fact being true.'

In *Re Jones* (1976) Buckley LJ in the Court of Appeal said that where a testator destroys his will, one would ask a series of questions. Firstly, did the testator destroy the will with the intention of revoking it? If he did not then there can be no revocation. If there was an intention to revoke, is the intention absolute or qualified? If it is qualified, what is the nature of the qualification? If the qualification is in the form of a condition or contingency, has the condition or contingency been fulfilled? If not, then the revocation is ineffective (6). In *Re Finnemore (dec'd)* (1992) the court held that an express revocation clause was conditional on the basis that such a clause could give a distributive meaning thereby enabling the court to interpret the clause as applying absolutely to some provisions, but only conditionally to others. In interpreting it in this way, the court was able to apply the doctrine of conditional revocation to save a gift in an earlier will, which had been struck down in a subsequent will owing to the effect of s 15 of the Wills Act 1837, in that the beneficiary had been a witness to the subsequent will. If, therefore, Susan could establish that Paul's intention in tearing up the will is qualified, and the nature of the qualification is such that the tearing up is conditional upon Paul's assumption being correct then the will would not be revoked and Susan could take all the property. Susan would, of course, have to establish proof of the contents of the will. The court would accept an authenticated completed draft copy of the will as secondary evidence as to contents (see, for example, *Re Webb* (1964)). The court would also consider statements by parties having a knowledge of the contents as to the contents of the will and even statements by Susan as principal beneficiary (see *Sugden v Lord St Leonards* (1876)) (7).

Formal Validity

Notes

1. In *Re Sinclair* (1985) the Court of Appeal construed 'lapse' to refer to the happening of an event such as divorce. The effect of this interpretation was not to trigger a gift in favour of a named charity where the precondition was the wife's predeceasing or failing to survive the testator for one month.
2. Marriage here would include a voidable marriage as in *Re Roberts* (1978) but not a void marriage as in *de Renville v de Renville* (1948).
3. In *Re Coleman*, Megarry VC held that the will was revoked by the subsequent marriage on the basis that the whole will was not made in contemplation of marriage, simply a gift in favour of the fiancée. This point is now dealt with by s 18(4) of the Wills Act 1837.
4. The action in *Cheese v Lovejoy* arose because the provision prior to the Wills Act 1837, in the Statute of Frauds 1677, referred to burning, tearing and cancelling the same. Did cancellation come within the wording in s 20 'burning, tearing or otherwise destroying the same'? – 'No' said the court in *Cheese v Lovejoy*, the words 'otherwise destroying the same should be construed in relation to burning and tearing'.
5. Even if Paul had married Susan, Susan would not necessarily have taken the whole of the estate, for this would depend upon the value and the possibility that Dan could share on the intestacy.
6. In *Re Jones* the court concluded that the testatrix had revoked her first will (by scratching out her signature) and this act was not qualified as being dependent upon the second will being valid; therefore, where the testatrix died before she could execute the second will the court ruled that the estate passed on the total intestacy.
7. The court concluded that Lord St Leonards, a former Lord Chancellor, held his will in such regard that this negated the presumption that he had revoked the will *animus revocandi* when the will could not be found at his death. The court then admitted evidence from one of his daughters who had acted as his secretary and was familiar with the phraseology of the will.

Question 11

'All the destroying in the world without intention will not revoke a will, nor all the intention in the world without destroying: there must be the two,' *per* James LJ in *Cheese v Lovejoy* (1877).

Discuss this statement.

Answer plan

The question is asking for a detailed analysis of s 20 of the Wills Act 1837 as to the meaning of revocation by destruction and the requirement that the act of destruction must be concurrent with the intention to revoke. One has to consider what is meant by destruction and consider examples of ways in which the intention is not clearly formed.

Answer

The key characteristic of the law of wills is that a will is revocable at any time prior to the death of the testator. A will cannot be made irrevocable (*Vynior's Case* (1609)). A will can only be revoked in one of the ways laid down by the Wills Act 1837. Apart from informal revocation where the testator may be in privileged status, the statutory power to revoke is contained in ss 20 and 18 of the Wills Act 1837. Section 18 is concerned with the revocation by marriage and is inapplicable here. The quote is concerned with the interpretation of that part of s 20 which refers to revocation by 'burning, tearing or otherwise destroying the same' by the testator or some other person in the presence and on the direction of the testator with the intention to revoke.

In order to effect a valid revocation s 20 requires an act of destruction coupled with a contemporaneous intention to revoke. How are the words 'or otherwise destroying the same' interpreted? Prior to the Wills Act 1837 revocation by destruction was governed by the Statute of Frauds 1677. This Act referred to 'burning, tearing and cancelling the same'. In *Cheese v Lovejoy* the testator drew his pen through some lines in the will and wrote on the back 'all these are revoked' and threw the will into a pile of waste paper. The will was subsequently retrieved by a housemaid and the court held that it had not been revoked. The court construed 'or otherwise destroying the same' in relation to the prior words 'burning and tearing'.

What does amount to destruction? Where the court construes the action as mere cancellation this will not affect the revocation as shown in *Cheese v Lovejoy* and in *Stephens v Taprell* (1840) where the testator crossed out certain dispositions and put a line through his name. The court asked the question is the act of destruction such as to impair the entirety of the will? So in a case prior to the Wills Act *Hobbs v Knight* (1838) the will had been so heavily scored over that the signatures of the testator and the witnesses could not be read. The court considered that this showed an intention to revoke the entire will. In *Re Adams* (1990) the testator had scribbled over his signature with a ball-point pen. The court considered the extent of the obliteration and by analogy with s 21 of the Wills Act which refers to the admission of unattested alterations asked the question could the signature be read with the normal aids to eyesight? The answer was no, and the court concluded that the intention was to revoke the entire will. If, therefore, the signature is still legible the will may still be regarded as admissible as in *Re Godfrey* (1893) (1).

The act of destruction must take place with a concurrent clearly formed intention to revoke. The will need not be destroyed by the testator, the act could be carried out by someone else provided this takes place in the presence of the testator and on his direction. In *Gill v Gill* (1909) the will was torn up by the wife of the testator in the course of a row with her husband. Although one had committed the act of destruction there was no concurrent intention (2). The testator in *Gill v Gill* did not take any steps to replace the will and it is likely that he subsequently agreed with his wife's action. However, the intention to revoke must coincide with the act of destruction, see for example *Mills v Millward* (1889) where the court rejected that one could have subsequent ratification of an act of destruction.

The intention to revoke must be clearly formed. Therefore, where the testator lacks the mental capacity to form the intention there can be no revocation. For example, in *Brunt v Brunt* (1873) the will was not revoked where the testator tore up the will in the course of suffering *delirium tremens* or in the goods of *Brassington*

(1902) where the testator destroyed the will whilst drunk. The test for mental capacity is the same as that required for the making of a valid will (*Re Sabatini* (1969)).

There can be no valid revocation where the will is destroyed by accident, see in the goods of *Re Taylor* (1890) or where the will had been destroyed in the belief that it had already been revoked as in *Scott v Scott* (1859) where there was a mistaken belief that a later will had already revoked it. Qualified revocation was considered by the Court of Appeal in *Re Jones* (1976). The court said one should ask a series of questions. When the testator destroyed his will was the intention to revoke qualified or unqualified? If it was unqualified the will is revoked. If the intention is qualified one then considers the nature of the qualification. If the qualification is in the form of a condition or contingency, has that condition or contingency been fulfilled? If it has not then the revocation is ineffective (2). The questions posed are asked where the court considers the doctrine of conditional or dependent relative revocation.

Where the original will was known to be in the possession of the testator there are two rebuttable evidential presumptions to consider. Firstly, where the original will cannot be found at death there is a presumption that the will has been revoked by the testator *animus revocandi* (*Allan v Morrison* (1900)). This presumption will vary according to the security surrounding the keeping of the will, the safer the security the stronger is the presumption, see *dicta* in *Sugden v Lord St Leonards* (1876) (3). This presumption is rebuttable by evidence, for example that the testator intended to adhere to the will (*Sugden v Lord St Leonards*). The court will also presume, where the will was known to be in the possession of the testator, and is found in a torn or mutilated condition at the death of the testator, that the testator has carried out the act of destruction *animus revocandi* (*Lambell v Lambell* (1831)). This again can be rebutted by evidence to the contrary. The burden of proof is on the balance of probabilities and would rest with the person seeking to propound the will as validly admissible.

Notes
1   There was commentary in *Re Adams* that the decision in *Re Godfrey* rested on the fact that all the interested parties accepted that the will was valid rather than on a formal ruling by the

Formal Validity

judge to that effect. An interesting case is that of the estate of *Nunn* (1936) where the testatrix cut certain beneficiaries out of the will, literally, and then pasted the will together again. If she had stopped there the will would have been admissible; however, she went on at a later date to cut off the part of the will containing her signature and the signature of the witnesses and the court concluded that the entire will had then been revoked.

2 On the facts in *Re Jones* the court concluded that the testatrix had mutilated the will herself with the intention of revoking the will prior to consulting her solicitor about making a new will. She died before instructions could be given for a new will and here estate was distributed on intestacy.

3 The court found that the will was not kept under close security in the *Sugden* case. The testator had been taken ill and it was known that the will was kept in a deed box close to him. The testator made a partial recovery and then there was a relapse and in the course of his being moved following these events the will disappeared.

Question 12

Patrick made a will in 1980 by which he left his property to be divided between his wife, Sarah, and his daughter, Ellen. Earlier this year, incensed by what he regarded as Ellen's wayward behaviour, Patrick decided to make a new will leaving all his property to his wife and the local cats' home.

Patrick took his new will to the golf club and asked two of his friends, Tom and Jerry, to witness it. He started to sign the will but before the signature was completed Patrick suffered a heart attack and collapsed. Tom tried to revive him whilst Jerry rushed outside to telephone for a doctor. Before Jerry returned Patrick revived and with Tom's help finished his signature. Tom immediately signed as a witness and on Jerry's return Tom said: 'Hurry up and sign before it's too late.' Patrick nodded weakly and Jerry signed. Patrick was then rushed to hospital where he recovered.

On returning home Patrick told his wife about the new will. She then tore up his earlier will and threw it in the dustbin saying: 'You won't need this old one any more then.'

Patrick has recently died.

Advise Ellen. (Ignore the possibility of claims under the Inheritance (Provision for Family and Dependants) Act 1975.)

Answer plan

This problem involves consideration of the rules as to formal validity in s 9 of the Wills Act 1837 and the provisions relating to revocation in s 20. In addition one should consider the possibility of the application of the doctrine of dependent relative revocation.

This is a popular area in the law of succession. The danger, when faced with problems on popular areas, is a tendency to write what one knows about the entire topic rather than applying the relevant law to the facts of the question.

Answer

The first consideration is whether the latest will is valid. Ellen, the daughter, will want to argue that this will is invalid and inadmissible to probate for she would then be able to take under the terms of the will made in 1980.

Is this latest will valid under the terms of s 9 of the Wills Act 1837? The formal requirements set out in s 9 are that the will should be signed or acknowledged by the testator in the presence of two witnesses present at the same time. The facts show that Patrick started to sign the will but before the signature was completed he suffered a heart attack and collapsed. Further, he went on to complete his signature but before the second witness, Jerry, had returned. In order to sign a will in the presence of the witnesses, the testator must do all he can. This is contrasting the cases of *Re Colling* (1948) and *In The Goods of Chalcraft* (1948). In *Re Colling* the testator had started to sign when one witness was called away from the bedside in such a way that he was no longer 'in the presence of' the testator. The testator continued to sign his name in the presence of the remaining witness and this witness signed before the other witness returned. The will was inadmissible to probate as it had not been 'signed' in the presence of two witnesses present at the same time. This is to be contrasted with the *Chalcraft* case where the testatrix started to sign her name in the presence of the witnesses but could not continue owing to declining health. The court ruled that the testatrix had done all she could in signing her name and therefore the will was admissible. Here we are told that Patrick revived and with Tom's help finished his signature. Although a will can be signed by someone else in the presence of the testator and on the testator's direction, the problem here is that the other witness, Jerry, had not returned. At that stage, therefore, the will would be inadmissible to probate by virtue of s 9 para B.

The interested parties propounding the latest will as valid could then argue that the testator's signature has been acknowledged in the presence of the witnesses. Section 9 provides that the testator can acknowledge his signature in the presence of two witnesses. The witnesses should then sign the will or acknowledge their signatures in the presence of the testator. (This is an application of the amended s 9 by s 17 of the Administration of Justice Act 1982 which seeks to overcome the 'mechanical' failure of wills as occurred in *Re Colling*.) The court would have to consider whether Patrick's weak response to Tom saying 'Hurry up and sign before it is too late' is a sufficient acknowledgment in the presence of the two witnesses. In order for there to be a valid acknowledgment the witnesses must be in a position to see the signature of the testator and the testator must give some indication either by words or gestures that that is his signature. Even if this is considered to be a valid acknowledgment the court would have to be satisfied as to the role of the witnesses before the will could be admitted under the terms of s 9. The facts show that Tom signed as a witness before Jerry's return. If the acknowledgment by Patrick is to be accepted, Tom should also acknowledge his signature in the presence of Patrick and Jerry given that Jerry had signed in the presence of all three. If it cannot be proved that Tom acknowledged his signature in the presence of Patrick and Jerry then the will is inadmissible.

If the latest will is admissible and contains an express revocation clause, then the earlier will of 1980 is revoked. Even if this latest will does not contain an express revocation clause, it will be placed alongside the earlier will and will revoke the earlier will to the extent of any inconsistency. This would again revoke the 1980 will for Patrick by his latest will leaves all his property to his wife and the local cats' home.

The latest will could be challenged for want of formal validity as explained above. In addition there is a possibility of a challenge on the basis of capacity in view of Patrick suffering a suspected heart attack and being weak when the purported acknowledgment occurs. One would have to show that Patrick fell within the test as to sound mind, memory and understanding, formulated in *Banks v Goodfellow* (1870). Even if there was some doubt as to capacity at the time of execution, it is possible the rule in *Parker v Felgate* (1883) could be invoked if it was the case that the latest will had been prepared by a solicitor and it could be proved that Patrick reasonably believed at the time of execution that the will accorded with the instructions he had given.

If the latest will is inadmissible for want of validity or capacity, is the 1980 will revoked? In order to effect revocation by destruction under the terms of s 20 of the Wills Act 1837, the testator must destroy the will by burning or tearing with the intention to revoke. The Act need not be done by the testator so long as it is done in his presence and on his direction. Did Patrick's wife tear up the earlier will in Patrick's presence? The implication is that she did so because of her saying 'You won't need this old one any more then'. One would have to prove that Patrick indicated by some act that he agreed with her action; if not then the will is not revoked.

An alternative line is that even if the act of destruction is considered sufficient within s 20, that is, Sarah destroyed the will in Patrick's presence and on his direction, Ellen could possibly argue that the revocation is flawed by applying the doctrine of dependent relative revocation. In order for this to succeed Ellen would have to prove that Patrick intended the earlier will to be destroyed only upon condition that the latest will would be admitted to probate. If that was the case and the latest will is inadmissible, then the court could rule that the 1980 will is not revoked and the property would be shared between Patrick's wife Sarah and his daughter Ellen.

Question 13

Last year, Alan, a bachelor aged 78, whilst recovering from illness refused the advice of his sister May that he should make a will. Alan told her: 'I haven't much to leave and in any event it will all go to you and our Ken'. Ken is the only child of Alan's deceased brother Tim. May resented this as she was not on good terms with Ken. Six months ago Alan won £300,000 on the national lottery.

Formal Validity

Alan then suffered a stroke which left him partially paralysed and unable to write. He asks May to prepare a will leaving his collection of sporting prints to the local golf club and the remainder equally between May and Ken.

May uses a will form and consults a book of will precedents from the library. After the gift of the prints there are a series of complicated clauses which have the effect of giving more of the residue to May. The form also appoints May as executrix.

Alan reads through the form in the presence of May and two friends. The form contains a printed revocation clause. May has written in Alan's name. May asks him if it is all right. Alan replies: 'I think so.' May then points to the attestation and Alan puts a tick against his name. May is then called to answer the door to visitors. When they have gone Alan tells her the friends had signed as witnesses and the will is locked in his deed box.

Alan died last week. May finds that Ken's name has been added alongside her name as executor. Ken is working overseas on a contract expected to last six months. When he learns of the contents he is unhappy about the unequal split of the residue.

May is anxious to prove the will as soon as possible. Further, representatives of the golf club want the will to be proved quickly as the prints prove to be valuable and the club needs funds to modernise the clubhouse.

Advise Ken on the validity of the will.

Answer plan

The question combines the areas of capacity to make a valid will with the formal requirements in s 9 Wills Act 1837. There is the general test as to capacity set out in *Banks v Goodfellow* (1870) together with the general proposition that the testator must know and approve of the contents of the will. Knowledge and approval can be challenged on the basis of suspicion. In addition probate may be refused for failure to comply with the formalities in s 9. The query is, if the will is in accordance with s 9 could it still fail wholly for want of capacity or could the gift to the golfclub be valid and the remainder fail? The court query the insertion of Ken's name as executor; is the insertion attested in accordance with s 9?

Answer

May will be anxious to prove the will as the last wishes of Alan. The court will query the apparent additional appointment of Ken as executor. Is the insertion attested in accordance with s 9 Wills Act 1837? In practice the court will accept the initials of the testator and the witnesses. Could Alan add his initials anyway, given that he could not sign his name to the will form but put a tick against his name? If there is no initialling then there would have to be proof that the name was added at the time of execution. It was not done when May pointed to Alan's name. If it was added when she left the room and before the witnesses signed did Alan acknowledge the insertion? The court would require affidavit evidence as to proof, sworn by the two friends who acted as witnesses. In any event would the court accept that Ken could act as an executor now, given that he is working on a contract overseas? If the appointment is valid it is more likely power would be reserved for Ken to act should he return. This presupposes Alan had the intention to appoint May as executor since he did not include this in his original instructions. May could argue he had read the will and seen the appointment.

Ken should be advised that the will could be challenged for want of capacity. The starting point is the general test laid down by Cockburn CJ in *Banks v Goodfellow* (1870). At the time of execution of the will did Alan have sound mind, memory and understanding? That is to say, did he understand he was making a will? Yes, he had given instructions and had testamentary intent. Did he appreciate the property at his disposal? This does not mean he had to know in detail the value of his assets: it is sufficient if it can be demonstrated he knew whether he was wealthy or of modest means. Here it would appear he appreciates the value of his estate save a possible query as to whether he knew the true value of the gift to the golf club. Did he intend to leave the club a high value gift? The third limb of the Cockburn CJ test is one of understanding, did Alan consider the persons one would expect him to consider? The answer here is clearly yes as he leaves the bulk of the estate to his surviving close relatives.

The issue as to capacity here is the discrepancy between wanting to leave the residue equally between May and Ken and the actual result where more is left to May. The problem for May is

Formal Validity

Ken could challenge the will on the general ground that Alan lacked the requisite knowledge and approval. Lord Penzance in *Guardhouse v Blackburn* (1866) stated the propositions for the court to consider where the will is put to proof. The court must be satisfied the testator knew and approved of the contents of the will. *Prima facie*, execution by the testator indicates knowledge and approval unless there is evidence of suspicious circumstances. The testator must have intended the document to take effect as a will, that is, to dispose of property on death. There must be no fraud. Here, Alan intended the document to be his will. The fact he read over the will would be *prima facie* evidence of knowledge and approval. However the court will weigh the complexity of the will together with evidence of the state of health and age of the testator (*Re Morris* (1971)). In *Re Morris* Latey J admitted that the question of determining knowledge and approval is not an easy one and, in past cases, has produced mental gymnastics. Was the attempt at drafting by May genuine? Did she appreciate the true meaning of the complicated clauses? If she did not understand them could Alan? Is he bound by what he has signed as in *Collins v Ellstone*? The strongest argument Ken could apply is one of suspicion given that May has prepared the will form and she is a major beneficiary.

May would have a problem countering the view of the court where a beneficiary is instrumental in preparing the will as expressed by Parke B in *Barry v Butlin* (1838). Baron Parke said in such circumstances the court should be vigilant in examining the evidence. In *Fulton v Andrew* (1875) the testator made a will in 1870 which was in the handwriting of one of his executors, W. The will contained long list of legacies, including one to W, and the residue equally between W and A, the other executor. Evidence showed that the will had been left with the testator a few days before execution. (The argument being that the testator had opportunity in that time to consider the will and give approval.) Further evidence revealed there were discrepancies between the testator's instructions and the will. The court refused probate of that part of the will relating to the disposal of the residue. The golf club could use the decision in *Fulton v Andrew* to contend that although the gift of the residue should be doubted on the ground of suspicion, the legacy to the club should stand. Ken and May would share the reminder of the estate on the resulting partial intestacy. However Ken could argue that, given Alan's age and state of health, coupled with the value of the collection, did Alan really intend to leave such a large legacy to the club? Ken would therefore be combining the general test as to capacity with the strong line the court takes where there are suspicious circumstances. A more recent case on suspicion, *Re Ticehurst* (1973) would support the argument to refuse probate of the whole will where the will was prepared with the assistance of the spouse of a specific legatee.

The degree of suspicion will vary according to the circumstances of the case (*Wintle v Nye* (1959) HL). *Wintle v Nye* shows that the onus of proof where there is suspicion rests with the person propounding the will. In this case the burden will fall on May to show the will does represent the last, free, wishes of the testator.

The will could be challenged on the grounds that it does not comply with the requirements as to form in s 9 Wills Act 1837. Assuming the two friends have signed as witnesses in the presence of Alan the problem is whether Alan has validly executed the will. What does amount to signature? A testator does not have to sign his name, the court will accept initials (*In b Christian* (1849)) and a thumb print (*In b Finn* (1935)). The problem concerns the placing of the signature. Prior to the 1982 amendments s 9 was strict as to the placing of the signature so that, for example, any words following or under the signature were inadmissible, see *Re Stalman* (1931). However s 9(b) now reads: '... the testator intended by his signature to give effect to the will.' Following the change made by s 17 Administration of Justice Act 1982 the courts have demonstrated flexibility in interpreting this subsection. In *Wood v Smith* (1992) the Court of Appeal accepted as a signature the handwriting of the testator when he wrote his name at the start of the document. (The will was inadmissible for want of capacity). In *Weatherhill v Pearce* (1994) the court applied *Wood v Smith* and accepted as a signature the name of the testatrix where she had written her name in the attestation clause. The problem here is Alan has not written his name. May would have to argue the tick, against Alan's name, is a signature. She could not argue the tick is an acknowledgement of the will for to acknowledge there must be a signature and Alan did not write his name, May did.

Although May would be hard pressed to overcome this degree of suspicion, the golf club could still be arguing the will should be admitted to give effect to the legacy, relying on *Fulton v Andrew*.

Formal Validity

Who would administer the estate? Is the appointment of May as executor valid? Evidence could be given by the witnesses and May as to the reading of the will and Alan's failing to object to her inclusion. Further, is the appointment of Ken valid? Assuming the insertion is not initialled to comply with s 20 Wills Act 1837 the witnesses could be put to proof as to whether the name was written in at the time of execution. If the appointment of Ken is valid, would he act given he is working abroad? The appointment of May could be accepted with power reserved for Ken to prove should he return. If the appointments are not valid and the will fails wholly or in part, May and Ken would be entitled to apply for a grant of Administration under Rule 22 of the Non-Contentious Probate Rules 1987. The grant would either be Administration (total intestacy) or Administration with will annexed if, say, the gift to the golf club was ruled to be valid.

Question 14

Alec died last month intestate. His estate consists of:

(1) A house with a total market value at death of £120,000. The house is jointly owned with his wife, Betty.
(2) A car value £10,000, used partly in his business as an accountant and also as his private car.
(3) Furniture, clothes and personal effects value £8,000.
(4) Investments, cash at the bank and proceeds of an insurance policy payable to his administrators on his death, total, after all liabilities have been paid, £245,000.

Alec is survived by Betty, his mother, Mabel (aged 84 and living in a nursing home), his son Paul aged 38 and Susan and Joy, aged 22 and 16 respectively, the daughters of Alec's son Michael who died two years ago. Last year, on the occasion of her wedding, Alec gave Susan £10,000.

Advise upon the distribution of the estate.

Who is entitled to a grant to the estate?

What difference, if any, would there be to the distribution if Betty obtained a decree of judicial separation three months before Alec's death?

Answer plan

This is a typical intestacy problem involving consideration of the rules of distribution on a total intestacy with the added twist of identifying possible administrators to the estate.

The approach should be:
1. Identify those who survive the intestate and who are entitled to share in his estate.
2. Consider the entitlement of the respective beneficiaries.
3. The effect of the gift to Susan upon the distribution of the estate.
4. The persons who are potentially entitled to a grant of administration to the estate.
5. Finally, one would deal with the rider question, the effect of a decree of judicial separation.

Answer

Alec has died totally intestate. Betty would receive the interest in the house by right of survivorship (1). The remainder of Alec's property will be held by his personal representatives on trust for sale with power to postpone the sale without being liable for loss so long as the personal representatives think proper, s 33 Administration of Estates Act 1925. The personal representatives must pay the funeral, testamentary and administration expenses and any debts and thereafter distribute the balance to those entitled on the intestacy (2).

The entitlement to share in the estate of the intestate depends upon the survivorship of individuals and the order of priority contained in s 46 Administration of Estates Act 1925. A surviving spouse has priority over all other categories. The extent of the share of the surviving spouse will depend upon the survivorship of others. In this case the property will be shared between the surviving spouse, Betty, and the surviving issue (3). The survivorship of Betty and issue means that no-one else can be entitled on the intestacy; therefore, Alec's mother will not be able to share.

Betty is entitled to the personal chattels absolutely, £125,000 free of tax and costs plus interest from the date of death until payment (this sum is called the 'statutory legacy') (4). In addition, Betty is entitled to a life interest in half the residue of the estate.

The personal chattels are defined by s 55(1)(x) of the Administration of Estates Act 1925. The furniture, clothes and personal effects belonging to Alec at death and value £8,000 would come within the definition. Section 55 also includes motor vehicles except those used for business purposes. Whether therefore Betty could take the car as a personal chattel would depend upon the degree of business use compared with private use. If Alec used the car primarily for his business then the value of the car will form part of the general estate available for distribution. Next Betty is entitled to the statutory legacy of £125,000. If it is the case that the business use of the car is merely incidental to the private use then the car would pass to Betty by virtue of s 55. Section 55 specifically excludes from its definition investments and cash; therefore the balance of the estate would be represented by the £245,000. If the statutory legacy is deducted this leaves a balance of £120,000 which would be divided as to one half to Betty for life and the other half held on the statutory trusts for the issue. Betty would therefore be entitled to the income yield on a fund of £60,000 for the remainder of her life. On her death the fund would be divided among the issue. By virtue of s 47(1)(a) Administration of Estates Act 1925 the surviving spouse has the right to redeem the life interest. Should the spouse so elect, by serving notice to the personal representatives, Betty would receive a lump sum and the balance of the fund which originally supported the life interest would pass to increase the entitlement of the issue (5).

The issue are Alec's son Paul, and the granddaughters, Susan and Joy. Distribution is on a *per stiripal* basis. Susan and Joy take the share their deceased father Michael would have taken had he survived Alec. The other half of the residue, £60,000, would therefore be divided two ways as to £30,000 to Paul and £30,000 shared equally between Susan and Joy. The issue take upon the statutory trusts, that is to say, their interests vest when the attain 18 or marry under that age. In this case Paul and Susan will obtain vested interests. Paul with therefore take £30,000. Susan will not have to account for the gift of £10,000. Although a gift made on the occasion of marriage is considered to be an advance by virtue of section 47(1)(iii). Section 47 only requires inter vivos advances to be brought in where they have been made to children. As Susan is a granddaughter of Alec she will not have to account. The remaining £15,000 will be held upon the statutory trusts for Joy and will vest when Joy attains 18 or marries under that age (6).

The order of entitlement to a grant of administration to the estate follows the order of priority of beneficial interest to the estate with the addition of creditors, see Non-Contentious Probate Rules 1987 rule 22. The order would therefore be Betty, Paul, Susan and Mabel. Where the intestacy rules create a life interest or there is property held on a contingent interest, for example, in this case the share held on behalf of Joy, the court usually requires at least two administrators to be appointed – s 114 Supreme Court Act 1981. There would have to be two chosen from Betty as priority, then Paul and Susan. It is not likely that Mabel would be considered in view of her age and being confined to a nursing home.

If Betty had obtained a decree of judicial separation then, provided the judicial separation is still in force at the death of Alec and the separation continued until the death, Betty would be treated as pre-deceasing Alec for the purposes of intestate distribution, s 18(2) Matrimonial Causes Act 1973. The effect therefore would be to pass the entire beneficial interest of the estate which passes on the intestacy (that is, excluding the house which would still pass to Betty by virtue of survivorship) to the issue. Therefore, the value of the car and the furniture, clothes and personal effects would be added to the £245,000 and divided into two equal shares, that is, the 'Paul fund', and the fund to be shared by Susan and Joy. There would still have to be two administrators because of the contingent interest passing to Joy. Betty would drop out and, in view of the age of Mabel and her being in a nursing home, administration could be granted to Paul and Susan. If either Paul or Susan were reluctant, Joy, as she is 16, could nominate someone to act as an administrator on her behalf (7).

Notes
1 The half value of the house, say £54,000 allowing for a 10% discount for occupancy of the surviving joint tenant would not be counted as part of the estate for distribution on the intestacy.
2 Personal chattels should not be sold without a special reason. There may, of course, be no choice, for example the chattels may have to be sold in order to pay debts.
3 In problems where there are a number of persons under the heading 'issue', for example where a son or daughter is pre-deceased survived by children and one of those children has

died leaving children, then it is useful to draw a family tree. Once you have identified those who are entitled then draw a vertical list in the order of priority of entitlement. It is useful to list all those who survive and could be on the list of priority rather than simply those who are potentially entitled because the list also then gives you the order of entitlement to a grant to the estate.

4 The statutory legacy was increased from £75,000 to £125,000 in December 1993. Where the intestate is survived by a spouse but no issue, but is survived by parents or brothers and sisters of the intestate and their issue, then the statutory legacy is £200,000 (increased in December 1993 from £125,000).

5 The amount which a surviving spouse receives where the surviving spouse elects to capitalise the life interest is calculated in accordance with the Intestates Succession (Interest and Capitalisation Order) 1977. The calculation is akin to a notional purchase of an annuity for the spouse. The younger the spouse, the higher the capital sum although it would never equal the full capital value of the fund supporting the life interest. A surviving spouse may wish to capitalise where the fund is so small that the administration charges to continue the trust do not make it worth while or, simply where the spouse needs additional capital rather than income.

6 The hotchpot provisions in ss 47 and 49 of the Administration of Estates Act 1925 were abolished by s 1(2) Law Reform (Succession) Act 1995; effective for deaths on or after 1 January 1996.

7 Betty would also lose her entitlement if Alec died on or after 1 January 1996 and Betty failed to survive Alec by 28 days including the date of Alec's death – s 1(1) Law Reform (Succession) Act 1995.

Question 15

Colin, a doctor, died in December 1995. Among his papers there is a will form signed by Colin and witnessed. The form appoints his wife Ruth to be his executor and leaves her the sum of £20,000 together with 'all my personal chattels as defined by s 55(1)(x) Administration of Estates Act 1925'. There is no other provision in the document. At death Colin's estate consists of:

1) A house, Blackacre, in the sole name of Colin with a market value of £95,000.
2) A car valued at £10,000.
3) A collection of commemorative coins inherited from an uncle. Colin has never found the time to display the coins but has kept them at his bank for safe-keeping.
4) Furniture, clothing and personal effects worth £8,000.
5) Investments, cash and insurances totalling £150,000 after all liabilities have been paid.

Colin is survived by Ruth, his son Michael, aged 32, Mary, aged 14 and Anne, aged 17, the daughters of his deceased son William, and Kate, Ruth's daughter from her previous marriage to Ben.

Six years ago Colin gave Michael shares worth £25,000 which Michael used as collateral to a loan to assist his cash flow and then to finance improvements to his joinery workshop. The business has now prospered and the shares are now worth £40,000.

Advise upon the distribution of the estate.

What would be the effect on the distribution if Colin died in February 1996?

Answer plan

The central point of this question is an application of the intestacy rules. There is a clear partial intestacy since the will form merely gives a legacy and personal chattels to Ruth. The question includes a consideration of the meaning of personal chattels approached, instead of by application of the intestacy rules, by the reference in the will form to s 55. One has to consider the beneficial entitlement on the intestacy, the effect of the gifts to Ruth on that entitlement and what appears to be an advance to Michael. The effect of Colin dying in February 1996 is that the hotchpot provisions would no longer apply.

Answer

The last wishes of Colin, the testator, have to be considered first in applying the provisions of the will form. On the basis that this is executed in accordance with s 9 Wills Act 1837 then Ruth is entitled to the pecuniary legacy of £20,000 together with all personal chattels as defined by s 55(1)(x) Administration of Estates Act 1925. Section 55 refers to furniture and effects provided they are not used for business purposes, motor cars but excluding those used for business purposes, and the section also excludes money or securities for money. Clearly the furniture, clothing and personal effects under item 4 at a value of £8,000 will pass to Ruth under the terms of the bequest. In the case of the car one would look at the primary use of the vehicle and given that Colin is a doctor it is likely that the car would have a predominant business use and therefore would not pass under the terms of the bequest.

The collection of commemorative coins in clause 3 is more difficult to determine. On the face of it coins would appear to come within the specific exclusion of money under the section. However, the coins as described would not appear to be currency, rather a collection which, akin to a hobby, could come within the general words of s 55 namely articles of personal use and enjoyment. The fact that Colin has not added to this collection and indeed has deposited it at the bank would not alter the view that the items could be considered to be personal chattels.

In *Re Crispin's Will Trusts* (1975) the Court of Appeal considered the definition in s 55 in respect of a collection of clocks and watches which had been inherited by the deceased. The collection had never been added to by the deceased and, although he kept the clocks in good working order, they were locked away in various rooms in the house. The Court of Appeal said that it was irrelevant that they had been kept locked away. The court considered that the clocks were articles of furniture and the watches were intrinsically articles of personal use and enjoyment. If therefore the coins are considered to be collectables rather than currency it would appear that they would pass under the terms of the bequest. The monies referred to in clause 5 would be specifically excluded under the terms of s 55.

The persons who would be included in order of priority on the partial intestacy under s 46 Administration of Estates Act 1925 are Ruth, the surviving spouse; Michael together with Mary and Anne who would all fall in the category of issue of the intestate deceased. Kate would not be included within the order under s 46 as she is not issue of Colin (1). Mary and Anne would take the share which would have gone to their father William if he had survived Colin.

Ruth is already entitled to the personal chattels as defined in accordance with the terms of the will form. On the partial intestacy she would be entitled to the fixed net sum known was the statutory legacy together with a life interest in half of the remainder. In view of the survivorship of issue the statutory legacy is £125,000. However, by virtue of s 49(1) Administration of Estates Act, Ruth must bring into account the legacy received under the will against the value of the statutory legacy. Therefore, the statutory legacy would be reduced to £105,000 (2). On the basis that the car would not be included within the definition of personal chattels, the value of the remainder of the estate would be £255,000 being the value of Blackacre plus the car and the investments, insurances and cash. After the deduction of the net statutory legacy, the value of the remainder would be £150,000. Ruth would be entitled to a life interest in half the value of the remainder, that is to say a fund of £75,000. The other half of the remainder would pass to the issue on the statutory trusts.

Ruth could serve notice on the administrators to capitalise the fund supporting the life interest. Instead of, therefore, taking a income from that fund for the remainder of her life, her entitlement would be translated into a lower capital sum. The amount would depend upon, *inter alia*, Ruth's age at the time of the capitalisation. If she did choose to take a capital sum then the balance remaining of the capital would pass to the issue. Blackacre, the former matrimonial home, will not pass automatically to Ruth under the terms of the partial intestacy. If Ruth wishes to take Blackacre she will have to do so against her entitlement under the will and intestacy. If Ruth did serve notice of appropriation of the house this would reduce her cash settlement of the statutory legacy to £10,000.

The half remainder of the residue going to the issue would be divided into two funds, the Michael fund and the William fund. The William fund would be further sub-divided into two equal shares for the benefit of Mary and Anne. The issue take the funds on the statutory trusts. In arriving at the division of the funds, one would have to consider whether the gift of shares four years ago would have to be brought into account under the hotchpot provisions under s 47(1)(iii) Administration of Estates Act 1925. Is the gift of shares an advance? An advancement must be distinguished from a mere gift *inter vivos*. An advancement is a payment whose purpose is to establish a child in life or make some permanent provision for the child – *Hardy v Shaw* (1975). A large gift is presumed to be an advancement, see *Taylor v Taylor* (1875).

The gift of shares would appear to be a substantial gift, therefore an advance. However, *dicta* in *Taylor* suggests that payments made by way of temporary assistance to help a business in difficulties are not regarded as advances. However, in this case there is a reference to the monies relating to improvements; therefore the gift would be considered to be an advance. Michael could possibly counter this by arguing that Colin had indicated a contrary intention either expressly or impliedly – see *dicta* in *Hardy v Shaw*. Michael would have to adduce evidence of Colin's intention that the gift should not be brought into account. The gift to Anne on the occasion of her marriage would automatically be considered to be an advance. However, this does not have to be taken into account as s 47(1) requires only advances to children to be brought into account and not remoter issue.

If Michael can establish evidence of a contrary intention on the part of Colin then the fund of £75,000 would be divided into two parts. Michael would be entitled to £37,500 and the remainder would be sub-divided as to £18,750 for Anne and £18,750 to Mary. Michael and Anne could take their shares as they are both of age. Mary would have to wait until she attains 18 or marries in order to take her share of the fund. If Michael could not prove a contrary intention, the value of the shares would have to be brought into account under the terms of s 47(1). The shares would have to be brought in at their value on the death of the intestate, that is £40,000 and not their value at the date the gift was made (3).

The £40,000 worth of shares would have to be added therefore to the £75,000 giving a total of £115,000 then divided equally between the Michael fund and the William fund giving values of £57,500 respectively. The hotchpot provisions would then require that the £40,000 be deducted from Michael's share leaving a balance to him of £17,500 and the remaining £57,500 to be divided equally between Anne and Mary. Mary again could not take her share until she attains 18 or earlier marriage.

If Colin died in February 1996 s 1(3) of the Law Reform (Succession) Act 1995 would apply. The section abolishes the hotchpot provisions in both ss 47 and 49 of the Administration of Estates Act 1925. Ruth would not have to account for the £20,000: therefore she would be entitled to the full amount of the statutory legacy of £125,000. Michael would not have to account for the value of the shares so the Michael and William funds would be divided equally. The William fund would then be further sub-divided as above.

Notes
1 The only way in which Kate could be included in the beneficial entitlement is if she had been legally adopted by Colin.
2 If the pecuniary legacy under the will had exceeded the statutory legacy Ruth would not have to account for the difference – s 49(1).
3 On the basis that this is an advance that would have to be brought into account, it would have been better for Michael if Colin had given the cash and let the donee buy the asset, thereby fixing the value of the advance at the time it was made.

Question 16

'The definition of "personal chattels" in s 55(1)(x) of the Administration of Estates Act 1925 (AEA) is defective and out of date and should be replaced.'

Discuss.

Answer plan

This essay question is not simply asking for a description of personal chattels followed by some case examples, but rather it is asking for a critique of the section. The essence of the section should be given, not necessarily in full detail, followed by examples in the way in which the section has been interpreted. Finally, a critique should be considered.

Answer

Where a person dies wholly intestate or partially intestate, the order of persons entitled to share under the intestacy is determined by s 46 of the Administration of Estates Act 1925. Where the intestate is survived by a spouse, the spouse is entitled, *inter alia*, to the personal chattels as defined by s 55(1)(x).

The section is somewhat dated in its tone as it is now nearly 70 years old. The section specified certain items, for example, carriages, horses, stable furniture and effects, domestic animals, linen, china, glass, books, furniture, jewellery and includes general words by reference to 'articles of personal use'. There are specific exclusions for items used for business purposes and the section excludes money or securities for money. The intention of the section is to cover items of personal and domestic use and ornament. Where an item falls within the definition, the item will pass to the surviving spouse absolutely. Litigation has arisen over particular items in view of their value. For example, in *Re Reynolds* (1966) the court was asked to consider whether a stamp collection made by the testator as a hobby came within the definition where the testator by his will had bequeathed the personal chattels as defined by s 55(1)(x). The case (heard by Mr Justice Stamp!) is a good illustration of the approach. Counsel for the beneficiary tried to argue that the stamp collection came within the reference to 'books'. The judge rejected this argument but did say that the collection came within the general words of 'personal use'. This interpretation was underlined by the fact that the testator had collected the stamps as a hobby. The judge did draw the contrast that if the testator had bought the collection in one lot and locked it away, one could argue that this had been bought for investment purposes rather than personal use and enjoyment.

An example where the chattel came within a specific enumeration is *Re Hutchinson* (1955) where the intestate deceased owned 12 race horses which were used entirely for recreation. A summons for direction was taken for the court to determine whether the race horses were personal chattels and therefore would pass to the surviving spouse absolutely. The court said that although the reference to 'horses' in the subsection was mentioned in the context of 'stable furniture and effects' there was nothing in the section to suggest the term should be confined to work horses; therefore horses used for domestic purposes, here race horses, could be included. There was no suggestion that the race horses were used as part of a business; therefore the court concluded that they were personal chattels. Another example of where a specific reference was queried in the context occurred in *Re Whitby* (1944) where the court had to consider whether a quantity of cut but unmounted diamonds fell within the word 'jewellery'. Did one link the word jewellery to adornment, therefore including only jewels which would be in a setting for example such as a brooch. The court referred to the *Oxford Dictionary* meaning of jewellery which referred to jewels as '... jewels collectively or as a form of adornment'. The court concluded that therefore individual precious stones could still be considered to be jewellery within the definition.

As referred to above, litigation has arisen in view of the high value of a particular item in relation to the remainder to the estate. In *Re Crispin's Will Trusts* (1975) the testator bequeathed all his personal chattels to his sister. The question arose as to whether the gift included a large collection of clocks and watches which the testator had inherited. The total value of the estate at death was £80,000 and £50,000 of this represented the value of the collection. At first instance the court doubted whether the testator intended to make such a high value gift to his sister and ruled that the collection fell into residue. On appeal, the court said that the judge had been swayed by the high value of the collection when the value was really irrelevant. The issue was whether the collection came within the definition. The testator had assisted his friend to build up the collection and the friend bequeathed the collection to the testator. The testator bought a larger house to accommodate the collection but thereafter never added to the collection. He ensured that basic maintenance work was carried out on the clocks and he occasionally wore one of the watches. The watch collection was normally secured in a large chest. The Court of Appeal held that clocks are articles or furniture in the ordinary sense of the word and it did not matter where the items were kept, whether in a locked room or in a museum. The court went on to rule that the collection of watches were personal chattels since they were intrinsically of personal use. Lord Justice Russell went on the query the example given by Mr Justice Stamp in *Re Reynolds* when he contrasted the situation where a person buys a stamp collection for investment. Lord Justice Russell said that this could still be considered an item of personal use within the section.

The section is clearly dated. The reference to horses, stable furniture and effects is redolent of an age gone by. Further, the structure of the section is such that litigation has sought to attempt to include items within specific references, *Re Reynolds* is a case in

Formal Validity

point, rather than using general words of personal use. The Law Commission recommended in its recent review of intestate distribution that the surviving spouse should take all the property of the deceased on the intestacy. If this recommendation had been taken up, this would have obviated the need for consideration of the section on intestacy. However, a common provision in wills, *Re Crispin's Will Trust* is a case in point, is where the testator bequeaths his personal chattels 'as defined by s 55(1)(x)'. One could still have interpretation problems therefore, unless the section was repealed and replaced by a much broader definition based upon articles of personal use and enjoyment. *Re Crispin's Will Trust* does indicate that the value of the item is irrelevant in determining whether or not it is a personal chattel. What is still perhaps left open is where items are bought purely for investment.

Question 17

Harry, aged 64, and his wife Anne, aged 62, died last week in a car crash. There are not children of the marriage. By his will Harry left £10,000 to his nephew Neil and the remainder of his estate to Anne, but if she should pre-decease him then to his niece Meg. Anne left all her estate to Harry with the proviso that if should pre-decease her then all her estate to her nephew Oliver.

Consider the entitlement to the respective estates of Harry and Anne in the following unrelated circumstances:

(a) where the evidence shows that Harry survived Anne by a few hours;
(b) where there is no evidence to show the order in which the deaths occurred;
(c) where there is no evidence as to the order of the deaths and Harry died intestate.

Answer plan

The issue in part (a) is straightforward. The main thrust of the question is a consideration of the statutory presumption as to survivorship in s 184 Law of Property Act 1925 and an application of the survivorship rule and intestacy.

Answer

As a general rule a beneficiary must survive the testator to take the benefit. The failure to survive the testator will, subject to certain exceptions, cause the gift to lapse. It is important, therefore to determine the order of deaths.

(a) Where there is clear evidence on the balance of probabilities as to survivorship this must be applied. The order of deaths would therefore be Anne and then Harry. Anne has therefore pre-deceased Harry and her property would fall into his estate and devolve as the £10,000 to his nephew Neil and the residue to Meg.

(b) At common law the courts would not presume survivorship in the absence of clear evidence. Therefore, if one could not establish which person died first, testator or beneficiary, the gift would fail. In *Underwood v Wing* (1855) a husband left all his property to his wife, stipulating that if she died in his lifetime then his property was to go to X. The wife left all her property to her husband but if he died in her lifetime the property was to go to X. Husband and wife were both killed when they were swept off the deck of a ship. The court said that X could not claim because he could not establish which out of the husband or the wife died first. The court would not apply a presumption as to order of deaths at common law. In *Wright v Netherwood* (1793) the court said that it was more reasonable to consider the parties as all dying at the same time rather than to 'resort to some fanciful supposition of survivorship on account of degrees of robustness'.

In order to remedy the unfortunate impasse created by decisions such as *Underwood v Wing*, s 184 Law of Property Act 1925 was passed. This provides that where two or more persons have died in circumstances where it is uncertain which has survived the other, then the order of deaths is presumed to have occurred in order of seniority. The word 'uncertain' was considered by the House of Lords in *Hickman v Peacey* (1945). Here two brothers had each made wills leaving legacies to one another. They were killed when the house in which they were sheltering during an air raid attack was hit by a bomb. The argument which prevailed in the Court of Appeal was that the

Formal Validity

statutory presumption as to order of survivorship could not apply because one would say in the particular circumstances that death had been instantaneous. The House of Lords reversed the decision of the Court of Appeal saying that all that was necessary to apply the statutory presumption was the slightest element of uncertainty. Here, although in lay terms, one would say death was instantaneous, one could not say for certain that the brothers died at exactly the same moment. Applying *Hickman v Peacey*, Anne would be presumed to have survived Harry with the result that Harry's estate would pass to Anne and the property thereafter pass to her nephew Oliver. In *Lamb v The Lord Advocate* (1976) the court said that if there is any evidence on the balance of probabilities as to the likelihood of survivorship, this should be applied rather than the statutory presumption. However, there is no indication on the evidence here; therefore s 184 would be applied.

(c) If Harry had died intestate, the statutory presumption in s 184 would not apply. Both spouses would be treated as having died at the same time – s 46(3) Administration of Estate Act 1925. Harry's property would therefore pass to Neil and Meg and Anne's property to Oliver. The reason for the exclusion of the rule is that if it were applied the whole of the property from Harry's estate and that of Anne would pass to Oliver to the exclusion of Harry's relatives.

A common provision in wills is the survivorship clause which not only refers to the beneficiary pre-deceasing but adds the stipulation that the beneficiary must survive the testator for say, one calendar month. That is long enough to resolve a common accident situation but not too long so as to hold up the administration of the estate. Inclusion of a survivorship clause which specifies a period of survivorship would obviate the need for s 184.

Question 18

Alice died on 1 May 1994, intestate. She was survived by her husband Bernard. They had three children, Christopher, 30, Emma, 17, and David who died in 1991. Unbeknown to Bernard, Alice also had another child Frank, 32, before they were married.

David was married to Gillian and they had two children, Ian, 6, and Jane who was born in 1991. Emma married Kevin on the 30 April 1994.

	£
Alice's net estate consists of:	
Clothes and personal effects	5,000
Car (valued at)	5,000
Chez Nous (the house in which she and Bernard lived and which she had inherited from her mother)	200,000
Bank accounts, cash, investments	350,000
	560,000

Explain fully how Alice's estate should be distributed under the intestacy rules. In your answer you should discuss the nature and extent of each person's entitlement. Also advise Bernard as to any special rights which he might have as surviving spouse. (Ignore the possibility of any claims under the Inheritance (Provision for Family and Dependants) Act 1975.)

Answer plan

This is a straightforward intestacy distribution question. Care should be taken when planning the question to set out those who are entitled to benefit from the intestacy. Here this would be confined to the surviving spouse and issue. One should then begin with the entitlement of the surviving spouse and then the issue making a distinction between those who take a vested interest and those who take under the terms of the statutory trusts. It is important in questions of this nature to clearly set out the law and then apply the relevant principles to the facts. It is not necessary to include the entire list of beneficial distribution on intestacy, for the question is confined to spouse and issue thereby making reference to, for example, parents or brothers and sisters irrelevant.

Answer

The persons entitled to benefit on Alice's intestacy are the surviving spouse (Bernard) and the surviving issue. Bernard, as surviving spouse, is entitled to the personal chattels, as defined by s 55(1)(x) of the Administration of Estates Act 1925, absolutely; the statutory legacy and a life interest in half the remainder of the estate. As there are surviving issue the statutory legacy is fixed at £125,000 (the Family Provision (Intestate Succession) Order 1993 SI 1993 No 2906).

The statutory legacy is taken free of tax and costs and carries interest at 6% per annum from the date of death until the date payment is made.

The remaining half of the estate would be divided four ways with Frank, Christopher and Emma all entitled to one quarter share. The remaining quarter would be split into one eighth each to Ian and Jane since they take the share their deceased father would have taken on a *per stiripal* basis.

Under the terms of s 55(1)(x), Bernard would take the clothes and personal effects absolutely. Whether he would be entitled to the car under s 55 depends upon whether the car is predominently used for private purposes or its predominent use is one of business. If the car is predominently used for business then the car will be distributed as part of the general estate. After deducting the value of the statutory legacy the remaining value of the estate would be divided in half and Bernard would be entitled to a life interest on one half of the residue. The house would form part of the value of the general estate since this was in the sole name of Alice. Bernard, as surviving spouse, has two special rights. The first of these is the right to capitalise his life interest in half of the residue under the terms of s 47A of the Administration of Estates Act 1925 and the second is the right to require the personal representatives to appropriate the matrimonial home towards his entitlement under the intestacy rules (see the Second Schedule to the Intestate Estate Act 1952). If Bernard decides to elect to capitalise the life interest he will convert the right to receive income during his life time into a 'one off' payment of a capital sum. The election must be made within 12 months of the grant of representation. Notice of election must be made to the personal representatives.

As Bernard was resident in the home at death he is entitled to file notice of appropriation of the matrimonial home against his entitlement under the intestacy rules. He must exercise the right of election within 12 months of the Grant of Representation, again with notice given to the personal representatives. Advice should be sought promptly following the death concerning the right to elect to take the home, for the value of the home is taken as at the date of appropriation. Therefore, where one is in a rising property market, any delay can prove costly. If Bernard does decide to appropriate the home he may well wish to serve notice of capitalisation of the life interest to provide him with capital to assist him in purchasing the interest. He is entitled to make up any balance in respect of the appropriation of the home 'in or towards part satisfaction' towards his absolute interest under the intestacy by virtue of the Court of Appeal interpretation of the words 'in *Re Phelps* (1979)'.

The surviving issue share the remainder of the estate on the terms of the statutory trusts contained in s 47(1)(i) of the Administration of Estates Act 1925. The terms of the trust are that the issue can take a vested interest if they have attained 18 at the death of the intestate or they have married. There is no distinction between illegitimate and legitimate issue for those dying intestate after the 3 April 1988 (s 18 Family Law Reform Act 1987). Frank and Christopher therefore take vested interest in one quarter of the half share of the residue by virtue of being over 18. Emma also takes a vested interest in one quarter for, although she is under 18, she has married at the date of the intestate's death. Ian and Jane as issue of their deceased father David, take their interest contingently on attaining 18. If one of them fails to meet the terms of the statutory trusts the one eighth share will pass to the survivor. Should both Ian and Jane fail to meet the contingencies then their share will fall back into residue and increase the shares going to Frank, Christopher and Emma. If Bernard does elect to capitalise his life interest and take a lump sum in lieu of the life interest, then the balance capital will increase the share going to the surviving issue.

Chapter 3

Family Provision

Introduction

The Family Provision Legislation should be studied in detail. Since the revision of the rules in the 1975 Act the wider category of dependants and the splitting of the standard of reasonable provision between the spouse standard and the other, maintenance cases have had an increasing influence on the pattern of succession to estates. Caution should be taken in considering older cases, that is to say before the 1975 Act. There has been recent judicial comment that following these cases can be misleading.

When faced with a problem on this topic one should first of all consider those who have potential *locus standi* before the court. The tricky points here concern former spouses under s 1(1)(b), the concept of 'child of the family' under subpara (d) and dependants in subpara (e). The Law Commission recommended under Category E where there is an application by a cohabitee that the requirement of prior proof of dependants should no longer be necessary.

A careful distinction should be drawn between the rights of the spouse and other claimants. The guidelines concerning the spouse provision are set out in *Re Besterman* (1984) and applied in the same year in *Re Bunning*.

There have been a number of interesting cases concerning provision for adult children and adult step-children. Mere proof that one is a child of the deceased is insufficient. The courts will look for evidence of moral obligation or other filial responsibility in considering the merits of an award.

Powers of the court in making awards should be noted carefully. The powers were greatly increased by the 1975 Act and include, for example, not only lump sum orders but transfers of property.

Finally, there can be some tricky questions concerning the application of the anti-avoidance provisions in ss 10 and 11.

Question 19

Alan was married to Bertha and they had two children Charles and Dora. Alan was frequently violent to Bertha and in 1988 Bertha obtained a decree nisi of divorce. At the time of the divorce Bertha had a nervous breakdown and still suffers from depression and other mental illnesses, necessitating continuous medical attention and frequent short stays in hospitals. The decree was never made absolute. Bertha received no property or financial provision from Alan on the divorce because Alan had no money or assets at the time. After the divorce Charles, aged 19, was taken into care and remains in a local authority children's home. Dora, aged 5, went to live with Bertha's unmarried sister Freda who has no children of her own. Freda tried to formally adopt Dora but the application was refused as her circumstances were thought to be unsatisfactory. Dora remains with her.

After the divorce Alan went to live with Gina, a widow, in Gina's house. He was demanding of her attentions and frequently needed nursing through illnesses which Gina lovingly provided. He didn't work and they initially lived on Gina's small widow's pension. In 1990 Alan inherited £150,000 from his father and he used the income and some of the capital for the living expenses of himself and Gina.

Alan has now died intestate leaving an estate of £100,000. Advise on the distribution of the estate and on any possible claims under the Inheritance (Provision for Family and Dependants) Act 1975 by any of the persons named above.

How, if at all, would your answer differ if Alan had made a will leaving his whole estate to Gina?

Answer plan

The answer should be divided into three parts. First, an explanation as to the distribution on intestacy. Secondly, the possible claims of each of the main parties under the Family Provision Legislation needs to be considered. Thirdly, the position on a partial intestacy needs to be considered and contrasted with the position on a total intestacy.

Answer

Given that Alan has died intestate, the whole of his estate would pass to the surviving spouse Bertha. The reasons for this are that Bertha is still regarded as the lawful spouse because the decree was never made absolute and she is entitled a statutory legacy of £125,000 in addition to the value of personal chattels absolutely, given that there are issue who also survive the intestate. Since the estate at death is under £125,000 the whole of the estate passes to Bertha.

The persons would could consider an application for provision under the Inheritance Act 1975 are the children Charles, Dora and Gina. The children would have automatic *locus standi* before the courts to apply under s 1(1)(c) of the Act. Given the events and the state of health of Bertha, it is unlikely that the children would be cared for by her. Given their young ages they could have a strong moral claim for an order for reasonable provision to be made to provide for their maintenance and education. Although the Court of Appeal in *Re Coventry* (1979) says that merely because one is a child does not of itself entitle an order to be made, the youth and circumstances of the children here would appear to give them a strong claim on some provision towards their living expenses and education.

In the case of Gina her rights would depend initially upon whether Alan died on or after 1 January 1996. If he did, it would have to be established whether Alan and Gina were cohabiting or merely living under the same roof. If they were cohabiting and the cohabitation had been continuous for a period of two years ending with the death of Alan then Gina would not be required to prove prior dependence in order to establish *locus standi* – s 2(1) Law Reform (Succession) Act 1995. Further, in considering an award, in addition to the general matters to be taken into account under s 3(2)(a)–(f) of the 1975 Act the court will take account of the length of time Alan and Gina have lived together and the contribution Gina has made to Alan's welfare.

If the evidence shows the cohabitation was not continuous for the two year period or the parties merely shared accommodation, then Gina would have to prove prior dependence. She would have to prove that she was being maintained either wholly or partly by Alan immediately before his death. Further it would have to be established that Alan was not receiving full valuable consideration for any maintenance he may have provided. The problem here is whether or not Alan was dependent upon Gina. Lord Justice Stephenson in *Jelley v Iliffe* in 1981 said:

> 'To discover whether the deceased was making such contribution, the court had to balance what she had contributed against what the applicant had contributed. If there was any doubt about the balance tipping in favour of the deceased being the greater contributor, the matter must go to trial. If however the balance was bound to come down in favour of the applicant being the greater contributor, or if the contributions were equal, there was no dependency of him upon her either because she depended upon him or there was mutual dependency between them and this application should be struck out.'

Gina would therefore have to establish that she was dependent upon Alan. In *Bishop v Plumley* (1990) in the Court of Appeal Lord Justice Butler-Sloss said that it wasn't a matter of detailed calculation but looking at the problem in the round and adopting a common sense approach as to dependents. Here, although one could argue until 1990 Alan was dependent upon Gina, since the inheritance in 1990 Gina could argue dependency to a degree upon Alan thereby giving her *locus standi*. It would assist Gina's case if she could produce some evidence of assumption of responsibility on the part of Alan following the inheritance.

In considering whether Alan has made reasonable provision for Gina, the court will want to know details of her assets and the standard of life Alan and Gina had assumed following the inheritance. Against this the court will consider the merits of the claims of the young children and Bertha. The court has wide powers to order transfer of property, lump sum orders or income provision for successful applicants.

If Alan had made a will leaving his whole estate to Gina then applications would be considered by Bertha as the surviving spouse under s 1(1)(a) and the children. The children's case has been considered above. The criterion in the case of Bertha would be one of the spouse provision rather than maintenance because decree absolute has not been granted. This provision enables the court to consider an award based upon an analogy if the partners were divorcing at the time of the application. The court will consider Alan's conduct and Bertha's state of health. The court will take account of the length of the marriage and the circumstances of the separation and subsequent decree nisi. See *dicta* in *Re Besterman* and *Re Bunning* both in 1984. The court will take account of Bertha's age, her health and the likelihood that she is not going to obtain a steady income from employment. There is a strong chance therefore that Bertha would be successful in obtaining either an income provision award or a lump sum. Against this the merits of Gina's claim would need to be considered and the standard of life to which she and Alan had become accustomed following the inheritance.

Question 20

Tom married Anna 20 years ago. They have a daughter, Kate, aged 10, and Anna has a son Robin, aged 19, from a previous, short-lived marriage to David who died 10 years ago.

Tom has always treated Robin as his son but their relationship became strained three years ago and this lead to arguments between Tom and Anna. Three years ago Anna discovered Tom was having an affair with his secretary Helen and later in the same year Tom left the matrimonial home, 'The Gables', and moved into an apartment with Helen. The lease was in Tom's name; Tom and Helen agreed to share the day to day expenses.

Anna refused to believe the marriage was over and would telephone Tom regularly at his office. After three months Tom persuaded Helen to leave her post as his secretary and paid her an allowance to make up for her loss of salary. Helen no longer shared the expenses of the apartment but looked after the accommodation and co-hosted dinners there with Tom and his business associates. In addition, Tom paid the expenses of 'The Gables' together with an allowance to Anna.

Tom had indicated several times to Helen he would like to leave city life and live in the country, and, in response to her enthusiasm, donated £5,000 to a wildlife sanctuary, and said he would buy her a cottage in the Lake District. Helen busied herself obtaining particulars and visiting several properties. However she grew impatient when Tom appeared reluctant to make his mind up. Eight months ago Tom returned to Anna at 'The Gables'.

However, six weeks before his death he started to stay at the apartment with Helen during the week, returning to 'The Gables' at weekends. Anna accepted this arrangement as all along she had hoped her marriage would continue and, despite the advice of friends, had not sought to take any matrimonial proceedings.

Tom died a month ago in a road accident. His estate is valued at £450,000 including 'The Gables', which is in Tom's name, personal effects, company shares and pension rights. The lease on the apartment has six months left and the landlords have served notice to quit. By his will Tom left 'The Gables' to Anna for life, the remainder to the World Wildlife Fund (WWF); shares in Glunk Limited which Tom believed to be worth £30,000 to Kate and Robin in equal shares; £10,000 to Helen and the residue to the WWF. After Tom's death the value of the holding in Glunk Limited falls to £6,000.

Consider the claims, if any, Anna, Kate, Robin and Helen may have under the Inheritance (Provision for Family and Dependants) Act 1975.

Answer plan

Problem questions on family provision can be quite long as you need to set the scene. In this question advice has to be given to four separate parties. The best approach is to divide the answer into four separate parts advising in turn Anna, Kate, Robin and Helen. In each case *locus standi* should be considered first and then, on the basis that reasonable provision has not been made, the factors which would be considered in the individual case. No hard and fast conclusion could be made because there are too many imponderables. The purpose of a question of this type is to elicit a knowledge and understanding of the Inheritance (Provision for Family and Dependents) Act 1975.

Answer

There is the initial presumption that Tom has died domiciled in England or Wales; therefore action could be contemplated under the Inheritance (Provision for Family and Dependents) Act 1975.

Anna is the lawful spouse. Although Tom and Anna separated three years ago there is no evidence that they have divorced. Anna would therefore have *locus standi* as the surviving spouse. The basis of an award for reasonable financial provision would therefore appear to be the spouse standard under s 1(2)(a) of the Inheritance Act. This section says that the provision is that that would be reasonable in all the circumstances, whether or not the provision is required for the maintenance of the applicant. Section 3(2) says that the starting point on this basis is the amount the applicant could have expected to have received on a divorce. Although the parties have separated there is no evidence that a decree of judicial separation has been made. The significance of such a decree is that the basis of reasonable provision is then be the maintenance standard (1).

What does the divorce analogy test mean? In *Re Besterman* (1984) Lord Justice Oliver said that the correct starting point was the likely provision which the applicant would have received if the divorce proceedings had been instituted (2). The court applied a three point test in saying one should consider first, the provisions of living accommodation for the spouse, secondly, income and capital to meet the costs of daily living and thirdly, there should be some provision for contingencies. The Court of Appeal stressed that each case depends upon its facts but the court did indicate guidelines in arriving at an award. Accounts should be taken of the length of the marriage and the relationship between the parties. Was it a happy marriage? The contribution made by the applicant to the welfare of the family should be considered. The age of the surviving spouse at the date of the application is relevant in considering whether the surviving spouse is young enough to either obtain employment or return to employment. Finally, the court would consider what the applicant would have received if the parties were divorcing (3). Although the Court of Appeal stressed that each case depends upon its own facts the principles enunciated in *Re Besterman* were considered and applied in the same year in *Re Bunning*. Here the parties had separated four years before the death of the husband and after 15 years of marriage. The court found that there were mitigating circumstances in the wife's favour leading to the separation and that on divorce the applicant wife would have received half of the estate taking into account gifts already made. The applicant wife was awarded £60,000 out of a total estate of £200,000 but allowing for some £47,000 which had been given to her during the deceased's lifetime.

There is no indication as to whether Anna has resources of her own save the reference to the fact that Tom has paid the expenses of the former matrimonial home together with an allowance to his wife. Anna has been left the former matrimonial home for life. Whether she will succeed in an application to have the title of the house made over to her is debatable. The fact that she has been left a life interest in the house does meet the first point of the three point test in *Re Besterman* that accommodation has been provided. Whether Anna would be better off in obtaining the freehold thereby having the flexibility of selling the house at a later date and receiving the proceeds would depend upon the extent of the provision in her favour and the merit of the claims of other parties. In *Re Clark dec'd* (1991) the court refused an application by a widow where the parties had been married for 12 years and, in addition to a lump sum of £25,000, the widow had been left a life interest in the former matrimonial home. Reference was made to the guidelines in *Besterman* and given that the widow had a lump sum provision coupled with the life interest the court ruled that provision was adequate. Again in *Davis v Lush* (1991) the Court of Appeal rejected an application by a widow where a life interest had been given in the house. The widow wanted the freehold title to be transferred to her on the basis that she wanted the security of owning her own home; the Court of Appeal rejected the claim saying that the trial judge had not erred in his judgment.

Kate would have no problem establishing *locus standi* as she is the lawful child of Tom and therefore qualifies under s 1(1)(c). A limited provision has been made for Kate and her stepbrother in the bequest of the shares. However, the shares do not prove to be as valuable as was believed. Kate would have to consider at the date of death whether reasonable provision has been made in order to consider making an application bearing in mind that application should be made within six months of the grant of title (s 4) and the question whether reasonable provision has been made is determined on the evidence available at the date of the application (s 3). The court could therefore take into account the fall in the value of the shares in Glunk Limited. The strongest factor in Kate's case is that she is aged 10. A key factor although not a pre-requisite is the moral obligation owed by the deceased to the applicant and in the case of a young child whose life and education is ahead of her the issue of moral obligation would be a strong one. The criterion on which an award would be considered would be one of maintenance; maintenance does not mean subsistence (4) but denote payments which directly or indirectly enable the applicant to discharge the recurrent cost of daily living. Provision for Kate's future education would clearly be an important factor in this regard. In *Re Coventry* (1979) the Court of Appeal said that reasonable provision was a question of fact, the judge making a value judgment. The courts do look for special factors and moral obligation would be the key issue in this regard. Further the court must take account, under s 3, of the merits and claims of other applicants as well as the beneficiaries under the will. A factor in this latter regard would be the residue going to an institution namely the charity, rather than individual beneficiaries.

Robin, as the stepson of Tom, would have to establish *locus standi* under s 1(1)(d) that is as a 'child of the family'. The most authoritative statement in regard to the meaning of child of the family is that of Lord Justice Slade in *Re Leach* (1985). He indicated that treating someone as a child of the family means more than a display of affection or the provision of birthday or Christmas presents. It denotes an assumption of responsibility which only a parent would assume. There is no indication as to what provision Anna's former husband made for Robin but it is given that Tom had always treated Robin as his son albeit that the relationship had become strained in recent times. Further under the terms of the will Robin is sharing the gift of the shares with Kate. The facts would seem to suggest therefore that Tom does treat Robin as a child of the family thereby giving Robin *locus standi* to apply. The criterion would again be the maintenance standard. Robin is aged 19 and evidence would need to be adduced as to whether or not he has completed his education or whether he is continuing in education thereby establishing a stronger obligation. The Court of Appeal in *Re Coventry*, reiterated by the Court of Appeal in *Re Harlow v National Westminster Bank plc* (1994) pointed out that the mere fact of a relationship of father to son or in this case an assumed son is not in itself sufficient to establish a claim. There must be some additional factor such as moral obligation. The fact that Tom, aged 19, has yet to make his way in life could establish the issue of moral obligation but without such an additional factor his claim would not be as strong, for example, as that of Kate.

The final possible applicant is Helen who could consider an application under s 1(1)(e). Although it would appear Tom and Helen were cohabiting, the problem for Helen is the cohabitation has not been continuous. By returning to Anna Tom has broken the period of two years laid down by s 2(1) of the Law Reform (Succession) Act 1995. The section states the period of cohabitation must be continuous for a period of two years ending with the death of the deceased. Even if Tom had not returned to Anna eight months ago, by living at the apartment in the week and returning to 'The Gables' at weekends, would the court consider this to be continuous cohabitation with Helen within the context of s 2? This is doubtful. If, as is likely, s 2(1) of the 1995 Act will not apply, this does not mean Helen cannot apply for provision. Helen would have to establish that she was being maintained, wholly or partially, by Tom immediately before his death. In addition, in order to establish *locus standi*, Helen would have to show that they had not entered into any bargain, that is, that Tom was not in receipt of full valuable consideration in return for any provision for Helen.

The leading case on establishing *locus standi* under sub-category (e) is *Jelley v Iliffe* (1981). Here the Court of Appeal referred to balancing the contributions between the respective parties. If the deceased was the greater contributor towards the well being of the applicant then *locus standi* is established and the matter could proceed to determine what should amount to responsible provision. In *Bishop v Plumley* (1990) the Court of Appeal said that in determining contribution one should look at the problem in the round and adopt a common sense approach rather than fine balance compensations. Dependence would appear to have been established here in Tom's persuading Helen to leave her employment, her receiving an allowance from Tom and co-hosting dinners. Dependence does not have to be simply in monetary terms but could be the provision of accommodation as in *Re Wilkinson* (1978).

Helen would have to establish dependence immediately after the death. Although their relationship appears to have become strained there is no suggestion that Tom has left Helen as was the case in *Kourgey v Lusher* (1982).

The criterion in making an award would again be the maintenance standard. The level of support is determined not only by reference to the applicant's financial circumstances but also regard would be had to the standard to which Helen had become accustomed, see for example *Re Inns* (1947) and *Malone v Harrison* (1979) (5). The court would take into account the legacy received under the will together with resources Helen may have on her own account, her age and the possibility that she could return to paid employment together with some provision for accommodation. The reference to the possibility of buying a cottage in the Lake District would assist her in claiming some provision for accommodation; however, she could not pursue the possibility for an action for proprietary estoppel, for example in *Re Basham* (1987), because Tom never actually purchased the cottage.

Provision for the respective applicants is out of the net estate; that is the gross estate less the bonified debts, claims and taxation. The court has power under s 10 to do claw back property where the deceased as made a disposition within six years of the death with a view to defeating the act. Whether one could apply s 10 to the donation to the wild life sanctuary is debatable. In *Re Bunning* the widow applicant sought to claim a gift to charity but the court rejected her claim on the basis that both the applicant and her husband had agreed to make the donation.

Notes

1 Had a decree of judicial separation been made and had it continued until the death of the deceased the application would not be treated as having been made by the surviving spouse. The standard applied is one of maintenance. However, under s 14 the court has a discretion to apply the surviving spouse standard in certain circumstances to judicially separated spouses.
2 In *Re Besterman* the parties had been married for 18 years during which time they enjoyed a high standard of living. The deceased husband left a net estate at death of £1.5 million. He left his widow (the applicant) a life interest in £100,000, personal chattels and the use of certain works of art. The residue of the estate was left to Oxford University. The husband had miscalculated as to the needs of his wife in maintaining the standard of living to which she had become accustomed. The court awarded her a lump sum of £378,000.

3   In some cases the divorce analogy test is of limited assistance. For example in *Winfield v Billington* (unreported) (1990) the Court of Appeal was unable to derive much assistance from the test because it was impossible to say which parent would have been awarded custody of the children of the marriage and the nature of the ancillary relief order which would have been would have hinged to a very large extent on the custody order.
4   See *Re Christie* (1979) which has been criticised by the Court of Appeal in *Re Coventry* (1979).
5   Cases under the earlier legislation should be viewed with caution. However, the cases can be constructive as the factors to be taken into account in making an award.

Question 21

How have the courts construed the meaning of maintenance in the Inheritance (Provision for Family and Dependants) Act 1975?

Answer plan

There is no statutory definition of maintenance. The intention of the question is to elicit a knowledge of judicial comment upon the meaning of maintenance.

Answer

The categories of person who can apply for financial provision from the estate of a deceased individual who has died domiciled in England and Wales are set out in subparas (a)–(e) in s 1(1) of the Inheritance (Provision for Family and Dependants) Act 1975 (referred to as the Inheritance Act). Section 1(2) referring to reasonable financial provision in the case of applicants other than the spouse of the deceased, means such financial provision as would be reasonable in all the circumstances of the case for the applicant to receive for his maintenance (s 1(2)(b)).

There is no statutory definition of maintenance. Various principles have emerged through the case law. It was said in *Re Christie* (1979) that maintenance does not mean subsistence. In *Re Christie* there was an application by an adult son who was able bodied and who had a steady job in the estate of his deceased mother. By her will, made in 1963, the mother had *inter alia* devised her interest in a house in Essex to her son. In 1971 after the death of her husband the mother executed a deed of gift of her share of a London house to her daughter and continued to live in the house in Essex. In 1976 she sold the Essex house and bought a smaller house. This had the effect of adeeming the devise of the house to the son. There was evidence adduced that she intended to execute a codicil, leaving the new house to the son but she died before doing so. The result was that the house fell into the residuary estate to be shared between the son and the daughter. The son then applied for reasonable provision out of the estate and won an order securing the transfer of the house to him. The decision has been criticised in particular in the judgment of Mr Justice Oliver in the first instance hearing in *Re Coventry* (1979) when he said:

'... it always has to be borne in mind that the 1975 Act, so far as it relates to applicants other than spouses, is an Act whose purpose is limited to the provision of reasonable maintenance. It is not the purpose of the Act to provide legacies or reward for meritorious conduct.'

The concept of maintenance, it has been said, denotes payments which directly or indirectly enable the applicant to discharge the recurrent cost of daily living. It does not generally include substantial benefits (see for example *dicta* in *Re Dennis* (1981)). In this case a wastrel son unsuccessfully applied for a hearing out of time when a death duty liability arose upon the gift he had received from his father of a farm when his father died within seven years of making the gift. Liability was to the extent of £90,000 payable to the revenue. The son had wasted his inheritance and was only prompted to seek approval of the court to apply out of time in order to obtain a lump sum award to pay the tax. The court rejected the application. The idea of maintenance is therefore one of income provision to enable the applicant to meet day to day expenses. However, the court will not simply look at the applicant's financial position but consider also the social standing of the applicant and that person's place in society, for example, the *dictum* of Mr Justice Wynn Parry in *Re Inns* (1947). This was one of the rare cases where there has been an application in a large estate where the net estate was in excess of £1,000,000.

Evidence may be adduced to the effect that the deceased had actively encouraged the applicant to adopt a certain standard of life. This is well illustrated in *Malone v Harrison* (1979). In this case there was an application by a mistress where the deceased had actively encouraged her to adopt a certain lifestyle and she had been tutored in becoming dependent upon the deceased. The deceased had purchased two apartments for the applicant, one in England and the other in Malta together with gifts of jewellery, furs and expenditure of somewhere in excess of £4,000 per annum upon the applicant. The applicant was therefore encouraged and received assistance by the deceased to adopt a certain higher lifestyle. The award was in the form of a lump sum payment calculated by reference to reflect the income to which she had become accustomed.

Although the decision in *Re Christie* has been criticised by the Court of Appeal in *Re Coventry*, *Christie* was not overruled and does stand for the principle that maintenance may well denote the well being, health and financial security of the applicant and his immediate family; the court recognised in this case that the only way that this could be achieved was by the provision of capital, namely the transfer of title of the newly purchased house in Essex. However, the further words of Mr Justice Oliver in *Re Coventry* should be noted in this context namely, 'the court has no *carte blanche* to reform the deceased's disposition or those which statute makes of his estate to accord to what the court itself might of thought would be sensible if it had been in the deceased's position'.

Question 22

Alan, a widower, died recently leaving an estate valued at £120,000 including a house worth £80,000. He left all his property by his will to his favourite charity. You are consulted by David, Alan's illegitimate son, aged 35. A few days after Alan's funeral, David was badly injured in an accident which is likely to leave him seriously disabled and unemployable for the rest of his life. In a letter found with the will, Alan stated that he was excluding David from his will 'because David had adopted a worthless existence'. David had been working as a college lecturer prior to the accident.

Family Provision 83

Answer plan

Alan has not made any provision for David. Is this reasonable in the circumstances? Consider David's age, the effect, if any, of the illegitimacy and the injuries to David after Alan's death as factors in building a case for David in an application for reasonable provision out of the estate of his father.

Answer

In an answer on possible applications under the Inheritance (Provision for Family and Dependants) Act 1975 one has to consider initially whether the will of the deceased or intestacy or a combination of both failed to make reasonable provision for the potential applicant. If this appears to be the case then one has to consider initially whether the applicant has the *locus standi* to apply. Then one has to consider the merits of the application.

In the case of David, as the biological child of Alan, David would be entitled to apply under s 1(1)(c) of the 1975 Act. There is no age restriction and 'child' for the purposes of s 1 clearly includes an adult child (see the *dicta* of Booth J in *Re Callaghan* where the court held that the reference to child refers not to age but to the relationship between the deceased and the applicants). However, a note of caution; the courts will not necessarily look sympathetically upon the able-bodied adult child either earning or well able to earn his or her own living (see the *dicta* in the Court of Appeal decision in *Re Coventry*). Note that although in *Re Christie* the court referred to the meaning of maintenance as referring to the well being of the applicant, in this particular case the decision is, in effect, correcting a will whereby the applicant received a legacy he argued he should have received but for a prior ademption. This *dicta* received unfavourable comment in *Re Coventry*.

The criterion on which to base a claim is one of maintenance; that is to say maintaining the applicant, as far as possible, at the standard of life to which the applicant has become accustomed. The court in *Re Leach* stated that the provision should keep the applicant neither in luxury nor in misery but comfortably in relation to his or her station in life. The Court of Appeal in *Re Coventry* said that maintenance does not mean subsistence.

One has to consider the attitude of the deceased and the reference in the letter. However, the court will not necessarily accept the deceased's reasons at face value. The letter can be admitted under the Civil Evidence Act 1968 but the court will reserve the right to enquire into the truth of such a statement. *Prima facie*, given the age of David and his employment, it would appear that he would have little chance of a successful claim bearing in mind the *dicta* in *Re Coventry*. Mr Justice Oliver said in *Re Coventry* that, subject to the court's powers under the 1975 Act and to fiscal demands, an Englishman still remained at liberty to dispose of his property in whatever way he pleases or indeed to leave the distribution of his estate to intestate succession. The court was reluctant to make an award based upon maintenance to an able-bodied adult child. However, in this case David has been seriously injured after the death of Alan. The test as to reasonable provision is an objective one and is to be considered on the basis of the circumstances prevailing at the date of the hearing (s 3(5)). The court can therefore take account of supervening events. In this case the instructing solicitor should draw the attention of counsel to the issue of moral obligation in the light of the accident to David. Indeed this was recognised in *Re Coventry* but there should be established some sort of moral claim over and above the mere fact of blood relationship. The case for David is further strengthened by the fact that the beneficiary under the will is a charity rather than another individual who may have a claim (see the *dicta* of the Court of Appeal in *Millward v Shenton*). Therefore it would appear that David, in the light of his unfortunate accident, would have a strong claim to an award (whether lump sum or income provision or a combination of both towards his future maintenance).

Question 23

Romeo died recently, leaving a net estate of £750,000. In his will he left a legacy of £30,000 to his aged mother and the rest of his estate to his son Caspar, 25. Romeo was survived by his mistress Juliet, 45, who is semi-paralysed following a road accident earlier this year; their three children, who are aged 22, 18 and 9; and his widow Diana, whom he deserted 20 years ago but from whom he was neither divorced nor judicially separated. Diana has been

Family Provision

living with William for many years and had been supported by him until his death a month ago.

Advise Diana, Juliet and the three children who wish to apply to the court for orders under the Inheritance (Provision for Family and Dependants) Act 1975.

Answer plan

In answers upon the Family Provision Legislation, one should consider first of all *locus standi* of the respective possible applicants and then go on to consider their claims and the merits of their claims. Given that there is a surviving spouse who has neither divorced nor been judicially separated, then one has to consider the two tests as to provision namely the spouse provision and the maintenance provision.

Answer

One is asked to advise Diana, the surviving spouse, Juliet the mistress, and the three children Romeo had by Juliet, that is to say excluding his other son Caspar who presumably survives and has been left the residue of the estate under Romeo's will.

In order to make a claim under the 1975 Act the applicants must prove that they have *locus standi* before the court. Diana would have this by virtue of s 1(1)(a) of the 1975 Act as the lawful wife of Romeo. The children would have *locus standi* by virtue of s 1(1)(c) and the mistress Juliet may have *locus standi* under the terms of subpara (e).

In order for Juliet to show that she has *locus standi* she would have to show that she was being maintained wholly or partly by Romeo immediately before his death. It would appear from the facts that Diana had been supported by Romeo immediately before his death, that is to say there had been no intention to end the relationship permanently prior to his death as in the case of *Kourgey v Lusher*. The meaning of 'maintained' is set out in s 1(3) of the Act which provides that a person will be treated as maintained if the deceased 'otherwise than for full valuable consideration, was making a substantial contribution in money or money's worth towards the reasonable needs of the person'. Given Juliet's condition it would appear that she was dependent on Romeo immediately before the death.

The respective parties entitled to make application under s 1 do so on the basis that Romeo's will did not make reasonable provision for them. Application must be made to the court within six months of the issue of the Grant of Representation. This is a substantive rule rather than merely procedural although the court does have a discretion to extend the time limit, see the guidelines laid down by Vice Chancellor McGarry in *Re Salmon* (1981).

Section 2 sets out two standards for judging whether provision is reasonable. There is the spouse standard whereby the court is asked to assess such financial provision as would be reasonable in all the circumstances. This has been considered analogous to provision that would be made if the spouses had been divorcing at the time of the death of the deceased, see the guidelines laid down in *Re Besterman* (1984) applied in *Re Bunning* (1984). The court would take account of the fact that Romeo and Diana had lived apart for 20 years and take account of how Diana had maintained herself throughout that period. Had she, for example, received any funds from Romeo or has Romeo been able to build up his substantial capital because he has failed to make provision over the years for Diana?

The test is an objective one, that is to say what the court considers reasonable in the circumstances and not what the deceased thought was reasonable.

In the case of the other potential applicants, the maintenance standard is applied. In the case of the children, clearly their ages would be taken into account, their state of health, employment and or education. *Dicta* in the Court of Appeal decision in *Re Coventry* (1979) indicates that the children do not have a claim to maintenance as of right. Rather, one would have to establish, for example, a moral claim. This would be easier in the case of the youngest child aged nine in considering the child's future education and dependence upon his semi-paralysed mother Juliet. In the case of the children aged 22 and 18 respectively, their chances of an award would depend again upon the stage they had reached in their education and future prospects as against the considerable size of the net estate.

Family Provision

In the case of Juliet the criterion would be one of maintenance. The court would have regard to the financial needs and resources of Juliet but bearing in mind her condition following the road accident. The question does not make it clear whether Romeo cohabited with Juliet, although one is given that he deserted his wife 20 years ago and the implication therefore is that Romeo and Juliet cohabited. The death of Romeo on or after 1 January 1996 would mean Juliet would not have to prove prior dependence – s 2(1) Law Reform Succession Act 1995. The purpose of the section is to bring claims by cohabitees closer to the rights of the spouse. Section 2(1) says that in addition to the general matters to be taken into account under s 3 (2)(a)–(f) of the 1975 Act, the court will have regard to the age of the applicant, the length of time the parties have lived together and the contribution made by the applicant to the welfare of the deceased and the contribution made in looking after the home or caring for the family. The criterion of award is still one of maintenance, however, in adding these factors, the cohabitee is set apart from other dependants under category (e). In addition to the amendment by s 2(1), in view of Juliet's condition, moral obligation in s 3(2)(a) will clearly be a strong factor in considering an award in her favour. Liability for Inheritance Tax will also be a factor in arriving at an award, see for example the *dictum* of Carnwath J in *Re Goodchild* (1996). Property passing to the surviving spouse will be exempt Inheritance Tax but property diverted elsewhere, in favour of other individuals, could attract tax. Inheritance Tax is charged on assets passing on death which are not exempt and where the estate exceeds £200,000 in value.

If it is the case that the parties have cohabited and Juliet has been dependent upon Romeo for that time, given that she has borne three children by him, the court could consider making a substantial award by way of lump sum and/or income payments calculated in relation to Juliet's condition following the road accident and her likely life expectancy, see *Malone v Harrison*. Orders made would include the provision of a home for Juliet and the child or children who are currently with her, together with possible provision for Diana and the children themselves given the considerable size of the estate.

Question 24

Bill, a successful actor, died in May, survived by his wife Alice, his former wife Betty, who is an invalid aged 53, and his unmarried son Charles aged 25. In the 10 years before his death, unknown to his family, Bill had been having an affair with Doris, an actress in the same company.

Five years ago Bill inherited some money which he used to buy a country cottage. In order that Doris should have some financial security the cottage was conveyed into the joint names of Bill and Doris. Bill also covenanted to pay £30,000 but the sum had not been paid. The estate at death was worth £300,000. Bill left £10,000 each to Doris and Charles and the residue to a named charity.

In September Alice made an application for reasonable provision under 1975 Act. Prior to the hearing of the application Alice and Charles were involved in a road accident in which Alice died and Charles was seriously injured.

Advise Betty, Charles, Doris and Alice's executors as to their rights, if any, in Bill's estate.

Answer plan

The question is asking you to consider the relative merits of the parties for reasonable provision under the 1975 Act. Each individual should be considered separately from the point of view first, of *locus standi*, and secondly, whether reasonable provision has been made, and thirdly, the particular factors one would consider as regards each individual applicant. This question has the interesting twist of the death of an applicant prior to the hearing of the case.

Answer

One has to consider the rights of application to the court and the merits of their respective cases under the 1975 Inheritance Act in respect of all those who survive Bill. This is on the basis that Bill died domiciled in England and Wales.

Alice, as the surviving spouse, clearly has *locus standi* under s 1(1)(a). However, Alice has died prior to the hearing of her application. In *Whyte v Ticehurst* (1986) the court held that in circumstances where an applicant dies before the hearing of the application the right to apply for reasonable provision under the 1975 Act is a personal right and not a right which survived for the benefit of the estate under the Law Reform (Miscellaneous Provisions) Act 1934. Therefore, despite the merit of Alice's claim as spouse and the fact that she was not left any property under the will, her estate would have no right to continue the application.

Betty has *locus standi* to apply under subpara (b) of the Act provided she has not remarried. The criterion in determining whether reasonable financial provision has been made for her is one of maintenance, s 1(1)(b). However, if Bill and Betty reached a financial settlement at the time of the divorce then Betty could be barred from applying under the Act. *Re Fullard* (1982) envisaged that claims by former spouses under the Inheritance Act would be relatively few. The reason is that the court now has much wider powers on divorce to make lump sum orders and appropriate capital adjustments. This does not necessarily rule out applications. The death may unlock assets which, during life, had limited realisable value, for example, insurance policies, or Betty may not pursue the rights to maintenance which she should have been awarded. For example, in *Re W* (1975), the former husband was able to build up the capital in his estate because his former wife had not pursued the question of maintenance at the time of the divorce owing to her 'gentle and compliant nature'.

Charles would have *locus standi* to apply under subpara (c) as a child of the deceased. There is no age limit, so the fact that Charles is adult would not prevent his right to apply and he would have six months from the date of the grant to the estate in order to lodge an application. Wherever one considers the right of the adult child, one has to bear in mind the *dicta* of the court at first instance and of the Court of Appeal in *Re Coventry* (1979). *Re Coventry* makes it clear that merely establishing oneself as the child of the deceased does not in itself merit an award being made. One has to establish some other additional factor or factors; for example, moral obligation or some physical or mental disability. Here Charles has been considered by the legacy of £10,000 under the will. However, since the death, Charles has been seriously injured in the accident.

The test as to whether reasonable provision has been made for an applicant is an objective test (s 3) and the time to consider this is the date of the hearing. If the court decides reasonable provision has not been made, account can be taken of supervening events. For example, in *Re Goodwin* (1968) after the death of the deceased it became clear a debt owed to the estate would not be repaid.

In addition, considering Charles's financial position and the financial position of the other applicants and beneficiaries in the estate the court will take account of the injuries Charles has suffered and the likelihood as to whether he could resume a normal life and the extent to which his earning capacity has been affected. The criterion by which an award would be considered is one of maintenance and if Charles is to be disabled for life then some contingency would be built into the award to take account, for example, of the erosion of investment income through inflation.

Doris could have *locus standi* to apply if she could establish that she was dependant upon Bill immediately before his death.

She would have to show that Bill was making a substantial contribution towards her maintenance in monies worth. Here the provision of the cottage and the covenant will be relevant. The criterion upon which the award is based is again one of maintenance, and regard to Doris's financial position and whether, for example, Bill encouraged Doris to adopt a particular lifestyle. One would need to know whether the cottage was held in their joint names, in which case the title would pass to Doris by right of survivorship. However, this could mean that the court could order Bill's share to form part of the net estate available for an award under the Act, see s 9 and for an application of s 9 *Jessop v Jessop* (1992). The fact of the covenant also shows an intention upon Bill to make some financial provision for Doris. In addition, if the covenant has actually been executed although not paid then it is possible that Doris could have a claim against the estate as a creditor prior to the determination of the meaning of net estate for the purposes of the Act. This application can be counted if it can be shown that Bill had entered into the covenant in order to thwart a possible application under the Act by, for example, members of his family, s 11. Doris would have to supply details of her financial position including the legacy of £10,000 under the will. The court may be more sympathetic in favour of individuals in their claims, particularly with regard to Charles if he is permanently disabled, where the residue is going to a charity rather than a named individual (see for example *dicta* in *Re Parkinson* (1975)). The court

Family Provision

has wide powers under the Act to make income and capital orders in making provision for maintenance.

Question 25

Consider the above facts as varied so that in the case of the road accident, although Charles is seriously injured, Alice escapes with mere cuts and bruises.

Answer plan

This question deals with the rights of the surviving spouse in applications under the Inheritance legislation. The surviving spouse can be in a stronger position regarding an application compared with others who may have *locus standi* in view of the criterion for reasonable provision being based upon the 'divorce' standard. Although the courts have stressed that each case depends upon its own facts, the Court of Appeal in *Re Besterman* (1984) did set down guidelines which have been followed.

Answer

Alice as indicated would have *locus standi* as the surviving spouse under s 1(1)(a). The criterion in the case of an application by the spouse is that reasonable financial provision means such financial provision as it would be reasonable in all the circumstances of the case for the applicant to receive, whether or not that provision is required for the maintenance of the applicant (see s 1(1)(a)). Section 3(2) indicates that the guideline for provision for spouses is to answer the question of what the spouse would have received if the parties were divorcing at the time of the death. Although this test can, in certain circumstances, be of limited assistance (see, for example, *Winfield v Billington* (1990)) the court has set down guidelines in *Re Besterman* (1984).

The starting point in considering an application by the spouse is a three point approach, considering, firstly, whether the spouse has provision of a roof over her head, secondly, sufficient income to maintain her standard of living and thirdly, some provision for contingencies. One would need to know what financial resources Alice has and that there is no provision being made for her in the will. The court would also consider the length of the marriage and the conduct of the spouses within the marriage and the contribution that Alice has made to the marriage (see *Re Besterman* and the principles applied in *Re Bunning* (1984)). In *Moody v Stevenson* (1992) the court said that the starting point is what a family judge would have ordered if divorce, instead of death, had divided the couple. The test as to financial provision for a surviving spouse is objective, that is, the decision of the court as to whether the disposition of the estate makes reasonable provision for the spouse. The test is not whether the testator acted reasonably in making the dispositions.

Question 26

On 1 May John died intestate. He was survived by his wife Meg, his mother Betty and his sister-in-law Donna. John and Meg had been married for six years. Three years ago John established a business as a garden designer working from his home, 'The Gables'. He asked Donna to assist him and, as she had few assets of her own, arranged for her to live in an apartment over the garage at 'The Gables'. He paid Donna low wages but the accommodation was rent free and she often took her meals with John and Meg. Meg worked part-time as a receptionist at a local optician's. Betty, widowed, lived alone in an apartment owned by her supported by investments and a pension which gave her a comfortable though not lavish lifestyle.

John devoted long hours to the business and this led to strain in the relationship with Meg. Eight months before John's death they separated but Meg returned two months ago. At death John's net estate is valued at £200,000 including 'The Gables' which was in his sole name. Shortly before his death John gave Donna a collection of rare sketches of gardens worth £35,000. Meg claims Donna influenced John into giving her the sketches and requests their return. Donna says John told her he thought he had cancer and would like her to have the sketches. It transpires John did not have cancer; he died of heart failure.

Donna consults you to defend her right to the sketches and her rights, if any, to remain in the apartment. Donna has never received anything in writing concerning the accommodation but John had always assured her he would see her housed.

What difference, if any, would it make if Meg died three weeks after John?

Further, if Betty died a month after Meg.

Answer plan

Distribution of the estate is according to the rules of intestacy. Consider the rights of Meg as surviving spouse and the rights of Betty. Donna may be able to claim Family Provision and/or estoppel.

The sketches – are they a gift *inter vivos* or a *donatio mortis causa*? Could the gift be challenged for want of capacity?

Effect of the death of Meg – possible revocation of a grant to her. Re-distribution in favour of Betty. What is the effect of this on a possible claim by Donna for Family Provision?

The death of Betty – how does this affect a possible claim by Donna?

Answer

John has died intestate: therefore his estate will be distributed in accordance with s 46 (1) of the Administration of Estates Act 1925. The potential beneficiaries are Meg as surviving spouse and Betty, John's surviving parent. Assuming that Meg is John's lawful spouse under a valid or voidable marriage and there is no decree of judicial separation in force at death then Meg will be entitled as surviving spouse. As there are no issue Meg will take the personal chattels absolutely, the statutory legacy of £200,000 with interest at 6% per annum and half the remainder absolutely. The other half of the residue would go to Betty. However, given that the total value of the net estate is £200,000 Meg will take the entire estate. Betty would only be entitled to share if the collection of sketches was clawed back into the estate thereby increasing the value to £235,000. Then there could be an argument on behalf of Meg that the sketches are personal chattels within the definition in s 55(1)(x) of the AEA 1925 and would therefore pass to Meg absolutely.

Donna may be able to make a claim for reasonable provision out of the estate under the Inheritance (Provision for Family and Dependants) Act 1975. In order to establish *locus standi* Donna would have to show she comes within s 1(1)(e), that is, assuming John has died domiciled in England or Wales, that she was dependant upon John either wholly or in part immediately before his death. She would also have to prove that John was not receiving full, valuable consideration for the maintenance he provided (s 1(3)). The purpose of this sub-section is to exclude claims where there is agreement between the parties on shared responsibilities.

Maintenance need not be in monetary terms but could be the provision of accommodation – *Re Wilkinson* (1978). The proviso in s 1(3) was considered by the Court of Appeal in *Jelley v Iliffe* (1981). Here, the applicant, a widower, and the deceased, a widow, related by marriage, lived together in the deceased's house for eight years ending with the death of the deceased. They pooled their resources, including their pensions, to meet common living expenses. He provided some furniture, looked after the garden and did some household jobs; she provided him with rent-free accommodation, cooked and washed for him. By her will the deceased left all her property to her three children in equal shares. The applicant successfully appealed against orders striking out his application. Stephenson LJ said:

> 'To discover whether the deceased was making such a contribution the court had to balance what she had contributed against what the applicant had contributed. If there was any doubt about the balance tipping in favour of the deceased being the greater contributor, the matter must go to trial. If however the balance was bound to come down in favour of the [applicant] being the greater contributor, or if the contributions were equal, there was no dependency of him on her, either because she depended upon him or there was mutual dependency between them and his application should be struck out.'

In *Bishop v Plumley* (1990) Butler-Schloss LJ said in considering whether someone was maintained within s 1(1)(e) and (3) the court should look at the problem in the round and adopt a common sense approach avoiding fine balancing computations. In this case, providing a secure home for the applicant was recognised as a substantial contribution. Assuming Donna established *locus standi* she would claim the distribution on intestacy has failed to make reasonable provision for her, in particular, in relation to the question of future accommodation. The court would take account of her needs, her age and the likelihood of her obtaining future employment. Against that the court would look at the entitlement of Meg.

The onus of proof in challenging the gift of the sketches would rest with Meg. If the collection was not considered to be a personal chattel, possible given its subject matter, Betty would have an interest as the value of the collection would take the total value of the net estate to £235,000. Betty may therefore be able able to claim half the £35,000 on John's intestacy.

Donna could defend by saying the collection was the subject of a gift *inter vivos*. She could claim it was handed over with the clear intention on the part of John that the gift was to have immediate effect. Where the gift is substantial in relation to the remainder of the estate the test as to capacity to make the gift moves closer to the capacity to form the clear *animus testandi* to make a valid will (see *Re Beaney* (1978)). In the absence of any prior evidence of illness or failing faculties which could impair intention, Meg would have to allege undue influence. Meg would have to prove Donna had exerted pressure on John to make the gift against his will.

If there is no evidence to challenge the gift on the ground of lack of capacity Meg could allege the purported gift was a *donatio mortis causa*, a gift made in contemplation of death and the conditions for a valid *donatio* have not been met. In order to establish a valid *donatio*, Donna would have to prove the gift was made in contemplation, although not necessarily in expectation, of impending death; the gift was conditional on death and there must have been delivery of the subject matter (see *Sen v Headley* (1991) and *Re Woodard* (1994)).

Given that John handed over the sketches and he has died two of the conditions have been met. The problem for Donna if it is considered the gift is a *donatio* is the first condition. Was John's belief he had cancer a reasonable one? Donna could be put to proof, initially by affidavit evidence, as to the circumstances of the handing over of the collection and the words used. The belief in impending death must be a reasonable one. The English courts suggest the test is subjective. So, for example, in *Re Miller* (1961) the court accepted a woman could make a valid *donatio* where she had a fear of flying. Commonwealth cases have adopted an objective test, the court deciding whether the contemplation is reasonable, see for example *Thompson v Mechan* (1958).

A further possibility may be challenge by Meg that the purported gift is a disposition caught by s 10 Inheritance Act 1975, that is, it is a disposition made within six years of the donor's death with a view to defeating a claim under the 1975 Act. Meg would have to prove that John gave away the sketches to deliberately reduce the value of the net estate available for an order for provision. On the face of it this intention is unlikely. John has died intestate: therefore the bulk of his estate passes to Meg in any event. If he had wanted to frustrate Meg's inheritance he would have made a will leaving his property to someone other than Meg.

Another consideration affecting the gift of the collection is the incidence or burden of Inheritance Tax. If John has not made any previous dispositions then the value of the estate passing to Meg would be free of inheritance tax by virtue of the spouse exemption. The remaining value, the gift of the collection, although caught for tax, would be charged at the nil rate as falling within the band zero to £200,000. If, however, the spouse exemption did not apply (see below regarding Meg's failing to survive) then tax could be payable as the value of the collection exceeds the small estates band and the liability to bear the cost of the tax would fall on the recipient, Donna.

Assuming Donna has established prior dependence, her chances of claiming more from the estate in addition to the sketches will rest on her ability to prove John has failed to make reasonable provision for her maintenance. The court would consider any moral obligation owed by John to Donna, the value of her existing assets including her right to keep the collection and the claims of Meg as surviving spouse. Meg would be in a strong position. She has the bulk of the estate on intestacy. In considering her rights in Family Provision the basis is the spouse provision, not simply maintenance. The court would consider the length of the marriage and the contribution Meg has made to the marriage. The onus would be on Donna to alter the distribution of the estate by claiming John has failed to make reasonable provision for her.

Family Provision

An alternative, if the apartment is regarded as separate accommodation from 'The Gables', itself is that Donna may have a claim in proprietary estoppel as used in *Re Basham* (1987).

In order to establish a claim Donna would have to prove that she reasonably believed she was going to receive the apartment on John's death. Further, that the belief was encouraged by John; that she has acted to her detriment and she has acted in the belief and reliance that she would be given the property on death. The claim would only be possible if the accommodation was held under a separate title to the remainder of 'The Gables' and, for example, in working for John for low wages she was acting on the reliance, in the light of his representations, that she would be left the apartment. Against Donna would be the argument that she was living rent-free and meals were being provided, hence the low wage and, if she is to proceed with a claim, she might have a stronger case applying for maintenance provision out of the net estate under the Inheritance Act 1975.

If Meg died three weeks after John she would lose her entitlement to the estate – s 1 Law Reform (Succession) Act 1995. If a Grant of Administration had been issued to Meg (she would be entitled under Rule 22 Non-Contentious Probate Rules 1987) the grant would be revoked. It is unlikely, indeed it would have been unwise, that any distribution of assets had taken place in view of the requirement of conditional survivorship of the spouse on intestacy and the possibility of a Family Provision application by Donna. The death of Meg would mean Betty would be entitled to the entire estate as surviving parent of the intestate deceased. The redistribution could improve Donna's chances of a successful application for reasonable provision from the estate for she will no longer be competing with a surviving spouse and Betty appears to be well provided for compared with Donna. There would be an inheritance tax liability on Donna in respect of the gift of the collection as the value would take the estate over the nil rate band threshold.

If Betty died after Meg the assets would pass according to any valid will made by Betty. However, if Betty died intestate and there are no surviving blood relatives the assets, including those from John's estate would devolve on *bona vacantia* to the Crown or the Duchies of Cornwall or Lancaster, depending upon where Betty lived. Donna could have no claim to the assets on intestacy as she is not a blood relative, merely a relative by marriage. Again any case for Family Provision may be stronger given there are now no relatives of John entitled to his assets. If Betty herself had been considering a claim for reasonable provision, as a dependant, the right would die with her – *Whyte v Ticehurst* (1986).

Chapter 4

Construction

Introduction

The rules concerning the construction of wills have been revised by s 21 of the Administration of Justice Act 1982 together with the limited powers of rectification of wills in s 20. The basic rules of construction should be studied carefully, but when one considers the admission of extrinsic evidence in the case of ambiguity, the older cases are not necessarily a guide here in view of the revision in the 1982 Act.

It is important to carefully distinguish between the different types of legacies and to understand the distinction between ademption and abatement. The cases concerning ademption and the giving of shareholdings, for example *Re Slater* (1907) and *Re Gage* (1934), are tricky but should be studied carefully. Mistakes are often made in analysing questions on gifts in wills by not defining clearly the types of legacy and unless this is done the full effects of ademption and abatement cannot be appreciated.

The effect of republication under s 34 of the Wills Act should be considered carefully in relation to gifts in wills where it is given there is a later codicil. Does that codicil confirm the will in which case it is likely it would effect an updating of the will under s 34 which could result in a different destination of the gift?

Question 27

Alice, a widow, and her daughter Meg, both died when the car, driven by Meg, crashed.

Alice's will reads as follows:
- 'I appoint one of my brothers to be my executor.' There was added below in pencil 'either Ned or George'.
Alice has three brothers who survive her – Ned, George and Jack.
- '£3,000 to my sister.' There is a line through the figure and £5,000 has been written above in ink. Alice is survived by her two sisters.
- 'My 2,000 shares in British Gas plc to my dear Jack.' At the date of the will Alice had exactly 2,000 shares. Subsequently Alice sold 500 shares; however, shortly before her death Alice received 200 shares in a rights issue.

- 'My house "The Gables", its contents, and my other effects to Meg provided she does not pre-decease me or our deaths coincide, if so, then to (a named) charity.'

  Meg is survived by her illegitimate son Philip.

  Advise Ned upon the appointments and dispositions contained in the will.

Answer plan

The way to approach a mixed construction question of this nature is to take each clause of the wills separately in advising Ned. There is no clear cut answer in each case: instead the purpose is to elicit and demonstrate the issues and potential difficulties. Principal points to be considered in this question are an understanding of the application of s 21 of the Administration of Justice Act 1982 on the admission of extrinsic evidence; an understanding of the distinction between the different types of legacy, in particular the definition of specific legacies; a possible application of s 184 of the Law of Property Act 1925 and the approach of the court to the interpretation of the wording in clause 4 as to 'my other effects'.

Answer

The first point to consider is who would administer the estate on behalf of Alice. The express appointment in clause 1 is patently ambiguous, that is to say that it is ambiguous on the face of the instrument. Prior to 1983 it was not possible to admit extrinsic evidence to resolve a patent ambiguity, save in the exceptional case of *Doe d Gord v Needs* (1836). However, by s 21(1)(b) of the Administration of Justice Act 1982 the court will admit extrinsic evidence in so far as the language used in any part of the will is ambiguous on the face of the will. Evidence would have to be sought therefore of any statements made by Alice which showed that she preferred one brother against another. Would the court take account of the word in pencil? Where a will is written in ink or typewritten, and words in pencil are included then there is an evidential presumption that the words in pencil are merely deliberative (see in the goods of *Adams* (1872)). The words may be testamentary but there would have to be clear proof that they were written prior to execution by the testatrix. Evidence could be adduced by the witnesses by affidavit of due execution (see r 12 The Non-Contentious Probate Rules 1987), in order to establish whether the interlineation was written prior to execution. If there is no clear proof, one is up against the presumption that any alterations or interlineations are made not only after execution of the will but after the execution of any codicils (s 21 Wills Act 1837). If it cannot be proved that the words are testamentary there is still the possibility, if it can be established that the writing matches the handwriting of Alice, that the words could be admissible as extrinsic evidence to at least eliminate Jack as a possible executor. Even if that was the case one would still need evidence to distinguish between the choice of either Ned or George. In the absence of extrinsic evidence to resolve the ambiguity the appointment of the executor would fail. It is not as if the court could, say, appoint Ned and George because the will says 'I appoint one of my brothers to be my executor'.

The legacy of £3,000 to 'my sister' is an example of a latent ambiguity. Extrinsic evidence was admissible prior to 1983 where the gift was not ambiguous on the face of the instrument (see, for example, *Re Jackson* (1933)) (1). The admissibility of extrinsic evidence where the ambiguity is latent is now encompassed in s 21(1)(c) of the 1982 Act. The extrinsic evidence which is admissible may be direct, that is, statements made by the testator including statements as to his or her intention, together with circumstantial extrinsic evidence, for example, which sister Alice favoured (2). Assuming the evidence can resolve the identity of the sister what is the value of the legacy which the sister could take? The alteration involves an application of s 21 of the Wills Act 1837. If the alteration is not attested in accordance with s 9 of the Wills Act then the new amount cannot take effect and one would look to see whether the former amount is 'apparent on the face of the instrument'. Here, since there is simply a line through the original figure one could presumably see what was there before and, assuming the identity of the beneficiary is resolved, the sister would take £3,000.

In the case of the bequest in clause 3 one has to identify what type of legacy is represented by the gift of the shares. If the legacy is specific, that is to say, Alice has identified those particular 2,000 shares in British Gas plc, then the risk is the application of the doctrine of ademption. A specific gift is one which refers to the testator's asset in such a way as to distinguish it from the other assets in the estate and indicate that the asset is to pass to the legatee *in specie*, see the *dictum* of Jessel MR in *Bothamley v Sherson* (1875). Is the gift a specific legacy? The inclusion of the possessive word 'my' in describing the shares, points towards a specific legacy. Also, the fact that at the date of the will Alice owned exactly 2,000 shares in British Gas plc. However, the courts are reluctant to hold as a specific legacy the gift of shares which are subject to fluctuation and have indicated that the mere fact that Alice owns the exact number of shares at the date of the will is not conclusive. It is said that the court leans against construing legacies as specific (see *Re Rose* (1949)). This reluctance is due to the effect of the doctrine of ademption so that here, if the gift is held to be specific, the sale of the 500 shares would cause a partial ademption and the 200 shares received in the rights issue could be construed as completely new shares which would not be included in the gift (See *Re Kuypers* (1925)). The difference here as against *Re Kuypers* (3) is that the shares do not appear to have changed in class and one could therefore possibly argue that the 200 shares are identical to the other shares and, in the absence of contrary intention, applying s 24 of the Wills Act 1837 which construes gifts of property in wills as applying to their description at the date of death, one could argue that the 200 shares could be included, therefore the beneficiary would receive 1,700 shares. The problem is if the intention is to regard the 2,000 shares specifically as those 2,000 shares then the 200 shares would be considered additional and not part of the gift. The distinction between specific legacy and general legacy is one of intention. One could argue here that as Alice sold 500 shares by the time the will was executed this could indicate a general intention to give 2,000 shares to the beneficiary in any event. This would point towards construction as a general legacy. Where, however, the legacy is construed as specific and ademption occurs, then the doctrine of ademption applies independently of the testator's intention. One looks then at the change of form of the asset and the key is whether the asset can be traced. In *Re Slater* (1907) (4) Cozens-Hardy MR said in relation to the test 'where is the thing which is given? If you cannot find it at the testator's death, it is no use trying to trace it unless you can trace it in this sense, you will find something which has been changed in name and form only, but which is substantially the same thing'. If the gift is construed to be a general bequest then the beneficiary will take the shares answering the description which are held by the estate at death, here 1,700, and the balance is construed as a direction upon the personal representatives to either require the remaining shares or give the beneficiary the equivalent in money.

To whom are the shares given? Is Jack Alice's brother or someone else answering the description? One would look at the circumstances surrounding the will at the date of death and then if there is some doubt, apply the 'armchair rule' where one looks at the circumstances as Alice saw them at the date the will was executed (see for example *Charter v Charter* (1874)) (5).

Clause 4 is the devise of the house together with the constructional issue as to the extent of the remainder of the gift. Who is entitled to the gift? If there is any direct evidence as to the order of deaths between Alice and Meg then this will apply. So if the evidence shows that Meg pre-deceased Alice even by seconds then the property would pass to the charity. If, on the other hand, the evidence shows that Meg survived Alice then the property will pass according to Meg's will or intestacy and it is possible then that her son Philip could be a beneficiary. He would not be prevented from taking merely because he is illegitimate since the 1987 Family Law Reform Act removes illegitimacy as a bar in any succession to property. If there is no clear evidence as to who has survived then the question arises whether the statutory presumption in s 184 Law Property Act 1925 should be applied. What is the effect of the proviso, in particular the words 'or our deaths coincide'? In *Re Rowland* (1962) the Court of Appeal, by a majority, held that the word *coincide* means no more and no less than dying at the same time. Since one could not prove that the parties died at exactly the same time the court rules that the statutory presumption should be applied. If this is the case then Meg, the younger, would be presumed to have survived Alice and again it could be possible that Philip could share depending upon Meg's will or intestacy. In a dissenting judgment in *Re Rowland*, Lord Denning argued that one should ask what the words meant to the particular testator and he construed the use of the word *coincide* as meaning death occurring in a common accident where both Dr and Mrs Rowland perished. He cited the support of the House of Lords in *Re Perrin v*

Morgan (1943) but the majority of the court in *Re Rowland* could also cite *Perrin v Morgan* when saying that one interprets a will by considering the meaning of the written word which the testator used in a particular case. In *Re Rowland* the majority construed the word 'coinciding' in its strict sense of simultaneous. Therefore, on the authority of *Re Rowland* the statutory presumption would apply and the property would pass to Meg's estate.

The will does not appear to include a general residuary bequest. The only doubt is in the construction in clause 4 in the words 'my other effects'. Are these words to be confined within the context of 'The Gables' and its contents or could one put a broader construction upon the words 'my other effects' to mean the residue of the estate? One would look at the words used in the context of the will to try to determine Alice's intention adopting the approach of Viscount Simon LC in *Perrin v Morgan* when he said 'the question is not, of course, what the testator meant to do when he made his will, but what the written words he used mean in the particular case ... what are the "expressed intentions" of the testator'. If the court adopts a narrow construction in confining effects to personal effects in the house then there would be partial intestacy in view of the failure to make a general residuary gift.

Notes
1 In *Re Jackson* (1933) the testatrix left property to 'my nephew Arthur Murphy'. When the will was placed in context at death it was discovered that there were three nephews all called Arthur Murphy. All three were known to the testatrix at the date she executed the will. Two of the nephews were legitimate and the third illegitimate. (If, as the law stood at that time, there had only been one legitimate nephew called Arthur Murphy there would have been no equivocation because the law would have only recognised the legitimate nephew.) Because there were two legitimate nephews called Arthur Murphy revealed by the surrounding circumstances, this created a latent ambiguity and extrinsic evidence was admitted which revealed that the testatrix intended the illegitimate nephew to benefit.
2 Suppose in the case of the two sisters referred to in clause 2 one of them was the natural sister to Alice and the other a stepsister. Then there would have been no ambiguity because, *prima*

facie, the court would have construed the reference to sister as meaning the blood sister since relationships are construed strictly; therefore, in saying '£3,000 to my sister' there would be no ambiguity. Therefore the court would not admit extrinsic evidence even though Alice really intended the step-sister to benefit. In *NSPCC v SNSPCC* (1915) the testatrix left property to numerous Scottish charities. In a final codicil she left a legacy to the National Society for the Prevention of Cruelty to Children. The gift was challenged by the Scottish National Society for the Prevention of Cruelty to Children on the basis that all the testatrix's associations were Scottish and that her intention was almost certainly to benefit the Scottish Society. However, in making the gift she had accurately described the NSPCC, the English National Charity, and therefore the gift was not ambiguous and as a result extrinsic evidence could not be admitted.

3 In *Re Kuypers* (1925) the testatrix made a specific request of 600 15% cumulative preferred ordinary shares of £1 each in a company. Subsequently, by virtue of special resolutions of the shareholders of the company, these shares were consolidated with certain other preference shares and were allotted to the holders of the 15% preference shares as shares in one class of 8% cumulative preference shares of £1 each. In place of her 600 15% preference shares the testatrix received £1,200 of the new 8% preference shares. The court held that the specific legacy should relate to the 600 8% preference shares as these were traced as the actual shares referred to in the will. The court said they remained the same shares with a continuous history since before the will was made. On the other hand, the additional shares were held to be wholly new shares subscribed and paid for out of the reserve fund. These new shares were in the form of a compensation for a variation of the class rights and could not be treated as coming within the description of the original gift.

4 In *Re Slater* (1907) there was a gift of stock in the Lambeth Water Works. After the date of the will the stock was taken over by the Metropolitan Water Board and Metropolitan stock was given in lieu. The question arose as to whether this new stock passed under the bequest or whether there been ademption. The court held the gift was in fact not specific but general.

However, in construing the terms of the statute pursuant to which the shares had been taken over the court concluded that the Metropolitan Water Board stock was entirely new and the Lambeth stock had disappeared; therefore there was nothing on which to fasten a value for the personal representatives to give the beneficiaries. There had therefore been an extinction of the interest and the bequest could not take effect.

5   In *Charter v Charter* (1874) the testator left property by will to 'my son Forster Charter'. Following the death of the testator it was discovered that his son Forster had died some years before the will was executed. Two other sons had survived the testator, William Forster Charter and Charles Charter. William claimed the property on the basis that his middle name was 'Forster'. However, the court applied the 'armchair rule' whereby they looked at the situation as at the date of the will, that is, looking at the situation as the testator saw it. The admission of evidence under the 'armchair rule' revealed that William rarely saw his father but Charles lived with his father and his father was in the habit of frequently calling Charles 'Forster'; therefore Charles Charter was able to take the property.

Question 28

Was Lord Atkin being optimistic in his observation on the construction of wills when, in *Perrin v Morgan* (1943), he anticipated 'with satisfaction that henceforth the group of hosts of dissatisfied testators who, according to a late Chancery judge, wait on the other bank of the Styx to receive the judicial personages who have misconstrued their wills maybe considerably diminished' [1943] AC 399 at 415 (House of Lords).

Answer plan

This quote is asking you to consider the judicial attitude towards the construction of wills. Is the approach today more liberal than it was, say, at the turn of the century? Where a will is unclear as to its meaning matter may be referred to the Chancery Division as a court of construction. The Chancery Division of the 19th century and the early part of the 20th century took a strict line on the grammatical meaning of words, then gave a short shrift to, albeit well meaning testators, where the court considered the words used in the will were unclear. The quote requires consideration through the cases as to whether the courts today are prepared to adopt a more flexible approach. Certainly this approach is encouraged in the wording of the judgments in *Perrin v Morgan* itself. In addition one has the more flexible approach to the admission of extrinsic evidence now contained in s 21 of the Administration of Justice Act 1982 and the statutory power to rectify wills contained in s 20 of the 1982 Act.

The way to approach this question is to illustrate through the cases the approach of the courts in the construction of wills.

Answer

The optimism of the Lord Atkin in *Perrin v Morgan* (1943) stems from what was perceived to be a more liberal view of the interpretation of wills. *Perrin v Morgan* itself was concerned with the interpretation of the word 'moneys'. The word money has changed in meaning over the centuries as society developed more sophisticated banking procedures and forms of investment. Where one is considering the interpretation of a word which has shifted in meaning then the word and the context in the will are considered at the time the will was made. In an often quoted extract from the judgement Lord Simon said:

> '... fundamental rule in construing the language of a will is to put on the words used the meaning which, having regard to the terms of the will, the testator intended. The question is not, of course, what the testator meant to do when he made his will, but what the written words he uses mean in the particular case. What are the "expressed intentions" of the testator?.'

These words are frequently quoted as evidence of a more liberal approach in the construction of wills. Lord Simon then went on to refuse to place any cast iron meaning on the word money but went on to consider the way the meaning of the word has changed over the years.

How do the courts go about construing the meaning of the testator's will? It will become effective on the death of the testator. The first step is to read the will and consider whether it is clearly expressed. One places the will in the context of the surrounding circumstances at the death of the testator. This is essential in order to determine the extent of the estate and whether particular references to property and persons correspond with the property and persons at the death of the testator. It must be borne in mind that the function of the court is to interpret the words which the testator used and not attempt to make the will itself. This approach is implicit in the above quote from the judgment of Lord Simon. The court can only interpret the testator's intention as expressed in the will and it is not the court's function as Lord Justice Jenkins said in *Re Bailey* (1951) 'to improve upon or perfect testamentary dispositions'. The will must be read as a whole. Words are given their ordinary grammatical meaning unless the context of the will indicates otherwise. If the testator uses words which are clear and unambiguous effect must be given to them however capricious they may appear to be. The testator is at liberty to adopt his own eccentricity and it may be that this could only be challenged on the basis that this may be *prima facie* evidence that the testator lacked capacity at the time he made the will or those persons who feel unjustly served by the will could consider an application under the Family Provision legislation.

If, by reading the will as a whole and placing it in the context at death, doubt arises as to the meaning of words then the court will adopt the so called 'armchair rule'. This entails attempting to look at the will in the context and through the eyes of the testator as he saw the will when it was made. *Thorn v Dickens* (1906), a case which is recorded as the shortest litigated will, is an example of this approach. The will said simply 'all to mother'. Evidence of the circumstances at the testator's death showed that the testator was well aware that his mother was dead when he made the will. This raised the question of what he meant. In looking at the context at the time the will was made it became clear that in referring to 'mother' he was in fact referring to his wife.

If equivocation is revealed in the context, in the form of a latent ambiguity, or indeed where the gift is ambiguous on the face of it, then the court is permitted to admit extrinsic evidence, including

Construction

evidence of the testator's intention, in order to resolve the ambiguity.

The court will approach a clause by looking at it in the context of the will as a whole. The approach is to deduce the intention of the testator from the will itself. To assist it, the court adopts 'rules of construction', that is rules of convenience in assisting the courts to arrive at a solution to the meaning of a gift. It is emphasised that the court will not attempt to write the will for the testator so where the words used are clear then, subject to the limited power of rectification in s 20 of the Administration of Justice Act 1982, the court will give effect to the words used even though it is likely that that is not what the testator intended, see for example *Scale v Rawlins* (1892) (1) and *National Society for the Prevention of Cruelty to Children v Scottish National Society for the Prevention of Cruelty to Children* (1915). In the *NSPCC* case the testatrix gave various legacies to Scottish charities. Included among these was a legacy to the National Society for the Prevention of Cruelty to Children, that is, the name of the English charity. The gift was challenged on the basis that the testatrix had lived all her life in Scotland and all her associations were with Scotland. However, she had accurately described the English society; therefore effect was given to that gift (2). The court can interpret words in their strict sense, therefore resulting in a narrower construction to a provision than was perhaps was intended by the testator, for example, in the approach by the majority of the Court of Appeal in *Re Rowland* (1963) (3).

The basic approach is that a word is given its ordinary grammatical meaning. This is to safeguard against wills becoming too general in expression. Where a word is used whose meaning has altered over the years then the meaning which is to be contributed is the meaning applicable at the date the will was made, as in the construction of the word money in *Perrin v Morgan*. The testator may however indicate a secondary meaning to a word. Exceptionally the will contains a definition clause. Alternatively when the will becomes effective, on the death of the testator, and is placed in the surrounding circumstances these circumstances may indicate a secondary meaning. *Re Davidson* (1949) is an example whereby the context of the will showed that the testator had applied a secondary meaning (4) as is *Re Smalley* (1929) where the testator left his property to 'my wife Eliza Ann Smalley'. His lawful wife was called Mary Smalley but surrounding circumstances showed that the testator lived with a woman called Eliza Ann. The court concluded that the testator had used the word wife in the secondary sense meaning common law wife.

A secondary meaning may emerge when the court applies the 'armchair rule' first described by Lord Justice James in *Boyes v Cook* (1880) when he said 'You may place yourself, so to speak, in the testator's armchair and consider the circumstances by which he was surrounded when he made his will'. So in *Thorne v Dickins*, referred to above, application of the armchair rule showed that the testator intended his wife to have the property and in *Charter v Charter* (1874) it indicated that the testator intended his son Charles Charter to benefit.

Words may have more than one meaning. *Perrin v Morgan* is a good example of the approach that the court will adopt the most probable meaning in the circumstances. Lord Simon said that it was a mistake to pick out one interpretation of a word and call it the 'legal meaning'. In *Perrin v Morgan* the House of Lords held that in the will form made by the testatrix without legal assistance the phrase 'all monies of which I died possessed' was intended to give the whole of the net personal estate (5).

Where a testator uses a word or phrase which has required a technical (legal or scientific) meaning then there is a strong presumption that the words will carry the technical meaning. This presents a danger particularly where the testator writes out the will without legal assistance and includes words which, unappreciated by the testator, carry a strict technical meaning. One has to distinguish between technical words and phrases and words which merely convey description, for example, 'male issue' is a technical phrase meaning the male descendants in the male line whereas the phrase 'male descendants' is not a term of art but a descriptive phrase meaning males descended through both the male and female line, see *Re Drakes WT* (1969). The dangers in *Perrin* in using legal phraseology are well illustrated in *Re Cook* (1948) where the testatrix, in a homemade will, gave 'all my personal estate whatsoever' to her nephew and nieces. The bulk of the estate consisted of realty and the court held that this had not been disposed by the phrase; therefore the bulk of the estate passed on intestacy (6).

'Next of kin' is not a technical phrase. It has been construed as the nearest blood relations but one would look at the context in which the phrase is used, so, for example, if the will referred to the next of kin who would benefit on an intestacy this would be construed as the statutory next of kin.

The testator may use special words or symbols which have a meaning only within his locality, trade, or business. In *Kell v Charmer* (1856) the testator, a jeweller, had indicated an amount of certain legacies in the form of a jeweller's code which could be interpreted by fellow jewellers. However, if the code is one known only to the testator then in the absence of evidence of incorporation by reference the gift would fail, see *Clayton v Lord Nugent* (1844) (7).

The meaning of a particular word or phrase may be resolved by admission of evidence of custom within a particular trade or group of persons which included the testator. *Kell v Charmer* is an example of a customary use of codes in the jeweller's trade. In *Shore v Wilson* (1842) the testator was a member of a dissenting religious sect and the term 'godly persons' was interpreted with reference to a meaning current among members of the sect.

The courts have always maintained that they will not attempt to write a will for the testator. However, prior to the passing of the Administration of Justice Act 1982, there were two circumstances where the court would alter a will in the absence of fraud. The court omits words included by inadvertence or mistake if the omission would give affect to the testator's intention as in *Re Morris dec'd* (1971). Alternatively, the court could in certain circumstances supply words to give the meaning to a clause where this would with certainty carry out the testator's intention.

In *Re Whitrick* (1957) the testatrix by her will left all her property to her husband but added 'in the event of my husband ... and myself both dying at the same time' then the estate was to be held for certain named persons. The husband predeceased the testatrix leaving a will in similar terms so that the testatrix inherited the whole estate. The question arose upon her death as to whether the trust would take effect. The Court of Appeal held that the testatrix had not expressed the whole contingency which she really intended and was prepared to add the proviso that the gift should take effect if the husband predeceased her. The court in *Re Whitrick* was not rectifying the will, rather, the court was adding words to overcome a defect.

By s 20 of the Administration of Justice Act 1982 the court has power to rectify a will in two alternative circumstances. First, where the will fails to carry out the testator's intention as a result of a clerical error, for example, where £50 is written instead of £500 or the name of X is erroneously inserted instead of Y (for an example of rectification as a result of a clerical error see *Wordingham v Royal Exchange Trust* (1992)). Secondly, where the testator and the transcriber are at cross purposes so that the transcriber is mistaken as to the true intentions of the testator. Section 20 would cover the situation which arose in *Re Morris* but it is to be emphasised that the statutory power to rectify is confined to these two circumstances and therefore the principle in *Re Whitrick* is still relevant. Also where the wronged beneficiary cannot recover under s 20 there is the possibility of an action for negligence against the draftsman under the principle in *Re Ross v Caunters* (1980).

The optimism expressed by Lord Simon has been given an added boost by the statutory revision of the powers to admit the extrinsic evidence now contained in s 21 of the Administration of Justice Act 1982. The armchair rule allows the court to admit facts which were known to the testator at the time he made the will. The application of this rule allows the court to admit evidence to illustrate that the testator intended a secondary meaning to a particular word or description as for example in *Re Fish* (1894) (8). Section 21 allows extrinsic evidence in so far as any part of the will is meaningless (s 21(1)(a)). This would cover, for example, situations such as *Kell v Charmer* where, at first glance the code was meaningless, and would now enable evidence to be admitted in a situation such as *Clayton v Lord Nugent*. However, it is doubtful whether the court would allow extrinsic evidence where the testator had left a gift in blank.

Subparagraphs (b) and (c) to s 21(1) allow the admission of extrinsic evidence in so far as the language used in any part of the will is ambiguous on the face of the will (para (b)) or in so far as evidence, other than evidence of the testator's intention, shows that the language used in any part of the will is ambiguous in the light of the surrounding circumstances (para (c)). These two subparagraphs represent a widening of the former *Wigram* rules on the admission of extrinsic evidence. Under the *Wigram* rules an ambiguity could be revealed by evidence of the material facts and cured by extrinsic evidence, as for example in *Re Jackson* (1933) (9).

The effect of subpara (b) is to admit extrinsic evidence to resolve the gift which is clearly ambiguous on the face of the will. This is the extension to the admission of evidence for, prior to the 1982 Act, such words would have to be construed upon the face of the will without the admission of extrinsic evidence and the gift would fail. Subparagraph (c) takes the admission of extrinsic evidence further in the case of latent ambiguities by allowing the admission of circumstantial extrinsic evidence, that is to say, evidence other than evidence of the testator's intention, to reveal the ambiguity. How far the courts will be prepared to go in admitting evidence in construing the will, will depend upon whether they adopt a narrow interpretation to s 21 or a wider interpretation. Does the extension by paras (b) and (c) mean that 'ambiguous' will be construed as possibly having more than one meaning objectively or subjectively? One cannot admit extrinsic evidence of the testator's intention in order to create the ambiguity. For example, if there had only been one legitimate nephew in *Re Jackson* that nephew would have taken as there would have been no ambiguity. Whether the extension of the rules on the admission of extrinsic evidence, particularly by subpara (c), alter the *NSPCC* case is debatable. By accurately describing the English charity there was no ambiguity. The material fact was that there was a charity answering the description given in the will. However, the purpose of the extension in para (c) is to use extrinsic evidence to make the disposition mean something other than it naturally appears to mean. Therefore, one could argue that by placing the gift in the context of the surrounding circumstances, the fact that all the other gifts were to a Scottish institutions and given the testatrix's connections, this would allow the court to adopt a subjective meaning to 'ambiguous' and allow the Scottish charity to take the gift.

As the time the legislation which became ss 20 and 21 of the 1982 Act were passing through Parliament the then Lord Chancellor, Lord Hailsham, recognised that the legislation represented a codification of the rules on the admission of extrinsic evidence. If the courts are going to construe s 21 widely then it would appear that Lord Atkin's optimism is well founded.

Notes
1 In *Scale v Rawlins* (1892) the testator left three houses to his niece for life and providing she should die leaving no children the houses were to pass to certain nephews. The niece died leaving children. The question arose did they take the property? The court ruled no; although this was probably the intention of the testator, the will did not say so, therefore, the houses passed to the nephews.
Note that if one could establish today that the drafting of the will was the result of a misunderstanding between the testator and the draftsman it is possible that application could be lodged for rectification of the will.
2 The description was not ambiguous. Whether this approach would be different in the light of s 21(1)(c) of the 1982 Act is debatable (see *infra*).
3 The majority of the Court of Appeal in *Re Rowland* interpreted the word 'coinciding' in its strict sense of simultaneous. Since it could not be proved the doctor and Mrs Rowland had died simultaneously the contingency did not take effect; therefore the majority applied the statutory presumption as to survivorship in s 184 Law of Property Act 1925. Lord Denning, in his dissenting judgment, argued that one should construe 'coinciding' in a wider sense looking at what Dr Rowland intended when he wrote the provision. Although one can sympathise with Lord Denning, the danger with this approach is that is can lead one down the path of writing a will for the testator. For a debate upon Lord Denning's approach and the way he countered criticism, see his Lordship's book *The Discipline of the Law*.
There is evidence of a greater flexibility on the part of the judiciary by judges no longer referring to the 'rules' of construction but instead making reference to 'guides'. Lord Denning has been the strongest critic of hard and fast rules and his approach is typified by his *dictum* in *Re Allsop (dec'd)* (1968): 'Eschewing technical rules and literal interpretation you must look to see simply what the testator intended. If you find that a literal interpretation gives rise to a capricious result which you are satisfied the testator can never have intended then you should reject that interpretation and seek for a sensible interpretation which does accord with his intention.'

(For a detailed consideration of the principles see 'The Wind of Change in the Law of Wills' by Professor C H Sherrin in *The Conveyancer* Vol 40 at p 66).

4   In *Re Davidson* the testator had earlier in the will referred to his named stepson as 'my son' and to one of the stepson's children as 'my granddaughter'. The court concluded that the testator had therefore adopted a secondary meaning to the word 'grandchildren' to include not only the blood line but the children of the stepson.

5   Lord Simon in *Perrin v Morgan* said 'in choosing between "popular" meanings, it seems to me that an interpretation which includes realty as well as personalty in the word "money" may often be going too far though of course, everything turns on the language and circumstances of the particular will. An amateur will maker, though using the word "money" loosely may be drawing a distinction between "my money" and "my land", and indeed, may mean to include leaseholds as well as freeholds in the latter expression, if he owns both'.

6   In *Re Cook* (1948) Mr Justice Harman said 'it seems unlikely that she intended to dispose only of the personal estate in the lawyer's sense of that word ... but this is the case that a layman had chosen to use a term of art. The words "all my personal estate" are words so well known to lawyers that it must take a very strong context to make them include real estate. Testators can make black mean white if they make the dictionary sufficiently clear, but the testatrix has not done so. It may well be that she thought "personal estate" meant "all my worldly goods"; I do not known. In the absence of something to show that the phrase ought to be so construed, I must suppose that she used the term "personal estate" in its ordinary meaning as a term of art'.

7   In *Clayton v Lord Nugent* (1844) the donee's in the will were described by letters which referred to a card index system maintained by the testator which was not incorporated by reference. It was not possible to admit extrinsic evidence as to the significance of the letters.

8   In *Re Fish* (1894) the testator bequeathed property 'to my niece Eliza Waterhouse'. When the will was placed in context at death it was discovered that the testator did not have a niece of

that name but his wife had a grand niece called Eliza Waterhouse. The court concluded that the testator had used the word 'niece' in the wider sense; therefore the grand niece took the property. The armchair rule has been applied to descriptions of property as in *Ricketts v Turquand* (1848) where the testator described the property in the will as 'my Ashford Hall Estate'. Evidence was admitted through the use of the armchair rule to determine what the testator meant by his Ashford Hall Estate.

9 In *Re Jackson* (1933) the testatrix left property 'to my nephew Arthur Murphy'. When the will took effect and surrounding circumstances were considered it was discovered that the testatrix had three nephews called Arthur Murphy. Two were legitimate, the third illegitimate. As the law stood at that time if there had only been two nephews, one legitimate the other illegitimate, there would have been no ambiguity for the legitimate nephew would have taken. However, since there were two legitimate nephews answering the description extrinsic evidence was admitted under the *Wigram* Rules which showed that the testatrix intended the illegitimate nephew to take the property.

Question 29

> 'If a man lies in extremities ... and not having the opportunity of making his will; but lest he should die before he could make it, he gives with his own hands his goods to his friends; this, if he dies shall operate as a legacy.' (*Per* Lord Cowper in *Hedges v Hedges* (1708).)

Explain by reference to the case law the requirements which must be established in order to make a *valid donatio mortis causa*.

Answer plan

This essay should start by clearly setting out the requirements which must be established to make a *valid donatio* and should then expand upon the three conditions, with illustrations, from the case law.

Answer

A *donatio mortis causa* is a gift made in contemplation of death. It is considered mid-way between a gift *inter vivos* and testamentary gift. To establish a *valid donatio* three requirements must be present: first, the gift must be made in contemplation, although not necessarily in expectation, of impending death; secondly, the gift is made on the condition that it is to be absolute and perfected only on the donor's death, revocable until that death and ineffective if death does not take place; and thirdly, there must be delivery of the subject matter or sufficient indication of title amounting to a parting with dominion over the property and not merely a parting with possession. The gift is conditional upon death; once the condition is satisfied it takes effect retrospectively from the date the gift was made (see *Rigden v Vallier* (1751)). It follows, therefore, that the donor must have intended the gift to be absolute once the condition is fulfilled (*Re Beaumont* (1902)).

The donor must be contemplating death in the near future and from some reason which he believes to be impending, for example, in *Re Craven's Estate* (1937), where a donor made a gift expressed in a general contemplation of death this did not amount to a valid *donatio*. It would be a question then of intention as to whether the donor intended the gift to take effect as a gift *inter vivos*. Evidence that the donor believed that death was impending may come from his words used, for example, 'I am done for' as in *Re Lillingstone* (1952) or can be inferred where the gift is made during illness and shortly before death as in *Gardner v Parker* (1818) (1). The donor does not have to die from the illness causing the specific contemplation unless the gift is made conditional upon death from that illness. In *Wilkes v Allington* (1931) the donor mortgagee knew that he was dying from cancer and handed over the mortgage deed to relatives. He subsequently caught a chill and died of pneumonia. The court held that this was a *valid donation* (2).

Does the contemplation of death have to be reasonable? English authorities appear to adopt a subjective approach, the belief in the mind of the donor, rather than the objective test of reasonableness. In *Re Miller* (1961) the court held that a *valid donatio* was possible where a woman had a fear of flying even though it was pointed out in the case that, statistically, air travel is safer than driving a car.

The donor must part with dominion over the property either by handing over the assets or the means to control. One has to consider whether control has passed. For example, where the donor hands over a cash box but retains the key this would not amount to a *valid donatio* (see *Redell v Dobree* (1839)). However, there will be a *valid donatio*, even though the donor has retained a set of keys, where in reality the donor no longer intends to use the asset. In *Woodward v Woodward* (1992) the donor father was gravely ill from cancer and gave his son the keys to his car. The son used the car on his journeys, with his mother, to the hospital to visit the father. A few days before his death the father said to the son 'You can keep the keys, I won't be driving it anymore'. The father had retained a duplicate set of keys but the court held that a *valid donatio* had been made on the basis that the father intended dominion to be transferred to the son. In *Sen v Headley* (1991) the Court of Appeal reversing the decision at first instance held that a gift of land by the constructive delivery of title deeds could amount to a *valid donatio*. Shortly before his death, in the last stages of a terminal illness, the donor told a friend 'The house is yours ... You have the keys. They are in your bag, the deeds are in the steel box'. At some stage unbeknown to the donee the donor had slipped the set of keys in the donee's handbag. The Court of Appeal held that the intention implicit in the act resulted in the personal representatives of the deceased holding the property as trustees for the donee under a constructive trust (3). *Caine v Moon* (1896), the authority which sets out the three requirements for a *valid donatio*, is an example of constructive delivery (4). One can have delivery to the donee's agent as, for example, the handing over of a parcel of stocks to a priest in *Mills v Shields* (1948) with instructions that in the event of the donor's death the parcel was to be given to relatives. If, however, the recipient is an employee of the donor then the person is construed as agent for the donor and dominion would not have passed (*Trimmer v Danby* (1856)). The evidence must establish that the donor has handed over the means by which possession can be obtained, for example, delivery of the only set of keys to a box containing the subject matter as in *Re Craven's Estate No 1* (1937). The means to possession can take several stages as in the handing over of the keys in *Re Lillingstone* (see note 1).

To be a *valid donatio* it must be clear that the gift is conditional upon the donor's death. If the real intention is that the gift is immediate and absolute then this would be construed as a gift *inter vivos* and not a *donatio*. So, for example, an imperfect gift cannot be saved by attempting to construe as a *donatio* if it was not intended as such (*Agnew v Belfast Banking* (1896)). The court will look at the circumstances at the time the gift is made, so, for example, where property is handed over in the last days of a donor's final illness the court is more likely to construe this as a *donatio* rather than simply a gift *inter vivos* (*Gardner v Parker* (1818)) (5). If the donor recovers, the gift is revoked. So in a situation where property is handed over prior to an air journey where the donor has a fear of flying the *donatio* is no longer effected if the donor returns safely. Where the death does occur the gift is effective at the date dominion was handed over; therefore, the subject matter of the gift passes to the donee and not to the personal representatives. So in *Sen v Headley* the personal representatives held all the house on trust for the donee. In these circumstances the personal representatives can be compelled to perfect the gift (see *Duffield v Elwes* (1827)). A *donatio* is subject to Inheritance Tax and liability for the tax falls upon the recipient donee, s 200(1)(c) Inheritance Tax Act 1984 (6).

Notes

1 In *Re Lillingstone* (1952) the donor (L) in poor health (bedridden), told the intended donee that she was 'done for'. She said, 'I'm going to give you all my jewellery. I'm giving you the key to the safe deposit box at Harrods and when I am gone you can go and get the jewellery'. She then handed over the keys to a trunk in her room and added that the donee would find the key to the Harrods safe deposit on the right hand side of the finger of a glove. The donee was told that the key to L's city safe was at Harrods. L added, 'I want you to have all my jewellery except my diamond necklace which is for my goddaughter. That is in my city safe'. She then took a packet from under her pillow saying, 'This is also for you'. L opened it; the packet contained more jewellery, which she placed in the trunk. She then locked the trunk and gave the key to the donee saying, 'Keep the key it is now yours'. The court concluded that there had been a *valid donatio* of all the jewellery.

2   The courts have held that where the donor has committed suicide there is no *valid donatio*. There has been no authority since 1961 when suicide was ruled to be no longer a crime. In *Agnew v Belfast Banking Company* (1896) the donor gave a bank deposit receipt book to the plaintiff saying, 'That is yours if anything should happen to me'. Nine days later the donor poisoned herself leaving a note dated the day of the gift showing her intention to commit suicide. The court refused to hold that there had been a *valid donatio* on the basis that it was against public policy since suicide was a crime. Although *Agnew* is an Irish case the principle was applied by the English courts in *Re Dudman* (1925) where envelopes containing money and letters were handed over and one of the letters clearly indicated that the donor intended suicide. However, it would appear (from an Irish authority) that a subsequent decision to commit suicide will not invalidate the gift. In *Mills v Shields* (1948) the donor was very ill and was considering going to Dublin to undergo what would been dangerous treatment. He gave his priest a parcel containing £600 worth of stocks telling the priest that if anything should happen to him while he was away that he should give the stocks to his brothers in South Africa. Before undergoing the treatment he hanged himself. The court held that a *valid donatio* had been made.
3   The deceased in *Sen* had retained a set of keys to the house but this was held not to prevent an effective transfer of dominion over the property retained. Nourse J said '... By keeping his own set of keys to the house (he) retained possession of it. But the benefits which thereby accrued to him were wholly theoretical. He uttered the words of the gift, without reservation, two days after his readmission to hospital when he knew that he did not have long to live and when there could have been no practical possibility of his ever returning home. He had parted with dominion over the title deeds. Mrs Sen had her own set of keys to the house and was in effect in control of it'.
4   In *Caine v Moon* (1896) Mrs Caine delivered a deposit note to her mother for safe custody. Later when she fell ill and did not expect to live she referred to the note held by her mother and said, 'Everything I possess and the bank note is yours, if I die'. The court held that this was an effective constructive delivery of the subject matter.

5 In *Gardner v Parker* (1818) the donor, on his death bed, said to the donee, 'There, take that and keep it', handing over a bond two days before his death.

Donatios are usually oral. If the gift is made in writing this raises a presumption that it was intended either as a gift *inter vivos* or testamentary. However, the mere fact that the gift is in writing will not necessarily invalidate the *donatio* if the intention can be proved. In *Wilkes v Allington* (1931) the donor delivered a mortgage deed as an intended *donatio*. He had written on the envelope containing the deeds of the property 'deeds relating to Astwood. To be given up at death'. The court, in holding that this was a *valid donatio* rather than an abortive gift *inter vivos*, said that the writing was simply identifying the subject matter of the gift.

Question 30

Gerald, a widower, died in May. His will, executed five years ago, contains (*inter alia*) the following provisions:

(a) To my sister Edith, my gold watch.
(b) To my dearest brother-in-law, my stamp collection.
(c) To my friend Arthur, a Mercedes motor car.
(d) To my nephew Eric, the £500 in my account with the Eastshire Building Society.
(e) To my godson Jeremy, £2,000 payable out of my account with the Northshire Building Society.
(f) To my uncle Samuel, my 1,000 ordinary shares in Pixons.
(g) £15,000 each to my daughters Kate and Emily.

You ascertain the following:

(i) Edith and Kate both predeceased Gerald, each leaving two daughters alive at the date of Gerald's death.
(ii) Gerald had two brothers-in-law, both of whom he visited regularly prior to his death.
(iii) At the date the will was executed Gerald owned a Skoda car which he replaced six months ago with a Ford Fiesta. He has never owned a Mercedes.
(iv) At the date of Gerald's death the balance of his account with the Eastshire Building Society stood at £200.
(v) The Northshire Building Society account was closed in 1990.

(vi) In 1990 Pixons had converted its £1 ordinary shares into two units of 50p ordinary stock. Gerald owned 2,000 units of Pixons ordinary stock at the date of his death.

Advise Gerald's executors in respect of the above gifts.

Answer plan

This is a classic form of constructional question based upon the application of the meaning of legacies and devises and the doctrine of lapse. It is important in a question of this nature to define the terms ademption and abatement and to identify the different types of legacy. Once the type of legacy is identified then one applies this to the individual beneficiaries to see whether or not to apply the doctrine of lapse. The best approach to avoid confusion in applying the law to the facts is to deal with each clause separately.

Answer

The advice to the executors is given by reference to each individual clause.

(a) The gift to Edith is a specific legacy, that is to say that Gerald identifies his gold watch in such a way as to separate it from other aspects of the estate. A precondition of the law of succession is that a beneficiary should survive the testator in order to take the benefit. There are exceptions to this doctrine of lapse. However, in this case, since Edith, Gerald's sister, has predeceased Gerald, the gift will lapse. The important exception contained in s 33 of the Wills Act 1837 will not apply since this section only applies to gifts to children and remoter issue and here we are given that Edith is the testator's sister.

(b) This gift is ambiguous given that there are two brothers-in-law. Section 21(1)(c) of the Administration of Justice Act 1982 allows for the admission of extrinsic evidence, that is to say evidence outside of the will, in order to identify for which brother-in-law provision is made. This evidence could include statements made by Gerald which would amount to direct extrinsic evidence, or the court could permit the admission of circumstantial extrinsic evidence to indicate which brother-in-law is to receive the gift. This could include, for example, evidence that one particular brother-in-law was always interested in the stamp collection. If the extrinsic evidence cannot resolve which brother-in-law Gerald intended to benefit then the gift could fail for uncertainty. The stamp collection would then fall into residue.

(c) The legacy here is a general legacy, that is to say it does not identify a particular item owned by Gerald at the date of death but is construed as a direction to the personal representatives to acquire the asset for the beneficiary. A problem here could be one of specifics given the possible uncertainty as to the particular model and type of Mercedes and given a possible discrepancy in value between a Mercedes motor car and the type of cars which Gerald had previously owned and owned at death. It would be a matter for the personal representatives to negotiate for Arthur, in relation to the value of the whole estate, whether to purchase a suitable car or to negotiate a cash settlement.

(d) The legacy here is demonstrative in nature (see *Ashburner v McGuire* (1786)). That is to say the legacy is general in nature but points to a specific fund. If there are sufficient monies in the fund then the legatee takes the full legacy from the fund. However, in this case, there remains a balance of only £200 in the fund. Eric would be entitled to the £200 and would then have to prove as a general legatee for the remaining balance of £300. Therefore, although the fund has abated to the extent of the reduction, Eric could still take the full amount of the legacy if there are sufficient funds remaining to meet the requirements of the general legatees.

(e) The gift to Jeremy is also a demonstrative legacy. Demonstrative legacies have been said to be something of a hybrid; that is to say they are specific in nature in pointing to a particular fund but where that fund is diminished or has gone, the legatee can prove as a general legatee. This would be the case here in that, although the account has closed, Jeremy could prove for the full amount of the legacy as a general legatee. The only danger then would be if there were insufficient funds in the estate to meet the requirements of the general legatees, then Jeremy's legacy would abate rateably accordingly to value.

(f) The wording of the gift here would suggest a specific legacy, that is to say, by using the possessive word 'my' in respect of the Pixon's shares Gerald is indicating the particular shares that he holds. The danger in construing a gift this specific is that the gift may no longer be identifiable at the date of death and therefore subject to ademption. Whether ademption has occurred here will depend upon whether the change in the nature of the shares is considered to be a change in one of form only as, for example, in *Re Kuyper's Trusts* (1925) or one of substance as, for example, in the case of *Re Slater* (1907). If it is the case that the Pixon's shares held at death are essentially the same in nature, then Samuel would be entitled to 1,000 shares.

(g) Assuming that Emily has survived Gerald, then she will take the pecuniary legacy of £15,000. We are given that Kate predeceased Gerald but was survived by two daughters who were alive at the date of Gerald's death. In this case then although the gift to Kate would appear to lapse, the gift is saved by the operation of s 33 of the Wills Act 1837 as amended by s 19 of the Administration of Justice Act 1982. The effect of this provision is that where a gift is made by a will to a child or remoter issue of the testator and that child or remoter issue predeceases the testator survived by issue, then, in the absence of a contrary direction, the surviving issue will take the gift that the beneficiary would have taken had he or she survived. Kate's daughters will therefore be entitled to share the gift of £15,000.

Question 31

Eric has recently been convicted of the manslaughter of his wife Frieda, during the course of a violet quarrel. Eric has been sentenced to six years' imprisonment. In her will Frieda made a gift of 'my piano' to her sister, Grace, and left the residue of the estate (valued at £40,000) to James, her son by her marriage to Eric. James pre-deceased Frieda, survived by his adopted daughter, Ruth. Shortly before her death Frieda had sold the concert grand piano that she had owned when making the will and bought a cheap, second hand upright piano. Discuss.

Would it make a difference to your answer if James had died childless?

Answer plan

The issues which should be addressed in the problem relate to the Forfeiture Act of 1982 and the operation of s 33 of the Wills Act 1837 to counter the doctrine of lapse and the meaning of specific legacies.

Answer

A number of issues arise here as to the nature of the gifts made by Frieda in her will and the consequences of the possible failure of the gifts owing to subject matter or beneficiary. The will appears to dispose of all the property belonging to Frieda since there is a general residuary gift. The course will have regard to the expressed intentions of Frieda in making this her last will.

The gift of 'my piano' would appear to be a specific gift (*Bothamley v Sherson* (1875)). The gift appears to distinguish the particular item, namely the piano, in such a way as to distinguish the property from other property belonging to Frieda. Further, the inclusion of the possessive prefix 'my' indicates a specific gift. The condition laid down in *Bothamley v Sherson* is that the gift must form part of the testator's estate and be specified in such a way as to be separable or distinguishable from the remainder of the estate. The use of the possessive word 'my' indicates that the property belonged to the testator at the time the will is made (*Re Wilcocks* (1921)). The problem concerning construing gifts as specific is the danger of an ademption; that is to say that if the particular property does not form part of the estate at death, for whatever reason, the gift is said to adeem and the beneficiary will lose the gift. The fact, therefore, that the original, apparently expensive, piano has been replaced by a cheaper version could mean that the original gift has been adeemed. In *Re Sykes* (1870), for example, the testatrix made a gift in her will of 'my piano' and after the date of the will replaced a seemingly inexpensive piano with a much more expensive instrument. The court concluded that the intention was to give the original piano, and therefore, by replacing the piano the gift was adeemed. On the other hand, if one applies s 24 of the Wills Act 1837 that, as regards property, the will is to be construed as if it were executed immediately before the death then, on the basis of s 24, Grace could argue that she should take the piano owned at the date of the death. However, s 24 does say that it is subject to a contrary intention and the prefix 'my' may indicate a contrary intention as in *Re Sykes*. On the other hand, the intention may be to give to Grace whatever piano is owned as at the date of Frieda's death (*Re Flemming* (1974)).

A pre-condition of the law of succession is that to take a gift a beneficiary must survive the testator. It would appear, therefore, that the gift of residue to James will lapse (*Elliott v Davenport* (1705)). However, an exception to the doctrine of lapse is that of the application of s 33 of the Wills Act 1837 as amended by s 19 of the Administration of Justice Act 1982. Section 33 says that where there is a gift to a child or remoter issue, and that beneficiary predeceases the testator survived by issue living or *en ventre sa mere* at the date of the testator then the gift is saved and, subject to a contrary intention, the property passes to the surviving issue (in this case Ruth). This would still apply where Ruth is legally adopted (s 1(3)(c) Family Law Reform Act 1987).

If James had died childless then the gift of residue would lapse and in the absence of a gift over would be distributed according to Frieda's intestacy. The property would pass according to the laws of intestacy to the surviving spouse, Eric. The problem here is that Eric has been convicted of the manslaughter of Frieda. At common law, on the grounds of public policy, the perpetrator of an unlawful killing cannot benefit directly (*Re Crippen* (1911)) or indirectly (*Re Sigsworth* (1935)) from the effect of the crime. However, the court has now a discretionary power under s 2(1) of the Forfeiture Act 1982 provided the conviction is not one of murder. Therefore, it is possible that the court could consider the exercise of discretion in allowing Eric to take on the intestacy of Frieda (*Re K dec'd* (1982)).

Chapter 5

The Administration of the Estate

Introduction

The administration of estates is a vast topic. One has to consider carefully the nature of the course that is being studied, syllabus content and the emphasis placed by the persons delivering the course on the different aspects of administration. This is the topic where the academic points meet the practical.

A useful approach in looking at the topic of administration of estates as a whole is to ask what are the duties of the personal representatives in their taking steps to obtain the grant to the estate. There are three principal types of grant which should be understood. Namely, probate, administration with will annexed and administration on intestacy. The other specialist forms of grant are mainly offshoots from these three core types.

A useful exercise is to draw up a questionnaire to determine the typical breakdown of assets and liabilities in a private individual's estate. Also at this stage in studies, one can see the subject as a whole and attempt exercises in will drafting. The study of precedents of complete wills forms a useful instruction in reminding one of the kind of problems that can arise from the commencement of the course in the requirements as to form through to constructional problems and the difficult points concerning the incidence or burden of debts.

Question 32

Personal representative or trustee? Is the distinction important when, as often happens, the same person is appointed to both offices?

Answer plan

This is a relatively confined topic but one that is important in practice. The differing duties between personal representatives and trustees should be explained followed by the differences in liability between personal representatives and trustees. The difficulties which can arise and the importance in drawing the distinction should then be illustrated by reference to the case law, in particular, the cases of *Attenborough and Son v Solomon* (1913); *Re Ponder* (1921); *Harvell v Foster* (1954) and *Re King's Will Trust* (1964).

Answer

It is important to distinguish in what capacity a person is acting, whether as personal representative or trustee. The functions of the respective offices differ and their authority differs depending upon the type of property being transferred.

The function of the personal representative is to gather in the assets of the deceased, value them; assess the debts that are owing from the estate, pay them together with the funeral testamentary and administration expenses; calculate death duties which may be payable and, out of the net proceeds distribute the estate according to the will or intestacy or a combination of both. Generally speaking, the office of personal representative lasts for life although, in practice, the role would end once the estate is wound up. The function of a trustee is to hold assets until a specified event occurs and act in accordance with the trust instrument and the general law.

There is no statutory definition of the end of the administration period. In practice administration would end when the personal representatives make their final distribution of property to the beneficiaries and sign and hand over the final estate accounts. An exception would be where a personal representative is holding a limited appointment, for example, where the testator has by will appointed X as his executor and when the will takes effect X is under the age of 18 and cannot therefore act. If X has been appointed sole executor, an application to the court would have to be made for a grant for letters of administration with will annexed (*cum testamento annexo*), limited during the minority of the infant (*durante minore aetate*) (1).

Where the same person has been appointed personal representative and trustee, administration ceases and trusteeship begins, in the case of land, when the personal representative assents to himself. In the case of pure personalty there would either be an assent or, more commonly, the trustee would take over the pure personalty when the administration period ends. The distinction is important for, in the case of the personal estate, the authority of the personal representatives is several whereas the authority of trustees is joint. Where there has been no formal assent of the personalty from personal representative to trustee it is a question of fact when the administration period has ended (*Attenborough and Son v Solomon* (1913)) (2). A sale by a sole, or sole surviving, personal representative will be sufficient to overreach equitable interests, whereas sale by a sole trustee will not, and, in the case of a sale by a trustee, the purchaser must insist on the appointment of a co-trustee in order to obtain a title free of over reachable equities (3).

A new trustee can be appointed to an existing trust by the existing trustees or by the personal representatives of the last surviving trustee (s 36 Trustee Act 1925). There is no such provision in the case of administration. Where an executor dies after obtaining the grant of probate but before completing the administration of the estate and that executor has appointed an executor by his will, then he becomes executor by representation to the first estate under the 'chain of representation' (s 7 Administration of Estates Act 1925). Where there is no proving executor to the estate of the deceased executor or where there is a grant of administration and the personal representative has died before completion of the administration of the estate, then a grant *de bonis non* must be obtained.

Although a person may be named both personal representative and trustee he cannot hold property in both capacities at the same time. Once the administration period has ended he will hold as trustee, but his role as personal representative will not cease, so that if, at some later date, further property falls into the estate (for example a gift saved as a result of the operation of s 33 of the Wills Act 1837) the person will hold that property as personal representative until it has been dealt with in accordance with the will or intestacy of the deceased.

In *Attenborough and Son v Solomon* the court said it was a question of fact when the administration period ended. Some 13 years had elapsed from the settlement of all the debts to the pledging of the plate by one of the sons. The court decided that the administration had long ended and, in pledging the plate, the son was acting as a trustee and therefore, acting alone, he could not give good title to the property. In *Re Ponder* (1921) a widow was granted letters of administration to her husband's estate. She paid the debts, ascertained the residue and divided the residue into separate funds as required by the pre-1926 Statutes of Distribution. The court held that she had assumed the character of trustee in respect of the property so advantage could be taken of the statutory power to appoint new trustees. The decision was queried in *Harvell v Foster* (1954) where the Court of Appeal allowed a daughter to take action against the sureties of an administration bond issued when the daughter's husband had obtained letters of administration with will annexed owing to the daughter being under age when her father's will took effect. The Court of Appeal in referring to *Re Ponder* appeared to suggest that the personal representative could hold the property in a dual capacity, criticising the judgment of Mr Justice Sargant, saying that where he stated the capacities of personal representative and trustee are mutually exclusive, he stated the proposition too widely. The court in *Harvell* refused to define exactly the moment at which the personal representative would become trustee. In *Re Cockburn's* (1957) Mr Justice Danckwerts, commenting on *Harvell v Foster*, said that the observations in the case were *obiter* in so far as they cast any doubt upon the decision in *Re Ponder*. *Harvell* could be construed narrowly as a case turning upon the interest of the administration bond.

In the case of title to land, prior to 1964, conveyancers had adopted a practice of following *Re Ponder* in accepting that a personal representative had the power to appoint trustees if he was acting in the capacity of a trustee. However, in *Re King's Will Trusts* (1964) the court regarded itself bound by s 36(4) of the Administration of Estates Act 1925 which provides that an assent in writing must be made by the personal representative naming the person in whose favour it is given in order to vest the legal estate in the person as trustee. Previously it had been believed that where the same person was named personal representative and trustee the transfer of the legal estate would occur on the appointment of trustees by the former personal representative. *Re King's Will Trust* shows that even where the same person is personal representative and trustee he should execute a formal assent to himself from his capacity as personal representative to that of trustee in respect of the legal estate to the land (4).

The contrast of the nature of the offices of personal representative and trustee and in particular the respective authority in the transfer of either personal or real estate shows that it is important to distinguish in what capacity the individual is acting at the time of the transfer.

Notes

1 When the infant becomes of age he or she will not automatically become executor and must apply for a cessate grant. Contrast the situation where the deceased has appointed two executors one of whom is an infant and the other one proves the will at the date of death, power would be reserved to the infant to prove when he or she came of age.

2 In *Attenborough & Son v Solomon* (1913) the testator appointed his two sons as executors and trustees and left part of his estate to them and part in trust for his daughter. The testator died in March 1878 and by March 1879 all the debts and legacies had been paid. A silver plate in trust for the daughter had always been in the custody of one of the sons. In March 1892 the son pledged the plate (the lender did not know it was trust property). The son died and his brother took action against the lender on the basis that the lender did not have title to the plate. The House of Lords held that the sons had done all they could as executors in 1879 and, as there was nothing more to be done as executors the chattels vested in them as trustees. As a result the son could not on his own account give a valid title to the lender and the plate was recovered.

3 An exception is a sale by a sole trustee, constituted as a trust corporation, for example, a bank. The trust corporation can give good title.

4 In *Re King's Will Trust* the executors did not execute an assent of the land in their favour as trustees. The sole surviving executor and trustee appointed a co-trustee and, five years later, when he died his will was proved by X who also became executive by representation in the estate of the original testatrix. Both original executors named in her will had now died and by failing to execute the assent the title became diverged and the real estate remained in the administration therefore, being held by the executor by representation.

Question 33

You are consulted by Eric, the principal beneficiary to the estate of his late brother, Frank, a bachelor, who died four months ago.

By his will Frank appointed Len to be his executor; he bequeathed £2,000 to his friend Sam; his collection of Dresden china to his sister May; his house and 'the remainder of my effects' to Eric. There are no other surviving relatives.

Eric informs you that Len, who has not as far as Eric is aware, taken out a grant of probate, has gone to live in France. Eric has discovered Len has paid the funeral account and entered into a contract to sell the house. Eric has asked Len to settle matters quickly and had indicated that he (Eric) did not want to enter into possession of the house. It transpires that the purchaser is Mike, a friend of Len's, and the agreed price is well below the market value. Mike admits that the intention is to redecorate, assisted by a loan from Len, sell at a profit and divide the proceeds with Len. Further, Len had handed over two pieces of the china to Mike to obtain a valuation and one piece was broken whilst in Mike's possession. Sam cannot be traced. Apparently he left the area five years ago and no one has heard from him since.

Eric seeks your advice on the steps he can take to recover the assets and complete the distribution of the estate.

Answer plan

The question is concerned with the nature of the office of executor and the rules concerning acceptance of office. One should then consider the duties and, briefly, the liability of the executor and the accountability of Mike as *executor de son tort*.

Answer

An executor named in the will does not have to formally accept the office. After the death of the testator, payment of a funeral account by itself may not constitute acceptance of office for this could be construed as an act of support for a friend. However, Len has also taken steps to sell the house and value assets. These steps would be taken as acceptance of office by Len.

The executor is obliged to proceed with the administration of the estate with due diligence. Delay in obtaining the grant, thereby causing potential loss to the estate, can amount to *devastavit*; that is, breach of trust by a personal representative. Eric should attempt to find Len with a view to issuing citation, calling upon Len to proceed with the administration of the estate or formally renounce the appointment. If Len cannot be found Eric should seek an order of the court revoking the appointment of Len (*In the Goods of Loveday* (1900)). The way would then be open for Eric, as residuary beneficiary named in the will, to apply for letters of administration with will annexed, *de bonis non administrative*, under r 20 of the Non-Contentious Probate Rules 1987. The estate will be bound by all *bona fide* acts carried out by Len, such as settlement of the funeral account. Len would be entitled to indemnity from the estate for payment of the account.

In the case of the contract for the sale of the house this amounts to misappropriation of assets under the general heading of *devastavit*. The personal representative is under a duty to obtain the best price possible for the assets whereas in this instance there is evidence of collusion.

The personal representative must ensure all reasonable steps are taken to ascertain the debts of the estate. Failure to do so can render the personal representative liable for any losses. Section 27 Trustee Act 1925 sets out the advertisements which must be placed for claims against the estate. However, the statutory advertisements will not protect the personal representative where a beneficiary cannot be found. Advertisements would have to be placed asking for information concerning Sam. In the absence of definite proof of decease one cannot assume that Sam's share has passed. If there is no response to enquiries application can be made to the court for an order in the terms laid down in *Re Benjamin* (1902) requesting a 'Benjamin Order' allowing the personal representative to distribute the estate on the basis that the beneficiary has died before the testator.

Where, as in the case of Mike, someone takes estate assets without authority, that person is constituted an *executor de son tort* or intermeddler in the estate. A person who is constituted an *executor de son tort* is liable, however innocently he has acted (*New York Breweries v AG* (1898)). Mike would be liable to the extent of the value of the estate assets which have come into his hands. Mike can be called to account including for losses which have occurred (*IRC v Stype Investments (Jersey) Limited* (1982)). If, however, Mike is a recognised valuer and Len has given Mike the china in good faith (unlikely in view of the deal over the house) then the power of delegation by a personal representative under s 23 Trustee Act 1925 could be pleaded. Mike could still be made liable for the breakages under the general principles of negligence.

Question 34

Consider the circumstances where, in dealing with the assets of the deceased, a grant to the estate may not be necessary.

Answer plan

This question can be divided into two main parts. (1) consideration of the assets which do not pass to the estate on the death of the deceased, and (2) assets which do pass but, due to their relatively small value, a grant is not required.

Answer

A basic rule of the law of succession is that one cannot distribute the estate of the deceased on the strength of the will alone or, in the case of undisposed of property, simply following the rules of intestate distribution. Generally, in order to distribute estate assets title to the estate must be obtained by an authorised person, either an executor or administrator, ie the person or persons obtaining the grant to the estate. However, there may be circumstances where a grant may not be necessary.

There may be assets which form part of the estate for Inheritance Tax purposes but pass outside the terms of the will or rules of intestacy. Where the deceased held property as a beneficial joint tenant. Here the interest to which the deceased was entitled will pass automatically to the surviving joint tenant(s) by virtue of the right of survivorship, the *jus acresendi*. The growth of home ownership in the UK since the late 1950s has seen an increase in the ownership of the matrimonial home on a joint basis. More recently the increase in parties cohabiting rather than entering into a lawful marriage has seen the added need for joint ownership as the best way to protect the interest of the cohabitee. On the death of the deceased the interest passes to the co-owner(s) on proof of survivorship, either through direct evidence or by virtue of the statutory presumption in s 184 Law of Property Act 1925, thereby by-passing the terms of the will or the rules of intestate succession. This means the statutory survivorship period for spouses taking on intestacy in s 1 Law Reform (Succession) Act 1995 will not affect co-ownership.

The value of the interest of the deceased will be subject to Inheritance Tax. In the case of realty the usual practice is to discount the value passing on death by approximately 10% to take account of the continuing occupancy of the surviving party.

The interest of the deceased in the joint property will pass according to the will or intestacy where the interest was held as a beneficial tenancy in common. In this situation the deceased can direct by will who should receive his half share or it will form part of his estate on his intestacy. In this situation a grant to the estate will be necessary. A beneficial joint tenancy can be converted to a tenancy in common *inter vivos* by a letter of severance.

There are some investments which may pass directly to a beneficiary by virtue of a statutory nomination. A nomination must be in writing and attested by one witness. Nominations are now confined to monies held in Friendly Societies and Industrial and Provident Societies, to a limit in each case of £5,000. The effect of the nomination is to pass the property directly to the nominee even if a will is executed after the date of the nomination. Again, a grant will not be required although the value of the property may be liable to Inheritance Tax.

Where the deceased has made valid gifts *inter vivos* these clearly do not form part of his estate at death but belong to the donee from the date of the gift. There are Inheritance Tax advantages in making gifts *inter vivos*. Most types of property will be potentially exempt from Inheritance Tax. That is to say, provided a valid gift *inter vivos* is made and the donor survives seven years from the making of the gift the property passes free of Inheritance Tax. Certain gifts do not qualify as potentially exempt transfers, for example, gifts into a discretionary trust. Also property where the donor has not divested himself of interest will mean the seven year period will not start to run. Also, where the donor must take care, for Inheritance Tax purposes, is ensuring the gift is not construed as a *donatio mortis causa*. In this case the gift only takes effect on the death; therefore advantage could not be taken of the seven year period. However, Inheritance Tax considerations apart, property which forms a *donatio mortis causa*, that is, a gift in contemplation of death, will not form part of the estate of the deceased; therefore a grant would not be needed.

It is a question of intention whether the gift is a *donatio* or gift *inter vivos*. The conditions which apply to make the gift donatio are (1) the gift is made in contemplation, although not necessarily in expectation, of death (a general contemplation is insufficient), (2) the gift is conditional on death and (3) dominion over the property must have passed to the donee or a person acting as agent of the donee. The subject matter must be capable of passing by way of a *donatio*, for example, the keys to a car coupled with a clear intention to give as in *Re Woodard* (1995) and land, as in *Sen v Headley* (1991) where the handing over of keys to a deed box were taken as intention to give the donor's house by way of *donatio*. (For a more detailed consideration of this method of giving see the answer to Question 29.)

The property referred to above does not pass to the personal representatives. There is another category of property which does not form part of the estate at death at all. The reason is beneficial entitlement has passed during the life of the deceased. No grant of representation is needed and this property does not form part of the estate for Inheritance Tax.

The beneficial entitlement to policies of life assurance can be assigned by the policy holder *inter vivos*. The person on whose life the policy is effected can create an implied trust in favour of his spouse and/or his children under s 11 Married Women's Property Act 1882. If the policy holder wishes to benefit any other person he or she can do so by declaring an express trust. It is the policy holder who assigns, that is, the person on whose life the policy is effected. In order to effect a policy on the life of another, the person who wishes to take out the policy must prove an insurable interest. On the death of the person on whose life the policy is secured the policy monies are payable directly to the beneficiaries and do not form part of the deceased's estate. The only way the policy monies could be clawed back for Inheritance Tax is where the policy is assigned but the person on whose life it is effected continues to pay the premiums. Each premium paid, to keep the policy valid, is considered to be a gift of rights under the policy; therefore the policy moneys could be caught for tax unless the payments were treated as exempt gifts.

Another significant source of funds concerns pension benefits, particularly death in service benefits. Many occupational pension schemes are drafted in such a way that death in service benefits which would normally accrue to the estate of the deceased can pass directly to beneficiaries. Usually the scheme will provide that should the employee die whilst still in employment, any lump sum is payable to the trustees of the scheme for them to apply the monies in their absolute discretion. Therefore the lump sum benefit will not form part of the estate of the deceased, no grant will be necessary, merely proof of death, and no Inheritance Tax will be payable.

The property considered above, whether it does not pass to the personal representatives, or to the estate at all, can represent a considerable portion of value passing as a result of the death of the deceased. It is the increase in the amount of property held as beneficial joint tenant coupled with the growth in life assurance and pension benefits which lead Professor Langbein to write in the *Harvard Law Journal* about the 'non-probate revolution'. That is to say the value of property which can pass with the minimum of formality (certainly not the formal requirements of the Wills Act 1837) and not requiring a grant to the estate (*Harvard Law Journal* no 97 at p 1108).

There are certain assets which my be paid out of the estate without the production of a grant. Each item must not exceed £5,000 in value. If this is exceeded a grant may be required in respect of the whole sum and not merely the excess. The provisions are contained in the Administration of Estates (Small Payments) Act 1965. Payment is made either to the person who would be entitled to a grant if one were obtained or to the person beneficially entitled; the only requirement is production of a death certificate. The type of property to which these provisions apply are, for example, monies in the National Savings Bank or National Savings Certificates and Premium Savings Bonds.

In addition, the 1965 Act provides for monies payable in respect of the wages, salary or superannuation benefits to civil servants or service pensions to the police or fire service may be payable on the production of a death certificate. Similar provisions apply to funds invested in building society accounts (Building Societies Act 1986).

Where the amounts exceed £5,000 or there are other assets then a grant will be required. For example, the deceased may have owned a small number of company shares, purchased many years ago. The motive may not have been one of investment but loyalty, for example, shares in a favourite football club. The modest estate passes without production of a grant and the share certificates are simply put with other family papers and ignored. Some time later they may acquire a more significant monetary value when someone emerges keen to buy the shares. In order to transfer them a grant must be obtained to the estate of the deceased holder of the shares. If a grant is not obtained and the company allows transfer, say, on proof of death only the company could be constituted an *executor de son tort*, however innocently it may have acted, see *New York Breweries v AG* (1899).

Where the estate is low in value but a grant is still required the Capital Taxes Office form is relatively simple. The form requires the personal representative to set out details of the value of the assets and debts including the funeral account. The CTO will check no Inheritance Tax is payable. Tax is payable where the value of the net estate (that is, the value of the assets passing on death plus non-exempt gifts made within seven years of the death, less allowable debts) exceeds £200,000. In addition to the estate account form the personal representative(s) must file the original will and any codicils together with the executor's or administrator's oath. The oath indicates the entitlement of the person applying for the grant and includes the estimated gross value of the estate. The person(s) completing the oath swear or affirm that they will administer the estate according to law. It is this oath which gives protection to the beneficiaries should they consider action should be taken for maladministration.

Question 35

Clem, a widower, died five months ago. By his will he appointed his former partner, Morgan, to be his sole executor and left the entire estate to his daughter, Gemma, who survived him. In the first four weeks following the death of Clem, Morgan arranged the funeral, collected insurance monies on Clem's life and paid the funeral account. Since then, Morgan, who spends long periods looking after business interests in New York, has done nothing within the estate.

Last week the Inland Revenue wrote to Gemma asking for the reason for the delay in view of the size of the estate, which includes extensive farmlands and a number of paintings including two attributed to Turner.

Gemma seeks the advice of her uncle, Dan, Clem's estranged brother, who is the stage manager of a local theatre. Dan informs her he will 'sort things out', and takes two valuable vases from Clem's farmhouse, which he sells to Nodder, an auctioneer friend. Dan keeps the sale proceeds 'to defray expenses' and pays the electricity and telephone bills relating to the farm out of the sale of some grain stocks.

Advise Gemma.

Answer plan

Gemma would want to know how to expedite the administration of the estate and in particular the rights she may have against Morgan and Dan. As Morgan is the legally constituted executor one has to consider liability as an executor. In the case of Dan one has to consider possible liability as an executor *de son tort*, and finally whether Gemma could take over the administration of the estate herself.

Answer

Morgan is the executor named in the will. The executor does not have to formally accept office (1). The court will consider that the office has been accepted if the person named as executor does some act which only a lawfully constituted personal representative would do. This is to be contrasted with carrying out acts of necessity such as arranging a funeral. Collecting assets or paying debts is sufficient to amount to acceptance of office (*Re Stevenson* (1897)) and it would therefore appear here that by collecting the insurance monies and paying the funeral account Morgan has accepted office. Since nothing further has been done to take out the grant of probate to the estate Gemma should be advised to issue citation against Morgan to compel him to take out the grant (see, for example, *Biggs's Estate* (1966)). A personal representative is under a general statutory obligation to administer the estate of the deceased in accordance with law (s 9 Administration of Estates Act 1971). In accepting office by his actions Morgan will render himself liable if he does not seek to obtain probate promptly. If citation is issued and Morgan fails to take action to obtain the grant having received the citation then he can be guilty of contempt of court. Morgan could reply to the citation by renouncing.

If Morgan renounces, Gemma could apply for letters of administration with will annexed under r 20 of the Non-Contentious Probate Rules 1987 provided she is of age. If Gemma is under age but has attained 16 she can nominate somebody to apply for a grant on her behalf. Where she is under 16 then an application to the court would be made for an application to administer on her behalf; the grant, in either case, being limited during her minority. If there is an outstanding liability to taxation and the Inland Revenue considers there has been unwarranted delay then the Revenue could apply to the official solicitor to obtain a grant *ad colligenda bona* in order to expedite outstanding tax (see, for example, *Re Clore* (1982)).

Whether Morgan continues with the administration of the estate or a grant is issued with will annexed the lawful personal representative should take action against Dan. Dan has no authority under the will but has taken it upon himself to deal with the estate's assets. Dan would therefore be constituted an executor *de son tort*. Dan can be liable, however innocently he has acted (see *New York Breweries Company Limited v AG* (1898)) (2) because the person is constituted *executor de son tort* if he obtains estate property or releases a debt without lawful authority (*Sharland v Mildon* (1845)). This is to be contrasted with acts of necessity such as arranging a funeral or taking care of deceased life stock. These acts of necessity or charity would not render a person liable as executor *de son tort*. However, Dan has taken estate assets and has acted in the way that a lawful representative would act. Dan will be liable to the extent of the assets he has received (s 28 Administration of Estates Act 1925). He can plead as a defence that he has only done what the lawful representative would have done in settling *bona fide* debts. If, however, he has sold the vases to Nodder at an under value then Dan would be liable to the estate for the difference between sale proceeds and the full market value. If Nodder reasonably believed that Dan had lawful authority to sell the vases (for example, his suspicion may have been aroused by a sale at an under value) then Dan's action will bind the estate (*Mountford v Gibson* (1804)) (3).

A personal representative is entitled to claim out of pocket expenses from the estate. Additional expenses or costs cannot be claimed unless there is a charging clause in the will or the beneficiaries agree. Dan, as *executor de son tort*, would have to account for the sale proceeds from the sale of the vases and could only plead in defence of legitimately incurred expenses, that is, expenses which the lawful personal representative would have incurred. Provided that the electricity and telephone bills were *bona fide* then Dan can plead due receipt of these as a defence.

Dan cannot be compelled to take out a grant to the estate where he is not entitled to a grant. There is a possibility, although there are insufficient facts, that as Dan is Gemma's uncle he could possibly be entitled to a grant of administration with will annexed limited during Gemma's minority if Gemma is under age. Otherwise Dan's obligation is merely to account for the assets he has received. He can be made to account to the lawful personal representative and to the creditors. In addition, Dan could be liable to the Inland Revenue for Inheritance Tax, due on any assets which have come into his possession (ss 199 and 200 of the Inheritance Tax Act 1984).

Notes

1   Compare acceptance of office with that of renunciation. Where a person wishes to renounce the appointment as executor this must be filed with the court and cannot be retracted without the consent of the court, see r 37 Non-Contentious Probate Rules 1987. The court will only consent to retraction of a renunciation

if it is in the interest of the estate (*Re Gill* (1873)). Renunciation as executor does not preclude a person from applying for a grant in another capacity, as for example, a creditor to the estate, unless the court orders otherwise in allowing the renunciation as executor.

2   In *New York Breweries Company Limited v AG* (1899) the deceased died domiciled in America but owned shares in an English company. The American executors did not obtain a grant of probate in England and had no intention of doing so. The English company knew this was the case but at the request of the executors the company registered the deceased's shares in the American executor's names and paid the dividends to that. The House of Lords held that the company had constituted itself *executor de son tort* and was liable to pay the death duty liability on the English estate.

3   In *Mountford v Gibson* (1804) the deceased had purchased, but not paid for, goods which had been delivered to him. The vendor asked the deceased's widow, shortly after his death for the return of the goods and she complied. The widow was not the lawful personal representative and in returning the goods she made herself liable as *executrix de son tort*. Letters of administration were subsequently granted to another person who sued the vendor. The vendor claimed that he was entitled to regard the widow as the lawful personal representative. The court held, however, that because the return of the goods was an isolated act and the widow had done no other act which would make her liable, the vendor had insufficient cause for believing that she had the authority to act, therefore the lawful personal representative recovered the goods.

Question 36

Explain the purpose and effect of the chain of representation.

Answer plan

This is a straightforward essay. The structure should consist of a clear explanation of the chain of representation and its effect. One should then consider the circumstances in which the chain of representation could be broken which would then result in an application for the *grant of administration de bonis non*.

Answer

The chain of representation is governed by s 7 of the Administration of Estates Act 1925. The chain applies where a sole or last surviving executor dies, before the completion of the administration of an estate having himself appointed an executor. The latter on taking out a grant of probate in respect of the executor's estate, automatically becomes the executor of the original testator.

Generally, the office of an executor is for life. If property falls into the estate many years after the completion of the administration the executor is duty bound to deal with it. Where the executor dies in office having taken out the grant of probate, s 7 provides that the duty is passed to his executor. Suppose, for example, A is named executor to the will of T. A proves T's will and then dies having appointed B to be his executor. Provided B proves the will of A, B becomes executor by representation to the estate of T. What happens where T appoints two executors X and Y? Suppose Y proves the will with power reserved for X to prove. If Y dies before completing the administration of T's estate having appointed Z to be his executor, Z should cite X to determine whether X wishes to prove the will of T. Z should use citation here because should he become executor by representation to the estate of T (by proving Y's will), X could subsequently have him removed when he, X, applies for probate to the estate of T. An executor faced with the chain of representation, such as B in the first example above, cannot pick and choose between estates so that where B does prove A's estate, he automatically becomes executor by representation to the estate of T. If B does not want to administer the estate of T but is entitled under some other capacity to administer A's estate, then B should consider renouncing the appointment as executor and applying in another capacity, as administrator, to administer the estate of A. This would be possible with the court's approval.

The purpose of the chain is to reduce delay in the administration of estates and thereby reduce the expense. The chain, however, can lead to complications and, in certain circumstances, can be broken. Where the chain is broken so a gap occurs in the administration of the estate, then those entitled under the Non-Contentious Probate Rules 1987 have to apply to the court for a *grant de bonis non-administrative*. The chain will be broken where, for example, the proving executor dies intestate or fails to appoint an executor or where the executor so appointed fails to obtain probate. The chain will also be broken where a general executor is followed by an executor whose duty is limited to a part of the estate. For example, suppose that A was T's general executor but B was executor only to a part of A's estate as literary executor. In this case, although B would prove as executor to the copyrights to manuscripts of A's estate, he would not become executor by representation to the estate of A. However, where one had the converse, a limited executor followed by a general executor, the chain would apply.

The chain has been criticised. An alternative would be to have similar powers as those held by trustees whereby the last surviving trustee or even the personal representatives of the last surviving trustee can appoint new trustees. However, the same rules do not apply in the case of personal representatives because of the personal nature of the office of executor.

Question 37

What do you understand by the term '*devastavit*'?

Answer plan

The word *devastavit* should be defined and then the main areas of liability, namely misappropriation, maladministration and failure to safeguard assets should be explained together with reference to authorities.

Answer

The personal representative is under a duty to gather in the assets, value them, assess the lawful debts and pay them together with any tax due on the estate and then distribute the estate according to the will, rules of intestacy or a combination of both. The term *'devastavit'* refers to breach of trust by a personal representative.

There are three main areas of liability within the heading *devastavit*: misappropriation of assets; maladministration; and failure to safeguard assets. Personal representatives can be liable for misappropriation where, for example, they use estate assets for personal use or enter into a collusive sale. Either way they are diminishing the value of the assets in the estate.

The general heading of maladministration divides into three sub-areas namely: misapplication of assets; unjustified expenses; and a wasting of the assets in the estate. An example of misapplication would be applying estate assets, albeit in good faith, otherwise than in the order provided by the will or statute. Personal representatives need to take great care in valuing the assets and liabilities. If it appears likely that the assets may not meet the liabilities, or the personal representatives are not sure, then they should proceed with caution and administer the estate as if it was insolvent. This means that the liabilities must be categorised into specially preferred debts, ordinary debts and deferred debts. If the personal representative pays an ordinary creditor before a preferred creditor then the personal representative could be personally liable for misapplication of assets. The personal representative could plead as a defence that he had no notice of the preferred creditor (*Re Fluyder* (1889)). However, he cannot plead this defence if he had no notice of the debt because he had not placed the statutory advertisement required by s 27 of the Trustee Act 1925 (see *Chelsea Waterworks v Cowper* (1795)).

Another example of maladministration would be incurring unjustified expenses. A personal representative can be liable if, for example, he incurs funeral expenses which are disproportionate to the value of the estate. Although in this case one would have regard to any wishes expressed by the testator together with wishes of the family, these must be balanced against the value of the estate and avoid diminishing of the assets.

The personal representative would be liable for maladministration if he has wasted assets in the estate. Examples would include giving away an asset of value or paying debts which he is not bound to pay because they are statute barred or the claim may be spurious.

In *Thompson v Thompson* (1821) the asset was a leasehold property which had a greater value than the rent payable. The personal representative was held liable when he surrendered the lease without consideration instead of selling the lease at a premium. The converse would apply where the personal representative failed to dispose of an uneconomic lease promptly, for example, where the rent exceeds the value as a result of onerous repairing covenants which the lease imposes on the landlord (*Rowley v Adams* (1839)).

The final area of liability is where the personal representative fails to safeguard assets. The duty of care of a personal representative in dealing with the estate is low. His position is akin to a gratuitous bailee and the personal representative cannot be held liable for loss in the absence of evidence of wilful default (*Job v Job* (1877)). So, for example, the personal representative would not be liable if assets were lost in a robbery. The burden of proof of loss by the personal representative rests with the person alleging the loss. Liability would result where, for example, the personal representative failed to pay a debt promptly so the creditors sued. The personal representative would be liable personally for any fees incurred and interest on the debt. Also, where the personal representative is slow to act in recovering assets so that they become statute barred, he could be liable for the loss in value of those assets. Delay in obtaining probate can also render the personal representative liable for *devastavit* (*Re Stevenson* (1897)) as, for example, where there are company shares in the estate and these cannot be dealt with until the grant has been obtained, so that where the personal representative is slow in obtaining the grant the opportunity to participate in rights issues may be lost.

The object of the rules relating to *devastavit* is to keep the value of the estate, after payment of proper debts and administration expenses, as high as possible for the benefit of both creditors and beneficiaries. By accepting office as personal representative a person also becomes liable as a trustee. There is therefore an overlap between *devastavit* and liability for breach of trust. A failure to take reasonable care of assets would render the personal representative liable both for *devastavit* and breach of trust. The concept of breach of trust is, however, wider; for example, the personal representative would be liable if he makes an unauthorised profit from the estate even though the estate itself does not suffer loss.

The acts of the co-representative will not make the other representative liable unless their default resulted in their failure to obtain the property into the joint control. Where personal representatives or trustees appoint agents, for example, a solicitor to apply for the grant or a surveyor to value property, they are not liable for the default of the agent provided they appointed the agent in good faith (s 23 Trustee Act 1925). The will itself may include a clause restricting the liability of the personal representatives to wilful wrong-doing. This will only protect the personal representatives as against the beneficiaries and will not affect the rights of the creditors of the estate at death. The debt must be paid promptly. In *Re Tankard* (1942) Mr Justice Uthwatt said that the personal representatives should have special regard to debts which carry interest and the personal representatives can be personally liable for any unnecessary order for costs against the estate. The personal representative can obtain protection against both creditors and beneficiaries in applying to the court under s 61 of the Trustee Act 1925. This section enables the court to grant relief where the personal representative or trustee has acted in good faith, reasonably, and ought fairly to be excused. Under this section the court has the power but not the duty to grant relief. The beneficiaries themselves may agree to absolve the personal representative or trustee from blame; however, the beneficiary must be *sui juris* and have full knowledge of the facts and must not be subjected to any undue influence.

Where mismanagement or misappropriation is alleged, a person who is interested in the estate may seek an order for an account. In commencing court proceedings in contract or tort creditors must commence the action within six years of the cause of action or within 12 years in the case of proceedings on a covenant. Beneficiaries must commence an action within 12 years from the date on which they became entitled and within six years to recover arrears of interest. The time period can be extended where the beneficiary had a future interest. The time period will not apply where the facts have been concealed by the personal representative by means of fraud.

Question 38

Martin died this year. His will contained the following dispositions:

- all his shares in Moonrock Limited (the family company) to his sister, Alice, 'subject to the payment thereof of all my just debts';
- the freehold farmhouse Whiteacre and the adjoining acreage to his brother Bert;
- the residue to his trustee on trust for his nephews Henry and Oliver in equal shares.

Oliver died a week before Martin. The remaining beneficiaries all survive Martin.

The family company shares are believed to be worth £60,000. There is other personality worth £40,000. Whiteacre is valued at £160,000 and the adjoining fields at £200,000. Both are charged by way of legal mortgage in the sum of £170,000. In addition there are general debts of £70,000.

Advise John, the executor, as to who should bear the burden of the debts.

Answer plan

This question is concerned with one of the most difficult areas in the law of succession, namely the incidence or burden of debts. Here there are two types of debt namely the general debts and the mortgage.

The approach should be to read the will and see if there is any direction regarding the payment of the debts and then to consider whether this direction alters the rules concerning the incidence of debts. The gift of the freeholding would appear to be subject to the mortgage by applying s 35 of the Administration of Estates Act 1925 as there does not appear to be a direction to the contrary.

The next step is to consider the incidence of the general debts and whether or not the direction varies the statutory order for the payment of debts contained in s 34(3) of the AEA 1925. If the direction does vary the order then the gift of shares will be primarily liable for the payment of the general debts. However, it is given that the shares are worth £60,000 whereas the general debts total £70,000. One has to consider therefore the incidence of the remaining £10,000. This involves considering application of the order in s 34(3) and consideration of the case law on the general variation of the order.

Answer

In advising John who should bear the burden of the debts one should first look to the wording of the will to see whether there are any clear directions as to the payment of debts. Where the will is silent as to the payment of debts or is unclear then payment is governed, in the case of general debts, by the statutory order contained in s 34(3) of the Administration of Estates Act 1925 and as regards debts on property by s 35 of the AEA 1925.

Bert is given a freehold farmhouse and adjoining acreage which are both charged with a mortgage. There is no direction in the gift as to any contrary intention regarding the payment of the mortgage and one would therefore apply the provisions of s 35 of the AEA 1925 to the gift. Section 35 makes the property itself primarily liable for the payment of the debt. There is no personal liability on Bert to pay the debt (*Syer v Gladstone* (1885)) since the debt attaches to the property. Here, the two properties, the farmhouse and the adjoining acreage, are given to the one beneficiary and therefore the total property, namely the farm and the adjoining fields, would bear the burden of the single mortgage. Section 35 applies to property which is charged 'at the time of his death'. The effect of this is that the section only applies to the extent of the debt charged and not to other debts incurred in respect of the asset. In *Re Birmingham* (1959) the testatrix contracted to buy a house but died before completion. The estate owned the equitable interest in the property subject to the vendor's lien for the unpaid purchase money. A codicil gave the house to X, residue to Y and Z. The court held that X took the property subject to the discharge of the lien but the legal cost of the purchase was a simple contract debt to be borne by the residue.

The effect of s 35 can be negated by a contrary intention provided this is in writing. A simple direction in the will that the debts are to be paid from the residue does not amount to a contrary intention of the rule in s 35. To effect an express contrary intention one would have to refer to the property itself and use some expression such as 'free from debt'. The contrary intention can also be indicated by implication (1). There does not appear to be any direction to the contrary in the will of Martin. The reference to the debts does not make specific reference to Whiteacre. John would therefore be advised to inform Bert that he could take Whiteacre and the acreage subject to the mortgage debt. If Bert wished to retain the properties he would have to take over the mortgage provided the mortgagees gave their consent. Alternatively the property or a part of the property could be sold to pay off the mortgage and the balance of the sale proceeds paid to Bert. The incidental costs incurred in disposal would be a general debt, applying the principle in *Re Birmingham* and not borne by Bert.

The advice as to the burden of the general debts again turns upon a reading of the will coupled with the question of whether or not the statutory order of the application of assets applies in the payment of the debts. John should first arrange a provisional categorisation of assets. The gift of the shares is a general legacy. The gift of the freehold farmhouse Whiteacre is a specific devise and the burden of the mortgage debt attaching to that property has been considered above. The gift of the residue divides into two funds. *Prima facie* Henry and Oliver are residuary beneficiaries. The property has been given to them as tenants in common. However, given that Oliver has died before Martin, his share lapses and, in the absence of a gift over in the will, becomes property undisposed of by the will. There are therefore four categories of assets within this will, namely: general legatee; specific devisee; residuary beneficiary (Henry); and the share, which would have passed to Oliver, which is distributed on a partial intestacy.

The burden of the general debts totalling £70,000 will depend upon whether the statutory order contained in s 34(iii) of the AEA 1925 applies or whether this order has been varied by the words of the will.

The statutory order envisages that the assets be placed into their respective categories, that is to say, the assets are 'marshalled'. The debts are then paid out of the assets in the order they appear in s 34 (iii). The first four categories in the statutory order are:

- property undisposed of by the will subject to the retention of a fund to meet any pecuniary legacies;

- the residue disposed of by will subject to gain to a fund for the pecuniary legacies;
- property the deceased specifically appropriated or devised or bequeathed at the payment of debts; and
- property the deceased charged with or devised or bequeathed subject to a charge for the payment of debts.

Does the will of Martin vary the order? An initial problem is that categories 3 and 4 in the statutory order, properties specifically devised or bequeathed, and property charged with the payment of debts would, one would think, appear as categories 1 and 2 in the order. This poses the question as to what it takes to vary the statutory order. Any variation must be in writing and an expression of contrary intention which is merely oral will not negate the order (*Perry v Hicknell* (1982)). Where the direction is in writing a mere direction to pay debts will not in itself vary the order because the personal representatives have got to pay the debts in any event. A mere appropriation or charging of property does not displace the statutory order because these are referred to in categories 3 and 4 in the order.

Do the words following the gift of the shares to Alice vary the statutory order? If the words are construed as a mere charging of property then the order in s 34(iii) is not displaced and the debts would be paid following the order laid down in s 34(iii) (*Re Gordon* (1940)) (2). In order to affect a variation based upon a direction, one would have to show that in using the words 'subject to the payment thereof of all my just debts' Martin has shown that he wishes the debts to be paid out of the bequest and has indicated an intention to exonerate the other property. The intention to exonerate was held to apply following an automatic gift of residue in *Re James* (1947) (3) and applied in *Re Meldrum* (1952) where the testator bequeathed to his daughter the money in a bank account after the payment of legacies and debts and left the residue of his property between his son and daughter. Mr Justice Upjohn, applying *Re James*, held that the direction to pay debts from the bank account showed an intention to exonerate the residue. The difference here is that the residue has been given to different people where as in *Re Meldrum* the daughter whose bequest of the bank account subject to debts was also included as a residuary beneficiary. There is no clear answer and it would be a matter of construction for the court to determine whether the bequest of the shares is to be primarily liable for the payment of debts.

If the conclusion is that the direction in the gift of the shares does not vary the statutory order then the general debts of £70,000 will be payable primarily out of the property passing on the partial intestacy ('the Oliver fund') and the share of residue to Henry. This will leave debts of £30,000 which will come out of the gift of the shares and the specific devise of the farmhouse applying category 6 in the statutory order. The debts will be borne ratably according to the value of the respective gifts so the majority of the remaining £30,000 would fall upon Bert and to a lesser extent Alice.

If the construction follows the interpretation in *Re James* and *Re Meldrum* then the statutory order will have been varied and the primary fund for the payment of the debts will be the gift of the shares thereby wiping out the gift to Alice. This will still leave £10,000 of general debts. Where these are payable from will depend again upon whether there has been a further variation of the order. If the statutory order applies then John will have divided the residuary personalty into two funds, the 'Oliver fund' and the 'Henry fund'. Each fund would be worth £20,000 and the burden of the balance of the general debts would be payable out of the Oliver fund. How could this be varied? The key to understanding the other line of authorities on the variation of the statutory order regarding the payment of debts lies in understanding the meaning of the expression 'residuary property'. The ordinary meaning of the term 'residuary property' is that one takes what is left after paying all expenses, debts, liabilities including taxation and a provision for the legacies. However, the purpose of s 34 is to place the assets in certain categories (that is, marshall them) with the intention that the debts are to be borne out of those categories in accordance with the statutory order (*Re Sanger* (1939)). The order may be varied by the testator directing debts to be paid from specified property as considered above. The alternative is for the will to include a direction to pay debts in such a way that the provisional categorisation of assets cannot be made until the debts have been paid. In *Re Kempthorne* (1930) the testator left all his property, after the payment of debts and legacies, to be divided among his brothers and sisters. Two of them predeceased him. At first instance the court held that the wording was a mere direction for debts to be paid and therefore did not vary the statutory order. The Court of Appeal disagreed saying that by using the word 'after' the testator had shown an intention that the debts should be paid before the residue was ascertained. Similarly, where the testator left residuary property 'subject to the payment of debts' in *Re Harland-Peck* (1941) the Court of Appeal held that the statutory order had been varied (4).

If there is some direction in Martin's will whereby the provisional categorisation cannot be made before the debts are paid then the order would be varied and the balance of the debts, the £10,000, would come out of the residuary personalty before division. This would leave a net £30,000 to be divided equally between the Oliver fund and the Henry fund. The decision as to the burden of the debts is important. Assuming that the gift of shares does vary the order then as regards the remaining £10,000 the Oliver fund would have to bear the burden leaving Henry to take £20,000 as against £10,000 to the Oliver fund. If, however, the order is varied then each fund will receive £15,000. There do not appear to be words of variation in this case and therefore, if the gift of the shares is to bear the debts, then the balance of £10,000 would be payable out of the Oliver fund passing on partial intestacy.

Notes

1. In *Re Valpy* (1906) there was a direction to pay all debts, except a mortgage debt on a particular property, and this was held to show an intention that all other mortgage debts should be paid from residue.
2. In *Re Gordon* (1940) the testatrix by her will gave a specific legacy, and a legacy of £5,000 with a direction to pay it from her debts, and to pay over the balance to another. The residue was undisposed of owing to the predecease of the beneficiary. The court held that the statutory order was not displaced with the result that the debts were paid from the undisposed of residue, rather than the legacy set aside for this purpose. There was no indication in the will of any intention to exonerate the residue.
3. In *Re James* (1947) the testator directed payment of his debts from a particular fund and left the residue to his wife. Mr Justice Roxburgh said, 'I should hold that the direction to pay debts out of a particular fund necessarily involved an intention to exonerate some other fund which the testator disposed of in some other part of his will – in other words, necessarily involved an intention to exonerate the residue of his estate which he devised and bequeathed to his wife absolutely'. Here,

the judge was saying, that the intention appeared to come automatically from the gift of the residue.

In *Re Meldrum* Mr Justice Upjohn said in reference to *Re Gordon*: '... as I understand Maugham J he is saying that, having regard to the presence of paras 1 and 2 (in the statutory order) an indication in the will that a particular piece of property is to be charged with the payment of debts is not sufficient to enable one to assume that the testator is intending to alter the order of application of assets, because, if that was so, one could never give effect to these paragraphs even where there was a partial intestacy bringing in para 1, or a gift of residue bringing in para 2. I think that Roxburgh J recognises that in *Re James*. Nevertheless, it seems to me to remain a question purely of construction of each will whether or not the testator has varied the order of application of assets or not.'

4 In *Re Kempthorne* (1930) the Court of Appeal had held that by referring to the residue 'after payment of expenses, debts and legacies' the testator intended that the debts should be paid before the residue could be ascertained.

In *Re Harland-Peck* the testator left his property 'subject to the payment of funeral and testamentary expenses and debts'. The Court of Appeal held that these words charged the debts on the whole residue and that they had to be discharged before the division was made.

These problems can be avoided in practice by careful drafting. A common provision in terms of the gift of the residue is to start the gift by saying 'subject to and after the payment of funeral testamentary expenses, debts, death duties and legacies I devise and bequeath the remainder of my property whatsoever and wheresoever ...'. This commonly used provision is a combination of the wording in *Re Kempthorne* and *Harland-Peck*. The effect of the clause is to prevent a provisional categorisation until the debts have been paid. This example also indicates that the categorisation cannot be made until the legacies are paid but that is another story.

Question 39

John, a widower, died in April. His estate consists of his freehold property Greenacre, valued at £250,000, but subject to a mortgage of £140,000; shares in ICI plc worth £50,000 and other personalty worth £80,000. At death John owed the Inland Revenue £80,000 together with other general debts of £10,000. By his will, made in 1988, John appointed Edward and David to be his executors, bequeathed the ICI plc shares to his son Ron, Greenacre to his daughter Kate and the residue of his estate 'after payment of all my debts of whatever kind' to his sisters Alice and Beth in equal shares.

In 1992 John wrote to his solicitor 'If it can be arranged I want Kate to have my home free from mortgage'. Alice died last year.

Advise Edward and David as to how the debt should be borne as between the beneficiaries.

Answer plan

The question involves the distribution of assets within the case of a solvent estate and the rules concerning the incidence or burden of debts. The question involves consideration of s 35 of the Administration of Estates Act 1925 and the statutory order for the payment of debts and liabilities contained in s 34(3) and Part II of the First Schedule of the Administration of Estates Act.

Answer

Edward and David are under a duty to pay the debts as quickly as possible. Failure to do so could render them liable for *devastavit*, that is, maladministration. The executors must act with due diligence (*Re Tankard* (1942)). Edward and David should first of all calculate that the estate is solvent, that is to say that the estate assets can meet the debts. Where it is uncertain, then the executors should administer the estate as if it were bankrupt. The danger is if debts are paid in the wrong order, the executors could again be personally liable for *devastavit*. In this case, however, the estate is solvent. The funeral, testamentary and administration expenses have the first claim on the estate.

The creditors will not be interested in how the debts are paid as long as they are paid promptly. The problem lies in determining the incidence or burden of debts and as to who, out of the beneficiaries entitled to the estate, should bear the burden of the debts.

The executors should look first of all to the will for directions as to the payment of debts. If the will is unclear then resort must be had to the statutory provisions contained in the Administration of Estates Act.

In the case of the mortgage debt, in the absence of a clear direction to the contrary in the will, s 35(1) of the Administration of Estates Act 1925 says that the freehold property on which the mortgage is secured should bear the primary liability for the debt. *Prima facie* therefore Kate would take Greenacre subject to the mortgage. She would face either taking over the mortgage with the permission of the mortgagees or seeing the property sold and the mortgage debt paid off, thereby becoming entitled to the balance. However, s 35(1) is subject to any contrary intention indicated by the deceased 'by will, deed or other document'. There is no direction contained in the will. What is the effect of the letter to John's solicitor? The direction would have to be clear. In *Re Bingham* (1959), the testatrix contracted to buy a house before her death and wrote to her solicitors directing them to execute a codicil leaving the house to her daughter 'free of all duties'. The testatrix died before completion and it was held that the property passed to the daughter subject to the unpaid vendor's lien. The direction in the letter was held to be insufficient to lift the burden of the debt from the inheritance.

In order to be effective the direction should indicate who is to bear the burden of the debt. Can one say that the residuary estate should bear the burden by implication? The problem here is that under s 35(1) a general direction to pay debts out of the testator's personal estate is not sufficient to indicate a contrary intention to the general rule in s 35(1). It would appear therefore that Kate would still have to bear the burden of the mortgage.

The general debts total £90,000. The Inland Revenue would not have any prior priority concerning the debt of £80,000 because the estate is solvent. In determining the burden of these general debts, Edward and David must first look to see if there is any direction which varies the application of the statutory order. If there is no direction, then the statutory order in s 34(3) must be applied. Does the direction 'after payment of all my debts of whatever kind' throw the debts on the residue as a whole? This depends upon the interpretation in *Re Harland-Peck* (1941) (see below).

The statutory order in s 34(3) means that the executors must place the assets in various categories. The first category is property undisposed by the will. Whether there is property undisposed of by the will will depend upon the terms of the gift of the residue. If this is given to Alice and Beth as tenants in common, then Alice's pre-decease will mean that her share will lapse and, in the absence of a gift over in the will, becomes property undisposed of by the will. If, however, the gift is to Alice and Beth as joint tenants then the surviving sister will take the whole of the residue. If there is a lapsed share then the residue, the personalty worth £80,000, must be divided: £40,000 to the Alice fund and £40,000 to the Beth fund. The Alice fund would be primarily liable for the debts and then resort would be made to the residue.

If the wording in the will is such that the assets cannot be placed in their respective categories until the debts have been paid, then the statutory order has been varied. It could be argued that the words 'after payment of all my debts of whatever kind' are sufficient, on the authority of *Re Harland-Peck*, to vary the order in respect of the general debts. Section 35(1) requires Greenacre to be specifically exonerated of debt. As this is not the case the mortgage will be paid out of the value of Greenacre leaving the other general debts of £90,000 to be borne primarily by the residuary estate before division. In practice, even if the residue was divided as to the Alice fund and the Beth fund this would make little difference since the general debts exceed the value of the residue. Whether the order is varied depends upon applying either *Re Harland-Peck* or the interpretation in *Re Lamb* (1929) that mere direction to pay debts out of residue will not vary the statutory order as the executors have got to do this in any event.

The Alice fund and the Beth fund will not, therefore, receive anything and the remaining £10,000 in the balance of the general debts will be paid out of the property specifically bequeathed; namely the ICI plc shares which are left to Ron.

Question 40

Advise in each of the following situations:

(a) Derek, who has just died, appointed Edward as executor in his will. Edward had agreed to be Derek's executor prior to the execution of the will in 1989 but no longer wishes to act. Advise him if he must do so.

(b) William has died intestate. His son Henry has said that he will deal with the estate. William's other relatives wish to know if he is entitled to do so.

(c) Probate of the will of Reginald was granted to Simon, one of the executors named in the will, power being reserved to Thomas the other executor. Simon has recently died and Victoria has obtained a grant of letters of administration of his estate. Yvonne (15) is the sole beneficiary under Reginald's will. Who is entitled to deal with the administration of Reginald's estate?

Answer plan

This question deals with a series of practical points on the administration of estates including the rules as to acceptance in renunciation; the order of entitlement to a grant under r 22 of the Non-Contentious Probate Rules 1987; r 20 of the Non-Contentious Probate Rules and the grant of double probate.

Answer

(a) The office of executorship is the personal choice of the testator. The office cannot be assigned (*Re Skinner*). However, an executor cannot be compelled to accept office and is free to renounce even where he has agreed to act as executor during the testator's lifetime. Edward could therefore file a renunciation with the court. The only bar to this would be if Edward had acted in the estate after Derek's death in such a way that would be deemed to be acceptance of office, for example, pursuing a claim for a debt or taking possession of chattels for the purposes of valuation rather than mere safe custody. If Edward has done such acts which would constitute acceptance, and still refuses to take out probate, he could be deemed liable as an intermeddler in the estate and notice served on him to take out a grant. If he then refused, he could be constituted liable as an *executor de son tort* to the extent of the value of the assets he has taken under his control. He can plead in defence that he has properly dealt with the assets.

Acts of necessity or humanity would not constitute a person an *executor de son tort* so, for example, if Edward had simply arranged the funeral or taken certain chattels into possession purely for safe custody this would not, in itself, amount to an acceptance of office. Edward must file his renunciation in writing to the Probate Registry. In practice this would be done by the persons subsequently applying for a grant and at the same time lodging Edward's written renunciation.

(b) In the case of a person dying intestate, a grant of letters of administration will issue. The order of entitlement to the grant is set out in r 22 of the Non-Contentious Probate Rules 1987. The order of entitlement follows the beneficial order of distribution on intestacy with the addition of creditors at the end of the list. One administrator is sufficient unless there is a minority interest in the estate or a limited interest in which case the court will require at least two administrators to be appointed.

The first person entitled under the order set out in r 22 would be William's spouse. If there is no surviving spouse then entitlement passes to the next category, the issue. This would include Henry but there may be others entitled within the same category; that is to say, any brothers or sisters of Henry or children of any deceased brother or sister. All those within the same class have an equal right to apply for the grant.

In order to apply for a grant an applicant must have a beneficial interest in the estate. If William did leave a surviving spouse then whether the issue would be entitled to benefit would depend upon the size of the estate. If the estate is valued at £125,000 excluding personal chattels, then the issue would not be entitled to benefit. However r 22(3) provides that a grant can be made to a person who would be entitled to a beneficial interest in the estate if there were an accretion to the estate provided that any person with a better right was cleared off. So, for example, if William's surviving spouse did not wish to take out the grant then those next in line, including Henry, could do so.

(c) Where an executor has died having taken out the grant but before completing the administration of the estate, then the entitlement to the grant of probate would pass to Thomas where power had been reserved to Thomas in the grant. The grant that would issue to Thomas would be double probate. Thomas cannot be forced to take the grant but should be cited as to whether he wishes to take out double probate or renounce. The chain of representation under s 7 of the Administration of Estates Act 1925 cannot apply in the case of Simon's estate because he has died intestate. If Thomas does renounce it will be necessary for a grant of letters of administration *de bonis non administrative* to issue to the estate of Reginald. Entitlement to a grant to Reginald's estate is governed by r 20 of the Non-Contentious Probate Rules 1987. Yvonne, as the sole beneficiary, would be entitled to a grant if she was of age. Since she is a minor, letters of administration would be issued on her behalf (*minore aetate*). In these circumstances a grant would normally be issued to Yvonne's parent or guardian. If Yvonne was aged 16 she could nominate someone to take out a grant on her behalf. If the administration of the estate is not completed by the time Yvonne attains the age of 18 then she can apply for a cessate grant and for the grant of letters of administration to be issued in her name.

Question 41

'It is the responsibility of the personal representatives to pay the just debts and liabilities of the deceased.'

Consider this duty with particular reference to the administration of the insolvent estate.

Answer plan

This is a straightforward essay requiring a knowledge of the classification of debts in the insolvent estate, distinguishing between secured and unsecured debts.

Answer

If the assets of the estate are insufficient to pay all the debts and liabilities (including funeral, testamentary and administration expenses) the estate is insolvent (s 228 Insolvency Act 1985). The debts must be paid in the order set out in the Insolvency Act 1985 and the Administration of Insolvent Estates of Deceased Persons Order SI 1986 No 1999. Priority given to reasonable funeral, testamentary and administration expenses even over preferred debts (r 2) and thereafter the order of debts in bankruptcy.

In *Re Palmer (dec'd) (a debtor)* (1993) the court considered the effect of an insolvency administration order upon property held on a joint tenancy. The court held that the effect of the insolvency administration was to vest the whole of the deceased's assets in the trustee as from the date of the bankruptcy. Further, since the order was to be treated as having been made on the same day as, but before the death, it was then held that the whole of the deceased's assets became vested in the trustee and a trust was imposed on the deceased's property for the benefit of his creditors. The effect therefore was to sever the joint tenancy before the death. The result was that the deceased's beneficial share in the property was available for his creditors. Vinelott J, in considering the new insolvency legislation, was clear that the effect was to impose upon the debtor's property, at the time when the bankruptcy order was made, a trust for the benefit of his creditors.

The creditor has loaned monies to the deceased on the security of property by way of mortgage, charge or lien. The usual course of action would be to realise the security to meet the debt. In cases where the security may be insufficient to meet the debt, other courses of action can be considered:

(a) To realise the security and prove for the balance of the debt.
(b) To set a value on the security and prove for the balance.
  If, for example, the creditor wishes to keep the property himself or, to dispose of the property, as in (a) above, would involve high costs.
(c) To surrender the security and prove for the whole of the debt.
  This would be done where, for example, the security proves to be worthless.

The order in bankruptcy is as follows:

(i) Funeral, testamentary and administration expenses.
  These take priority over all debts owed to unsecured creditors. As between the expenses themselves the funeral expenses have priority.
(ii) Specially preferred debts.

Where the deceased held money or property belonging to a friendly society in the capacity of an officer of the society such monies take priority over all other unsecured debts listed below.

(iii) Preferred debts.

These are listed under five categories:

- Debts due to the Inland Revenue.

  Pay-as-you-earn (PAYE) deductions owing in the 12 months preceding the death where the deceased was an employer and any sums due as a result of deductions from the pay of sub-contractors in the construction industry.

- Debts due to the Customs and Excise.

  These include *inter alia* value added tax due in the six months before the death and outstanding motor vehicle tax due in the 12 months before the death.

- Social security contributions.

  Sums due under Class 1 or Class 2 contributions under the Social Security Act 1975 for the 12 months ending with the death; sums assessed under Class 4.

- Contributions to occupational pension schemes.
- Remuneration of employees.

  Wages outstanding for the four months before death to a maximum (at present £800) and accrued holiday pay are the main items under this head.

  All categories of preferred debts rank equally as between themselves. If the assets are insufficient to meet them they will abate proportionately according to value.

(iv) Ordinary debts.

All debts not falling within any other category. This category will include moneys owed to the Inland Revenue and Customs and Excise which exceed the preferred category debts.

(v) Deferred debts.

They are debts owed in respect of credit provided by a person who was the spouse of the deceased at the latter's death; it is immaterial whether this was so at the time the credit was provided.

The order of priority set out above cannot be varied by the will of the deceased. Where a personal representative pays a debt out of order he can be personally liable. If the personal representative is in any doubt as to the solvency of the estate he should administer as if it were insolvent.

Question 42

'The effect of the Administration of Estates Act 1925 has been to produce lasting uncertainty as to the property out of which pecuniary legacies are payable.'

Discuss.

Answer plan

This quote is inviting a discussion of the incidence or burden of pecuniary legacies out of the solvent estate of the deceased. The topic is complex involving a mine field of permutations. Professor Mellows in the fourth addition to *Mellows on Succession* says that prior to reading the appropriate section in the text one should place a cold towel over one's head before proceeding.

The issue is whether or not the statutory order for the application of assets in the payment of debts contained in s 34 (iii) and Part II of the First Schedule to the Administration of Estate Act 1925 also applies in the payment of the pecuniary legacies. The problem is when one reads the statutory order the only reference to pecuniary legacies is in connection with the retention of a fund for the payment of the pecuniary legacies mentioned in numbers 1 and 2 in the order in an attempt to preserve the pecuniary legacies until certain other assets are exhausted. The pecuniary legacy fund can only be resorted to in category 5. Because there has been no clear reference to the incidence of burdens of legacies the cases have gone either way; for example *Re Worthington* itself supporting the idea that they should not be treated differently but against that *Re Thompson* (1936) followed by *Re Wilson* (1966).

Answer

The rules as to the incidents or burden of debts were changed after 1925 by s 34(3) of the Administration of Estates Act 1925. The pre-1926 legislation was based upon the preservation of real property which passed to the heir of law. Section 34(3) makes both the real and personal estate subject to the payment of funeral, testamentary and administration expenses, debts and liabilities. Personal representatives are required to make a provisional categorisation of assets in accordance with the order laid down in Schedule I Part II to the AEA 1925. It is not easy to determine whether the will has made a variation of this statutory order as regards the payment of the debts. For example, a mere appropriation of property for the payment for debts will not vary the statutory order as an appropriation is category 3 in the order after property undisposed of by the will and the residuary estate. The difficulties faced by the court of construction are compounded when it comes to considering the incidence or burden of legacies. The difficulty is that there is no clear reference to legacies in s 34(3) thereby making it uncertain whether they are to be treated in the same way as the debts. The only direct references are to the preservation of a fund for the payment of the pecuniary legacies to be retained out of categories 1 and 2 in the order, that is property undisposed of by the will and the residuary estate. The pecuniary legacy fund can only be resorted to in category 5 of the order. The lack of a clear direction has left the question uncertain as to whether the statutory order should be applied in the payment of the legacies. If it is the case that a court of construction thinks that the 1925 legislation does not apply then resort is had to the position before 1926.

Before 1926 the legacies were payable out of the testator's general personal estate, that is, those parts of the estate not otherwise specifically devised or bequeathed, *Robertson v Broadbent* (1883), there was no distinction in the general personal estate between that which was undisposed of and residue. Both were liable rateably for the payment of the legacies. The purpose of the pre-1926 legislation was in effect to 'ring fence' the realty. If the general personal estate proved insufficient the *legacies* abated proportionately and in general the realty was exempt. Realty could only be resorted to in exceptional circumstances. For example, the testator might make a unitary gift of realty and personalty. This would raise a presumption of the intention that the residuary realty could be resorted to after the residuary personalty had been exhausted, *Greville v Browne* (1859). If the residuary personalty and realty were given together and the testator added an express direction that the fund was to be subject to the payment of pecuniary legacies then the legacies were paid from both the realty and personalty rateably, *Roberts v Walker* (1830) (1). Very exceptionally, the testator could provide that the legacies should be paid out of realty in priority to personalty but to do this the testator not only had to clearly charge a specific fund of realty with payment of the legacies but had to show a clear intention to exonerate other property, *Elliott v Dearsley* (1881).

The failure to make any specific reference to the incidence of pecuniary legacies in the 1925 legislation has left a number of conflicting judicial decisions. In *Re Worthington* (1933) the testatrix left a number of pecuniary legacies and then disposed of the residue to two named beneficiaries one of whom died before her. At first instance it was held that the legacies were payable out of the general estate before categorisation of the shares of the residue. On appeal the Court of Appeal said that the legacies were payable primarily out of the undisposed share of residue; as regards the realty and personalty, this was to be used rateably to meet the pecuniary legacies. Lord Hanworth MR said that in the absence of a contrary indication in the will itself s 34(3) applied to the incidence of both debts and legacies (2). *Re Lamb* (1929) applied the statutory order to the payment of legacies also *Re Gillett's WT* (1950); however in *Re Thompson* (1936) the court ruled that s 34(3) was meant to apply to expenses, debts and liabilities alone Mr Justice Clauson took this view on the basis that there was no direct mention of legacies and he could see no grounds to suggest that the law had been altered from the pre-1926 position.

Confusion has arisen because the incidence of debts has not been clearly referred to in the AEA 1925. If the statutory order effected by s 34(3) is to be applied then the assets have to be provisionally categorised into their respective funds, including the pecuniary legacy fund, before any debts and liabilities are paid. However, where there is a lapsed share of residue, that is to say, property undisposed of by the will (category 1 in the order) s 33(2) AEA 1925 imposes a statutory trust for sale on the undisposed of property. Section 33(2) contains a direction to the personal representatives to pay off the debts and liabilities first and only after this payment should the balance be used to constitute a pecuniary legacy fund. In other words there is a direct clash between the terms of s 34(3) on Provision Categorisation of Assets and s 33(2).

Section 33 applies to the situations where a statutory trust for sale is imposed by s 33(1). This will occur for example where there is a total intestacy and by s 33(2) where there is a lapsed share of residue devolving on a partial intestacy. In *Re Worthington* the court made the lapsed share of residue primarily liable for the payment of legacies after debts and liabilities had been met and did not draw any distinction between realty and personalty. Had the pre-1926 rules been applied then *Greville v Browne* would have made the residuary personalty primarily liable for the payment of legacies with residuary realty available only in the event of a shortfall. *Re Worthington* therefore suggests that s 33(2) has altered the pre-1926 situation, throwing the primary burden of legacies on to property undisposed of by the will without differentiation between realty and personalty. Certainly this would accord with the general thrust of the 1925 property legislation, albeit, it would have helped if there had been a clearer reference to the burden of legacies.

The problems have only just begun however for s 33 cannot apply where the testator has created an express trust for sale. Section 33 takes effect subject to the terms of the will; therefore an express trust for sale would take priority. One cannot have to subsisting trusts for sale in respect of one and the same fund, *Re McKee* (1931). Section 33 applies where the deceased dies not having fully disposed of his property by will. If therefore the deceased dies fully testate then s 33 cannot apply. What happens therefore if there is a lapsed share of residue but the will contains an express trust for sale? In *Re Beaumont's WT* (1950) the will contained an express trust for sale, the court held that the pre-1926 rules applied and the pecuniary legacies came out of a proportionate payment of both realty and personalty and not out of the property undisposed of by the will (3). The decision in *Re Beaumont* is supported by *Re Thompson* (1936) and *Re Anstead* (1943).

Another line of authority has taken the view that s 34(3) makes pecuniary legacies payable out of the property undisposed of by will as far as possible. In *Re Midgley* (1955) the will contained an express trust for sale but there was a lapsed share of residue when the testatrix revoked a gift to one of the six named beneficiaries. Mr Justice Harman held that the legacies should be payable out of the lapsed share referring to the obligation in para 1 and 2 to retain a fund for the payment of pecuniary legacies (4). Where the will imposes an express trust for sale the case law has gone either way and is difficult if not impossible to reconcile.

The final consideration is whether realty should be treated in any way differently to personalty. One view is that realty and personalty should be treated identically. The schedule uses the word 'property' which is defined by s 55(1)(vii) of the AEA 1925 as including any interest whether real or personal. This approach was adopted in *Re Harland-Peck* (1941). The alternative view is based upon the position prior to 1926 when legacies were normally payable out of personalty and in the absence of a clear direction the schedule was not meant to alter the rules on the incidence of legacies within a particular category of property. This view was adopted in *Re Anstead* (1943) and *Re Wilson* (1967). The only relief from this confusion is that where a statutory trust for sale applies realty is converted into personalty rendering the discrimination between the two classes of property unnecessary, *Re Martin* (1955).

It would certainly save a great deal of tortuous construction if the view in *Re Worthington* prevailed, that is, that the statutory order of application of assets should apply not only to debts but to legacies. However the difficult path through the various cases referred to above arises because the wording of the legislation is by no means clear. The draftsman should therefore take care when it comes to the gift of the residuary estate to make sure that this is not ascertained until not only the debts and liabilities have been paid but to include also the payment of the legacies.

Notes

1. An example of the mixed fund such as in *Roberts v Walker* would be where the residue of realty and personalty is left upon trust for sale with a direction to pay the pecuniary legacies from the fund.
2. In *Re Worthington* Lord Hanworth MR referring to ss 33(2) and 34(3) queried whether there should be a distinction between debts on the one hand and legacies on the other. Referring to the judgment at first instance of Mr Justice Bennet the Master of the Rolls said: 'The learned judge seems to have read the will as providing for the payment of the legacies first and to have thought that the residue was not be ascertained until after they had been paid. But the provisions of the statute indicate that unless there is some provision in the will which negatives the prescribed order of administration, that order of administration must apply to both legacies and debts. The learned judge seems to have thought that because of the specific reference to legacies

in the will there was an indication of an intention that the statutory order should not apply to them. But, after all, if legacies are given by a will, there must be a specific reference to them, and I do not see how that can be sufficient to alter the statutory order of administration.'

3   In *Re Beaumont's WT* the testatrix left a number of pecuniary legacies and then left a real and personal estate not otherwise disposed of upon trust for sale, after payment of debts and expenses, to four named persons. One of the named persons predeceased the testatrix. Had the statutory order for the payment of debts been varied? Where did the burden fall for the payment of the pecuniary legacies? The court held that the statutory order had been varied by the will, the pecuniary legacies fund was to be set aside and the debts paid before the division of the residue into four equal parts. However, in the absence of a clear direction in the Administration of Estates Act 1925 Mr Justice Danckwerts held that the old law applied to the payment of the pecuniary legacies citing in support the decision in *Re Thompson*. Mr Justice Danckwerts said 'It seems to me ... in the present case the pecuniary legacies ... are all payable out of the whole estate before coming to what is divided into four equal parts and given to four named persons, so that the lapsed share is simply a lapsed share of the estate after those burdens have been cleared.'

4   Mr Justice Harman in *Re Midgley* (1955) in holding that the pecuniary legacies were payable primarily out of the property in category 1 being property undisposed of by the will said: 'Therefore, one has first to retain out of the property undisposed of a fund sufficient to meet any pecuniary legacies, and one has to pay the debts, testamentary expenses and so forth out of the rest of the undisposed of property. What is one to do then with the fund that has been retained thereout? The answer it seems to me, is that one must pay the pecuniary legacies because it has been retained to meet them. It is, if I may say so, a tortuous way of legislation, but that is what I should have thought it inevitably meant and so, indeed, Danckwerts J concluded recently in *Re Martin* (1955). It is quite true that in that case there was undisposed of real estate, and no trust for sale which applied to it. Any trust for sale would have failed because of the failure of the gift.'

In *Re Martin* the testator bequeathed two pecuniary legacies and then left all his real estate to his daughter. There then followed the gift of the residue of the personal estate to trustee on trust for sale with a direction to pay all debts and expenses and divide the balance among named beneficiaries. The testator subsequently revoked the gift of real estate to his daughter but did not make any further disposition of the property; therefore it was under disposed of at death and fell within para 1 of the statutory order. Did the pecuniary legacies fund come out of the undisposed of realty in para 1 or out of the residuary personalty in para 2? Mr Justice Danckwerts held that the pecuniary legacies fund should be retained out of the realty out of para 1. He said: 'It seems to me that here I am dealing simply with one asset, the undisposed of real estate and out of that undisposed of real estate a fund is to be raised to provide for the pecuniary legacies and if the fund is not to be raised for the payment of the pecuniary legacies, it is difficult to see what reason there is for setting aside the fund. Therefore, I am necessarily driven to the conclusion ... the proper fund to meet the legacies in the present case is the undisposed of property.'

Mr Justice Danckwerts drew a distinction between the situation in *Re Martin* and the decision of Mr Justice Clauson in *Re Thompson*. He said that in the *Thompson* case there was no question of an intestacy. There was a common fund comprised of real and personal estate and there was no direction in the will as to how the legacies were to be borne, that is, whether the AEA 1925 threw the burden on the legacies rateably between real and personal property or whether the pre-1926 law applied. It was held in *Thompson* that as regards the primary fund for the payment of legacies the law had not been altered; therefore the personal estate must bear the primary liabilities. Mr Justice Danckwerts pointed that in *Thompson* the judge was dealing with an interpretation of para 2 whereas in *Re Martin* the lapsed share brought into play para 1 which it was held applied in the case.

Question 43

Discuss the powers of personal representatives to delegate and the extent of their liability for any losses occurring as a result of such delegation.

Answer plan

This question requires consideration of the statutory powers of delegation under the Trustee Act 1925 and the Powers of Attorney Act 1971.

Answer

Personal Representatives cannot generally delegate their powers unless they have authority to do so. Statutory powers to delegate may exist unless they are specifically excluded by the will.

Section 23 of the Trustee Act 1925 gives an express power to personal representatives to appoint agents instead of their acting personally. Agents can include, for example, a solicitor, a banker, stockbroker or other persons to transact any business or to do any acts required to be transacted in the execution of the trust or administration of the estate. The power is wide enough to allow personal representatives to appoint agents to do acts which they themselves could have done. The personal representative is not liable for the default of an agent provided the agent has been employed in good faith. How far this absolution of responsibility applies is unclear given s 30 of the Trustee Act provides that a trustee, and this includes a personal representative, shall be chargeable only for money and securities actually received by him, and shall not be responsible for any other loss 'unless the same happens through his wilful default'. One could argue, therefore, that a failure to exercise a firm control over an agent may amount to wilful default.

The beneficiary or creditor who loses as a result of a lack of good faith on the part of the personal representative may sue all the personal representatives jointly or any of them individually. There are rights of contribution from other personal representatives unless the fault occurs solely through the act of the one who is sued and the others have not been guilty of wilful default, or where there has been fraud (see *Bahin v Hughes* (1886)). Where mismanagement or misappropriation is alleged, a person who is interested in the estate may seek an order for an account.

Where a personal representative would otherwise be liable to beneficiaries or creditors, he may, in certain circumstances, be relieved from liability where:

- there is a relieving clause in the will;
- where the court makes a relieving order; or
- where there is an agreement with the beneficiaries.

The usual clause in a will restricts liability to wilful and individual fraud. Section 61 of the Trustee Act 1925 enables the court to grant relief to a trustee or personal representative where he has acted honestly, that is, in good faith; reasonably; and ought fairly to be excused.

Where a beneficiary has agreed, or concurred, in a breach of trust he cannot afterwards bring an action in respect of it. However, the beneficiary must be *sui juris* at the time and have full knowledge of the relevant facts. A beneficiary will not be able to take action if, having learned of the wrongful act, he or she acquiesces in it or gives the personal representative a release.

Section 9 of the Powers of Attorney Act 1971 allows personal representatives to delegate by power of attorney the exercise of any of their powers and discretions. They may do this for a period not exceeding 12 months. The personal representatives remain liable, however, for the acts of the delegate as if they were their own acts.

Question 44

Advise each of the following:

a) Jake, who is the executor of Christine's estate. He is ready to distribute the estate but is concerned that he may not know of all of the claims against the estate.
b) Connie, who is the executrix of Frank's estate. She has settled all liabilities of the estate apart from one debt which is still the subject of legal proceedings. Until the proceedings are resolved she does not know the exact amount of the debt.
c) Kevin, who is the executor of Maxwell's estate. In his will made in 1990, Maxwell provided that his estate should be divided

amongst 'my children'. Kevin completed the administration and distributed the estate amongst Maxwell's four legitimate children. A fifth, illegitimate child, Ian, has now made a claim for a share in the estate.

Answer plan

This question requires an understanding of the statutory protections of personal representatives and the ability to apply the rules to the practical situations and, in particular, the use of the statutory protection afforded to personal representatives under s 27 of the Trustee Act 1925 regarding claims by creditors to the estate.

Answer

(a) In many cases it would be impractical for personal representatives to know of all possible claims that there may be against a deceased person's estate. In order that the personal representative can be protected and the distribution of the estate be expedited, s 27 of the Trustee Act 1925 provides that so long as the personal representatives place an advertisement in the statutory form giving notice of claims against the estate to be made not less than two months from the date of the notice, the personal representatives will be protected in any future distribution of assets. The notice must be published in the *London Gazette*, in a newspaper circulating in the district in which the land in the estate is situated, and by giving such other notices as would have been directed by the court. This would depend upon the size of the estate and the nature of the deceased's business. It may be necessary, for example, to file notices in newspapers abroad where the deceased had business interests or holdings overseas. Provided the notice is given in the correct form, Jake would be protected in any future claim by a creditor outside of the period stated in the notice. However, Jake could not plead lack of notice if he had failed, or failed within the correct minimum time, to file the correct notices. In such a case Jake could be liable for *devastavit*, that is to say, a misapplication or maladministration of estate assets. In such a case Jake would be personally liable and would not be entitled to an indemnity from the estate.

Section 27(2) requires that Jake should undertake searches or obtain official certificates of search similar to those to which an intending purchaser would be advised to make or obtain. These would include, for example, Land Charges Registry Searches.

Provided the correct notices and steps have been taken, Jake will be free to distribute the estate. If a creditor subsequently comes forward and proves his claim then the creditor could proceed against the beneficiaries.

(b) Filing a s 27 Trustee Act notice will not protect a personal representative where the personal representative knows of a specific claim. In these circumstances, Connie could not therefore claim the protection of s 27 and simply distribute the balance of the estate. In order to expedite distribution she should set aside a fund sufficient to meet the claim and any likely costs (she should be careful to set this figure on the conservative side to avoid the possibility of any shortfall) and pay the balance of the estate funds to the beneficiaries. Any excess once the debt has been resolved could then be paid to the beneficiaries. An alternative, though less attractive possibility, is to distribute the whole of the estate and take an indemnity from the beneficiaries that they will agree to pay the amount of the debt once it is fixed. The risk here is that the beneficiaries may not have the resources when the debt is finally resolved and the indemnities in such a case would prove to be worthless. Insurance against such a possibility could be considered but because of the risk factor the premium is likely to be high and this would only add to the costs of the estate. By far the best course of action is to retain funds from the estate to meet the potential liability.

(c) The Family Law Reform Act 1987 removed all barriers regarding illegitimacy and relations. Section 20 of the 1987 Act removed the previous protection given to personal representatives in respect of illegitimate children. Where the estate is distributed without regard to the possibility of an illegitimate child, the personal representative could be personally liable to that child. In order to obtain protection, Kevin should ensure that the statutory notices under s 27 are filed. Once time limits have expired Kevin would be free to distribute the estate amongst the children of which he is aware. When the fifth illegitimate child becomes known, that child would then have recourse against the other children for his or her share but Kevin would be protected against personal liability.

Question 45

When a personal representative assents to certain property passing in accordance with the terms of the will or intestacy he is indicating that he no longer needs the property for the purposes of the administration and the property can pass to the beneficiary. How is the assent made?

Answer plan

This essay requires a knowledge of the effects of an assent and the problems that can arise where the personal representative does not execute an assent in the course of the final distribution of the assets.

Answer

There is no set form as to how the assent is to be made. The personal representative can indicate orally, in writing or by conduct that the asset is no longer required for the administration (see *Attenborough v Solomon* (1913) (below)).

The transfer of property does not occur by reason of the assent but by virtue of the dispositions in the will. The assent merely makes the dispositions operative.

The effect of the assent of personalty:

(a) The gift relates back to death; therefore the beneficiary has the right to the income and profits arising from the death. The assent is operative in respect of the legacy and not the legatee. The significance is that in a situation where the legacy has been given to the wrong person (for example, a later will is found altering the destination of the gift) the assent perfects the title to the rightful legatee from the death.

This is illustrated by *Re West* (1913) where the executors assented to the person named in a codicil. A later codicil was subsequently discovered bequeathing the legacy to a different person. The beneficiary under the later codicil successfully sued. The fact that the assent had been made to the wrong person made no difference for the assent was to the bequest and not the beneficiary.

(b) The assent vests the property in the beneficiary and he becomes responsible for it thereafter. A consequence is that any costs of transport or packaging of the chattel together with insurance in transferring the asset must be born by the beneficiary; for example, in a delivery of china in *Re Sivewright* (1922).

(c) *Re West* (above) shows that the beneficiary is entitled to take legal proceedings for the recovery of the chattel. However, this right only exists in respect of specific gifts and not in the case of general or residuary legacies.

Title to the property passes when the assent is made. In the case of a chattel, such as a painting, title will pass immediately. In the case of a chose in action, shares in a limited company, for example, the personal representatives become trustees for the beneficiary where it is necessary to comply with other requirements of the transfer. For example, in the case of company shares the title will only pass to the beneficiary when his name is entered upon the share register (*Re Grosvenor* (1916)).

Section 36 Administration of Estates Act 1925 governs assents to land and applies to estates or interests in real estate which devolve on the personal representatives. If land is conveyed to the personal representatives after the death, for example, where the deceased died between contract and completion of the purchase, then an assent will not suffice and the land will have to be transferred to the personal representatives by deed (*Re Stirrup's Contract* (1961)).

The main circumstances in which an assent can be used are:
- to transfer the legal estate to a beneficiary in accordance with the terms of the will;
- to transfer the legal estate to trustees under the terms of the will;
- where a beneficiary has survived but the testator died before an assent could be made in his favour, an assent can be made to his personal representatives;
- where a beneficiary has predeceased the testator but the devise does not fail, an assent can be made to his personal representatives (for example, where s 33 Wills Act 1837 applies);
- where the deceased contracted to sell realty before his death but had not conveyed the property to the purchaser, the personal representative may make an assent to the purchaser.

The assent must be in writing, signed by the personal representatives and must name the party in whose favour the assent is effected (s 36(4)). Prior to 1964, conveyancing practitioners thought that the provisions of s 36(4) did not apply where the personal representative and the beneficiary were the same person because there was no 'passing' of the legal estate, merely a change in the capacity in which the estate was held. However, this view was held to be incorrect by the court in *Re King's Will Trust* (1964) (below).

The assent operates to vest the legal estate in favour of the person named in the assent. Section 36 contains provision designed to protect the purchaser in whose favour an assent is made. If the personal representatives have to sell realty in the course of the administration of the estate they are likely to use an assent to effect the transfer in order to save stamp duty on the transaction. In the case of a purchaser for money or money's worth, s 36(7) gives protection by providing that an assent is sufficient evidence of title unless notice has been placed or annexed to the probate or letters of administration.

Section 36(5) is intended to protect beneficiaries and entitles them to require the personal representatives to enter a notice of the assent upon the probate or letters of administration at the expense of the estate. This gives protection to the beneficiaries if the personal representatives subsequently try to sell the property to another. In such a case the purchasing party would not have the protection afforded by s 36(7). On the other hand, if the beneficiaries have not insisted upon a s 36(5) notice they will not be protected against a subsequent sale.

If the personal representative is slow to make the assent then the beneficiary can apply to the court of directions under s 43(2) Administration of Estates Act 1925.

Where a beneficiary has been left a large general legacy it may be expensive for the personal representatives to sell off estate assets to provide the legacy. Section 41 of the Administration of Estates Act 1925 gives the personal representatives power to appropriate any part of the real or personal estate towards satisfaction of any legacy or other interest in property given by the deceased.

The appropriate must not prejudice any specific gift. A personal representative could not appropriate a specific legacy in satisfaction of a pecuniary legacy.

Section 41(1)(ii) provides that where the beneficiary is absolutely entitled to the gift he must give his consent before appropriation can be effected. Where the interest is settled, consent must be obtained from the trustee or person entitled to the income.

If the person who should give consent is incapable through being under age or a mental patient then consent can be given by a parent, guardian, friend or the court.

The personal representative must employ a qualified valuer to value the property which is to be the subject of the appropriation. The time of value is the date of appropriation and not the date of death (s 41(3)).

Once the appropriation has been made it becomes in effect the substitute for the gift in the will. It binds all those interested in the property whose consents were not necessary. A subsequent purchaser from a beneficiary who has received the property as the result of an appropriation is protected for s 41 deems all requisite consents to have been obtained.

The power to appropriate in s 41 can be modified or even excluded by the provision of the will.

Question 46

Under what circumstances is a general legatee entitled to interest on the legacy?

Answer plan

This is a straightforward essay on the rules concerning the payment of interest on legacies.

Answer

A general legacy carries interest from the time it is payable (the rate is 6% per annum (RSC Order 44 r 10)). The time for payment may be fixed by the testator in his will, for example, by directing that the interest be paid immediately following the death. However, if no time for payment is stated then the time for payment of a general legacy is fixed by law.

The normal rule is that an immediate legacy, for example, '£2,000 to my brother Henry' is payable one year after the testator's death, that is, the end of the executor's year. If the legacy has not been paid by the time the year expires, interest will then become changeable, until such time as the legacy is paid. If, after that date, there is a part payment on account, this sum is treated as being made first in respect of arrears of interest (unless the will directs otherwise) (see *Re Morley's Estate* (1937)).

A contingent or deferred legacy carries interest from the time at which it becomes payable, for example, £3,000 to Paul provided he attains 18, only carries interest from the date of Paul's 18th birthday; where there is a direction in the will to sever the legacy then the legacy will carry interest from the end of the executor's year. For example, where the will leaves a general legacy to trustees to hold the legacy and the investments representing it on trust for Alice provided she attains 18, interest is payable from the end of the executor's year.

There are four situations where, exceptionally, a general legacy carries interest from the date of death of the testator; firstly, where the legacy is given in satisfaction of a debt (see, for example, *Re Rattenbury* (1906)). However, the will may direct a later time for the payment of interest. The second exception is where the legacy is charged only on realty, provided the legacy is vested. However, the normal rule applies where the will directs the legacy to be paid from the proceeds of sale of realty devised upon trust for sale (*Turner v Buck* (1874)).

The third exception is where the testator gives a legacy to his infant child or to an infant to whom he stands *in loco parentis*. Here the legacy carries interest from the date of death in order to provide maintenance for the child, for example, *Re Bowlby* (1904). This rule does not apply where the will has made other provision for the maintenance of the child nor does it apply where the legacy is given to trustees upon trust for the child (*Re Pollock* (1943)). The instances where this rule would apply will therefore be rare where the modern, professionally drawn will usually includes gifts to trustees on behalf of the child. The rate of interest in this case is 5% per annum provided there is sufficient income.

The fourth exception is where a legacy is given to an infant and the testator, by his will, shows an intention to provide for the infant's maintenance or education (*Re Selby-Walker* (1949)). Here, the legatee need not be a child or quasi-child of the testator, provided the legatee is an infant.

Where by his will the testator gives a legacy to his nephew provided he attains 18, then interest is payable once the nephew attains 18 (*Re Raine* (1929)). Interest in this case, would be payable from the end of the executor's year if the legacy had been severed from the general estate for some purpose connected with the legacy. The legacy would carry interest from the death of the testator if the testator stood *in loco parentis* to the nephew. Unless the will made some other provision for the maintenance of the nephew. Given the complexity of these rules in relation to infants, it is good practice to include in the will a clear direction as to the time of payment of interest on the legacy.

Question 47

What rights, if any, do beneficiaries have to the assets of the deceased pending distribution?

Answer plan

This question addresses the rights of the beneficiaries prior to the completion of the administration of the estate.

Answer

Prior to distribution of the assets to the beneficiaries under the will or intestacy the personal representatives hold the assets on a limited trust. As a general rule a beneficiary under a will or intestacy has no legal or equitable proprietary interest in the unadministered assets of the deceased's estate (see the decision of the Privy Council in *Commrs of Stamp Duties v Livingstone* (1965)). Ownership of the unadministered assets is in the hands of the personal representatives. Viscount Radcliffe in Livingstone said:

'... whatever property came to the executor by virtue of his office came to him in full ownership, without distinction between legal and equitable interests ... He held it for the purposes of carrying out the functions and duties of administration, not for his own benefit ... Certainly, therefore, he was in a fiduciary position with regard to the assets that came to him in the right of his office, and for certain purposes and in some aspects he was treated by the court as a trustee.'

Although Viscount Radcliffe refers to a 'fiduciary position', equity does not treat the unadministered assets as if they constituted a trust fund held upon trust for the beneficiaries.

The trust is limited in scope. It does not as a general rule give the beneficiaries an equitable interest in their entitlement in the same way as a beneficiary under an express trust has an equitable interest. The reason is that the personal representatives held the estate not merely for the benefit of the beneficiaries but also to ensure due payment of debts to creditors until the administration is complete; no one is in a position to say what terms of property would need to be realised for the purposes of the administration.

Pending distribution the beneficiary has a *chose* in action to ensure that the estate is properly administered (*Livingstone*, applied in *Re K (dec'd)* (1985)). The *chose* is assignable to the beneficiary in the same way as any other *chose* in action (*Re Leigh's Will Trusts* (1970)).

The nature of the residuary beneficiary's interest in the unadministered estate has been considered in *Crowden v Aldridge* (1993). The residuary beneficiaries agreed to increase the amount of a legacy to the testator's housekeeper. The memorandum directed to the executors, was intended to take effect as a binding variation of the will. Later, one of the residuary beneficiaries returned to sign the deed which had been prepared to formally effect the variation. If all the residuary beneficiaries had signed the deed, this would have been effective to vary the executors' obligations to administer the estate. However, the variation did not take effect because one residuary beneficiary had a change of mind, what was the interest of the residuary beneficiaries in the estate? Applying *Livingstone*, when they signed the memorandum, they had no defined interest in the unadministered estate. If, however, they had all signed the deed, this would have amounted to an effective variation of the will. The beneficiaries had a right, in the nature of a *chose* in action, enforceable in equity, to compel the executors to carry out their obligations even though they had no beneficial interest in the estate. A beneficiary could, for example, transfer his right under the will to another by formal assignment, notwithstanding that they did not yet have any equitable interest in the estate (see the Court of Appeal in *Gray v IRE* (1950)). However, there had been no formal assignment in *Crowden*. The memorandum was merely evidence of any intention to benefit the housekeeper by subsequently executing a deed of variation. The single change of heart by one beneficiary prior to the execution of the deed was sufficient to deny the housekeeper the increase in legacy.

A possible exception concerning ownership of the unadministered estate is in relation to a beneficiary entitled under a specific bequest or devise. Authorities suggest that the specific legatee or devisee takes an equitable interest in the subject matter of the gift at the death of the testator (see *Re Neeld* (1962) and *Re K* (1985)). The legal estate vests in the personal representative and the personal representative cannot be prevented from resorting to the specific gift for the payment of expenses, debts and liabilities. However, this exception does appear to run contrary to the *dicta* in *Livingstone* where the court stated that the property in the estate comes to the personal representative by virtue of his office without distinction between legal and equitable interests. If *Livingstone* is applied to all interests then the specific legatee or devisee would, like any other beneficiary, only have a *chose* in action to have the estate properly administered.

Question 48

What action may a creditor or beneficiary take where he or she is dissatisfied with the administration of the estate?

Answer plan

In the majority of cases the administration of the estate of a deceased proceeds smoothly from consideration of the terms of the will or rules of intestacy to the final distribution of assets to the beneficiaries. There may be instances, however, where the personal representatives need to seek the guidance of the court as to the validity or meaning of the will or the beneficiaries wish to call the personal representatives to account. Resort will therefore be made to the court for assistance. Problems and situations where personal representatives, beneficiaries or creditors can resort to the court for a remedy will be considered.

Answer

Any person interested in the estate may issue proceedings for administration by the court. The applicant may be, *inter alia*, a personal representative, beneficiary or creditor. Application would be to the Chancery Division of the High Court under s 61 Supreme Court Act 1981. There must be a duly constituted personal representative before the court would consider taking the administration. The reason is that there must be a defendant to the proceedings. This person cannot be an *executor de son tort* because his duty is not to administer the estate, merely to account for what he has received.

If no grant of administration has been made, creditors and beneficiaries interested in the estate may apply to the court for the appointment of a receiver to protect the estate pending the appointment of a personal representative. If there are proceedings pending in the estate, a better course of action is to apply for the appointment of an administrator pending suit under s 117 Supreme Court Act 1981.

Administration by the court is expensive and the court will not make an order unless it considers it absolutely necessary. An example would be if the deceased had died bankrupt and it appears that it would be a complex estate for the personal representatives to administer, then, in the interests particularly of the creditors, the court would take on the administration. In many cases, application to the court to take on administration will have been brought by creditors or beneficiaries by way of calling the personal representatives to account, claiming they have not acted properly and the court will make an order against the personal representatives to account. The types of orders include:

- An account of property not specifically devised or bequeathed which has come into the hands of the personal representatives.
- An account of the debts, funeral and testamentary expenses.
- An account of legacies.

The Administration of the Estate   183

- An account of any property of the deceased which remains outstanding.

Apart from an order calling to account, the court could appoint a person to act as a judicial trustee. He is an officer of the court who can act with the personal representatives or alone.

A person considering applying for the court to administer should heed the Limitation Act 1980. In the case of creditors the limitation period is six years for a debt due under a simple contract; the period runs from the date the right accrued (s 5 Limitation Act 1980). In the case of a judgment debt the period is 12 years from the date the judgment became enforceable (s 24). The periods may be extended by acknowledgement of the debt by the personal representatives, either by part payment or in writing.

The personal representatives themselves may apply to the court for specific relief, for example, on the meaning of a particular clause in the will or on a summons for the court to pronounce on the validity of the will. An example of the latter is the privileged will case of *Re Jones* (1981) where the court was asked to consider the validity of the words uttered to the warrant officer.

If a personal representative commits a breach of duty whilst in office he will be liable to the creditors or beneficiaries under the principles of *devastavit*. The nature of *devastavit* and examples were considered earlier in the chapter.

A personal representative is personally liable where *devastavit* is proved. However, certain defences may be raised; certain of these were considered earlier in the chapter but can be summarised as follows:

(a) The protection afforded by the s 27 Trustee Act 1925 notice.

(b) The discretion of the court under s 61 of the Trustee Act to excuse a personal representative who has acted 'honestly and reasonably'. The onus rests with the personal representative to establish that his conduct should be excused.

(c) Section 6 of the Trustee Act can order a personal representative to be indemnified for loss where a beneficiary or creditor has consented to the breach of duty.

(d) Where a beneficiary or creditor who is *sui juris* and with full knowledge of the facts acquiesced in the breach, the onus of proving acquiesence rests with the personal representative. The personal representative can protect himself by obtaining a deed of release from the beneficiary for acts done in the course of the administration of the estate but this release is ineffectual if it has been obtained fraudulently or with the application of undue influence.

(e) The right to take action may be barred by the Limitation Act (above).

(f) A personal representative may plead that he had duly administered all the assets which have come into his hands by entering the plea *'plene administravit'*.

(g) A modified form of the defence in (f) is to plead *'plene administravit praetor'*, that is, he had duly administered the assets which have come into his hands with the exception of assets of a stated value which he still holds.

(h) Under s 48 Administration of Justice Act 1985 the personal representative can plead that he has relied upon the opinion of a barrister on any question as to the meaning or interpretation of the will. The opinion must be written and given by a barrister of at least 10 years' standing. The opinion cannot be acted upon until the court so orders and the court will refuse where there are contentious issues which need to be aired before the court.

Action against the personal representative will be the first court of action by the creditor or beneficiary. However, the personal representative may not have sufficient assets of his own to cover the value of a claim. In that case the choices are:

(i) To pursue those who have received assets wrongly by way of a personal claim, as in *Ministry of Health v Simpson* (1951). Enquiries must be made to see that the recipient is solvent and the claim is worth being pursued.

(ii) Alternatively, a tracing action can be pursued to follow the assets into the hands of those who have received them other than a *bona fide* purchaser for value without notice of any defect. This action does not depend upon the solvency of the recipient, rather, it is an action against the asset in question. In order to succeed, the asset must be in a traceable form and it must not be inequitable to trace in the circumstances.

A leading example of tracing is the lengthy judgment of the Court of Appeal in *Re Diplock* (1948) where property was left by will to named charities for charitable or benevolent purposes. After distribution of many of the assets the will was successfully challenged on the basis that the gift should have read charitable and benevolent. As a result a succession of tracing actions commenced. The court said that where, for example, property had come into the hands of an innocent volunteer who had mixed the property with his own, perhaps, for example, extending a house, it would be inequitable to allow a tracing action to succeed. Tracing is not barred by limitation but, being an equitable remedy, the party seeking the relief must act promptly and, if guilty of *laches* (delay), the right to take action will be lost.

Question 49

Sam died a month ago. By his will he gave his estate to Eric and Dan on trust for sale and conversion, the beneficiaries being Sam's wife Tessa and their son James, aged 12. The residue includes a wholesale electrical equipment business. Tessa has asked Eric and Dan to carry on the business.

Answer plan

This question deals with the duties of personal representatives. The executors should endeavour to settle debts and distribute the estate at the earliest opportunity. They have to be careful concerning personal liability where a business, formerly run by the deceased, is included in the assets. The question entails specific consideration of the contractual liability of the executors.

Answer

Eric and Dan do not have to formally accept the appointment as executors. Should they do any act which an executor would normally do, this will constitute acceptance of office, for example, collecting assets or paying debts would be sufficient to amount to acceptance rendering the person or persons liable as executor (see *Re Stevens* (1897)). Care should be taken where, included in the assets there is a business formally conducted by the deceased. The personal representatives are under a duty to realise the assets to their best advantage. In the case of a business it can be important to preserve the value of the goodwill. Goodwill is defined as the likelihood that the customer will return; therefore any gap following the decease of a sole proprietor can seriously diminish the capital value.

In the course of the administration of the estate the personal representatives may enter into contracts. Provided the personal representative clearly contracts as personal representative, then his liability is limited to the net assets of the estate. However, this limited liability only applies where the contract is authorised, that is to say, within the powers of the personal representative in dealing with the administration of the estate. One area where the law is restrictive on powers is the ability of the personal representative to borrow money. This power is limited to the arranging of a loan to pay death duties where payment is necessary prior to the issue of the grant. In the case of funeral expenses, if no other person is liable (as a result of arranging the funeral), the personal representative is liable to the extent of the assets in his hands by virtue of an implied contract with the undertaker to provide a funeral commensurate with the station in life of the deceased.

In the case of trading contracts where, as in this case, the deceased carried on a business on his own account, the personal representative is entitled to carry on the business, if the goodwill is of value, to such an extent as to enable the business to be sold to the best advantage of the estate. If the personal representative does so the expenses incurred count as administration expenses. The personal representative is liable to the trade creditors but can be fully indemnified from the estate.

Debts incurred prior to the death of the deceased in respect of the business are liabilities of the estate in the normal way. If the personal representative prolongs the trading and is entitled to indemnity from the estate (that is, so long as he has authority either from the will or agreement of the beneficiaries), this right is postponed to the rights of the creditors at death, unless the creditors give express sanction to continue the business at their risk (see *Re Oxley* (1914)).

Where Eric and Dan have to be careful is that for debts incurred after the death of the deceased, whether they carry on the business for early realisation or on a longer term, authorised or not, they are not personally liable to the creditors. This applies even though they expressly trade as personal representatives. Provided they have the requisite authority they will be entitled to be indemnified from the estate. The indemnity ranks after the payment of liabilities but before the beneficiaries. If there is, however, a deficiency of assets to meet the indemnity, the personal representatives will stand the loss personally.

Where the personal representative has a right of indemnity the post-death creditors have a claim against the estate by way of subrogation but only against those assets over which the personal representative could exercise the right with the same degree of priority. The only situation where the post-death creditors would have rights over the pre-death creditors is where the latter expressly authorised the personal representatives to continue to trade.

Eric and Dan would therefore need the express authority in the will to continue the business beyond mere realisation. There is no indication in the question whether the express authority is included in the will. There may be an implied authority, if the trust for sale confirmed in the will contains a power to postpone sale. In *Re Crowther* (1895) it was held that a power to postpone carried with it by implication a power to carry on the business during the period of postponement.

If there is no express power in the will and there is no power to postpone the sale, the personal representatives have no authority to carry on the business except for the purposes of administration. If they do carry on the business beyond mere realisation without authority they will be personally liable for any loss without the right of indemnity. If they wish to agree to Tessa's request, they could seek an indemnity from Tessa or obtain a court order authorising them to carry on the business beyond mere realisation. The problem of a personal indemnity from Tessa is that it may prove valueless if she dissipates her assets.

A further problem is that personal representatives cannot profit from the trust. Where they carry on a business they are only entitled to remuneration if the will expressly provides for suitable remuneration or all the beneficiaries agree. To agree the beneficiaries must all be *sui juris*. The problem here is that James is under age. Eric and Dan could consider limited liability status for protection but they would need the consent of the court to effect this.

Eric and Dan should seek advice before they agree to Tessa's request to carry on the business beyond merely completing the administration of the estate.

Question 50

Consider why application may be made for a grant:
- *ad collingenda bona;*
- *administration durante minore aetate;*
- *de bonis non administratis.*

Answer plan

This is a straightforward question. Each separate grant should be defined and the reasons given for its purpose together with illustrations from the case law or statute.

Answer

Ad collingenda bona

One might call this the 'tomato' grant in that where an estate consists of perishable or other assets which need quick attention and nobody has applied for probate or administration then a grant *ad collingenda bona* may be obtained. The grant is limited to dealing with the assets which are the subject matter of the application. The grant enables the applicant to do what is necessary to preserve the asset and does not *per se* give the applicant power of sale over the asset. Where, however, the asset is in danger of wasting then application can be made to the court at the time of applying for a grant for an order for sale.

An interesting illustration of the use of this type of grant occurred in the litigation surrounding the death of the late Sir Charles Clore. An action was brought by the Inland Revenue to expedite the payment of capital transfer tax arising on the death of Sir Charles. Shortly before his death he had conveyed an estate in England to his nominees Stype Investments (Jersey) Limited to hold as bare trustees for Sir Charles. The company entered into a contract of sale of the estate and prior to completion Sir Charles died. When contracts were exchanged the company remitted the deposit monies to their bank in Jersey. On completion of the sale the company remitted the balance sale proceeds to Jersey. They then did nothing regarding the settlement of capital transfer tax liability arising on the English estate of Sir Charles. The Inland Revenue brought an action to constitute the company *executors de son tort*. This action failed at the first instance but the Revenue appealed and at the same time the Official Solicitor applied for a grant to the estate *ad collingenda bona* specifically to deal with the outstanding capital transfer tax. This action, *Re Charles Clore (dec'd)* (1982) was heard at the same time as the appeal by the Revenue and on appeal Stype Investments were held to be *executors de son tort*.

Administration durante minore aetate

Where, by his will, the testator appoints an executor who is under age at the time of the testator's death when the will takes effect then the minor cannot apply for a grant of probate (s 118 Supreme Court Act 1981). Where the person has been appointed sole executor then an application must be made for a grant of administration with will annexed limited in time to the minority of the named executor hence the title *administration durante minore aetate*. Where the minor is appointed sole executor and has no interest in the residuary estate the person entitled to the residue is entitled to apply for the grant (see r 32(1) Non-Contentious Probate Rules 1987. Where the minor has a beneficial interest in the residue the parent of the minor who has parental responsibility for him will be entitled to the grant (r 32 (1)). If the minor's parents were married when the minor was born then both parents will have parental responsibility (Children Act (1989) s 2) and either or both of them are entitled to take out the grant. If the parents were not married when the minor was born the mother has parental responsibility but the father can obtain parental responsibility by a court order or by agreement with the mother (ss 4 and 5 Children Act (1989)). Alternatively, the court may appoint a guardian for the minor under r 32(2) of the 1987 Rules.

An administrator under this limited grant has all the powers of an ordinary administrator; therefore he can proceed to sell assets and complete the administration (*Re Cope* (1880). The minor can, however, call the administrator to account whether or not the minor has a beneficial interest in the estate (*Harvell v Foster* (1954)).

The grant is usually limited expressly until the minor attains 18. When the minor attains 18 the grant automatically ceases and then the minor can apply for probate.

Where the testator has appointed A and B to be his executors and A is a minor but B is of age and able to prove this then probate will be granted to B with power reserved for A to prove when he attains majority. There would be no need, therefore, for a grant of administration *durante minore aetate*. However, if B is slow in making up his mind whether to take out the grant of probate then those acting on behalf of A should issue citation to B to make up his mind whether to take out the grant of probate and if not then whoever is entitled would apply for a grant of administration with letters annexed *durante minore aetate*.

De bonis non administratis

This form of grant translates literally as 'of the goods not yet administered'. The grant may be applied for where a grant of probate or letters of administration have already been issued to someone but the representative has not completed the administration of the estate and there is no representative by operation of the change of representation under s 7 Administration of Estates Act 1925. The grant *de bonis non* may be issued where a previous grant is revoked, for example, where the personal representative has disappeared. In *Loveday* (1900) the deceased died intestate leaving a widow and six children by a former marriage. The widow obtained letters of administration but subsequently disappeared before completing the winding up of the estate. The grant to her was revoked and a *grant de bonis non* was issued to one of the children. The grant *de bonis non* has also been issued where a grant was revoked, when the original administrator permanently left the jurisdiction (*Re French's Estate* (1910)).

The grant is most commonly issued where a sole administrator has obtained the grant but has died before completing the administration of the estate. A *grant de bonis non* would also be issued where a sole surviving executor, having obtained probate, dies in the course of the administration of the estate in circumstances where the chain of representation is broken. Section 7 of the Administration of Estates Act 1925 provides that where an executor who obtains the grant of probate dies in the course of the administration having appointed by his will an executor who proves his estate, then, this proving executor becomes executor automatically by representation to the estate of the original deceased. The chain can be broken by the original executor dying, not having made a will or failing to appoint an executor or the executors named predeceasing the appointor.

Suppose the testator, by his will, names A and B to be his executors and A takes out a grant of probate but B does not and so the power is reserved to be proved at a later date. Then A dies having appointed C to be his executor. If C accepts the appointment to A's estate it would appear that he would become executor by representation to the estate of the original testator. However, before taking over the estate by representation, C should cite B to force B to make up his mind as to whether he wishes to take out probate to the original estate. If C does not do this then he faces the risk that he may become executor by representation with the additional work that this entails only for B to come along at a later date and exercise his right to take out probate. If B, in response to the citation, does take out a grant of probate and he then dies before completing the administration a grant *de bonis non* would have to be issued.

If there are two personal representatives who take out the grant and one dies during the course of the administration all the powers of probate or administration pass to the surviving personal representative. If he should die before completion of the administration then a grant *de bonis non* will again be necessary. A grant *de bonis non* can only be made to the persons who would have been entitled to the original grant either of administration or administration with will annexed following the orders of entitlement laid down by rr 20 and 22 of the Non-Contentious Probate Rules 1987.

Index

A

Abatement	99
Accommodation	94, 95, 97
Acknowledgments	23
revocation and	23-34
signatures and	26-27, 29
witnesses and	29, 30, 32-34
Ademption	
construction of wills and	99, 102, 105, 124, 125
intention and	102
Administration of estates	127-191

See also Executors, Personal Representatives

account of and	147, 182-183
acquiescence and	183-184
ad collingenda bona and	188-189
administration durante minore aetate and	189-190
Administration of Estates Act 1925 and	163-169
administration on intestacy and	127, 145
administration with will annexed and	127, 128
administrators pending suit and	182
beneficiaries and	181-185
Capital Taxes Office forms and	138
chain of representation and	142-144, 160
children and	128, 189-190
cohabitees and	135
court by	181-185
creditors and	181-185
de bonis non administratis and	190-191
debts and	148-157, 160-169
delay in	139-142, 143-144, 157
devastavit and	144-147, 155, 172, 183
dissatisfaction with	181-185
distribution and	134, 145, 155-157, 179-181, 184-185
donatio mortis causa and	136
end of period of	128
failure to safeguard assets and	146
gifts and	125-136
grants and	188-191
inheritance tax and	134, 135-138
insolvency and	160-162
intention and	136
joint tenants and	134-135, 137
life assurance and	136-137
maladministration and	145-147, 172
misappropriation of assets and	145-147, 172
nominations and	125
oaths and	138
pensions and	137
potentially exempt transfers and	135
probate and	127
receivers and	182
remedies and	181-185
shares and	138
survivorship and	135
tenancies in common and	135
time limits and	183, 184
title to the estate and	134
tracing and	184
trustees and	127-131
trusts and	135, 136
wasting of assets and	145-147
Administration of Justice Act 1982	28-31
acknowledgments and	29, 30
signatures and	28, 29-30
witnesses and	28-29
Advertisements	133, 145, 172
Affidavits	20-21
Alterations	1
codicils and	101
construction of wills and	101
courts by	17-20
intention and	19
knowledge and approval and	17
omissions and	17-18, 19
rectification and	18, 19
revocation and	34
signatures and	27
witnesses and	27

Anti-avoidance provisions	69
Attestation clauses	32-34
Animus testandi	
See Intention	

B

Beneficiaries	
actions by	181-185
administration of estates and	179-181, 181-185
assignment and	179-181
distribution and	179-181
preparation of wills by	49-50
witnesses and	27
Benjamin orders	133
Blindness	20-21
Bona vacantia	97

C

Capacity	
See also Mental Capacity	
construction of wills and	108
donatio mortis causa and	95
fraud and	12-16
gifts and	92-98
intention and	14, 50
knowledge and approval and	14, 46-51
misrepresentation and	15
suspicion and	50-51
undue influence and	12-16
Capital Taxes Office forms	138
Chain of representation	142-144
administration of estates and	142-144
executors and	144, 160
intestacy and	144
personal representatives and	144
purpose of	143-144
trustees and	144
Charging clauses	141
Children	
administration of estates and	128, 140, 141, 173, 177
adult	69, 81, 83, 84
assent and	173, 177
education of	71
executors and	131, 160, 189-190
family provision and	69
illegitimate and	68, 82-84, 103-104, 116, 173
Inheritance (Provision for Family and Dependants) Act 1975 and	76-77, 81, 82-84
intestacy and	68, 71-73
legacies and	178
locus standi of	71, 77
maintenance of	71, 178-179
step	69, 77, 104-105
Codicils	
alterations and	101
assent and	174
construction of wills and	99, 101, 105
Cohabitees	
administration of estates and	135
family provision and	69, 71-72
Inheritance (Provision for Family and Dependants) Act 1975 and	78, 85-87
intestacy and	71-72
locus standi and	71-72
Conflicts of interest	17
Construction of wills	99-126
abatement and	99
ademption and	99, 102, 105, 124, 125
alterations and	100-101
ambiguities and	101, 104-105, 108-109, 113-114
capacity and	108
codicils and	99, 101, 105
context and	108-110, 112, 116
devises and	122-124
donatio mortis causa and	116-121
evidence and	99-100, 103, 04-116, 122-123
forfeiture and	126
illegitimacy and	103, 104, 116
intention and	101, 102, 104, 108-109, 111-114, 125-126
intestacy and	126
judicial attitude towards	106-116
lapse and	122-126
legacies and	99-100, 122-124
demonstrative and	123

general	102, 105, 123
specific	100-102, 105, 122, 123-126
mistake and	111-112
'moneys' and	107-116
rectification and	112, 114
rules of	109, 114
shares and	99-106
step-children and	104-105
survivorship and	114
tracing and	102-103
uncertainty and	123
unlawful killings and	126
Contracts	6-10

D

Debts	133, 148-154
administration of estates and	148-157, 163-169
devastavit and	155
executors and	155-157
expenses and	155
insolvent estates and	160-162
intention and	149-154, 156, 164-165
legacies and	150-151, 178
general	150
pecuniary	163-169
specific	153
marshalling of assets and	150
mortgages and	149-150, 153, 156
personal representatives and	133, 163-164, 185-188
priorities and	162-163
shares and	148-149, 150-152
trusts for sale and	165-166
uncertainty of	163-169
Decree *nisi*	70-73
Deeds	1
Dependants	35-40, 43-46
family provision and	69
Inheritance (Provision for Family and Dependants) Act 1975 and	73-80
locus standi and	72
maintenance and	96
Devastavit	144-147, 155, 172, 183
Devises	122-124

Distribution	
administration of estates and	134, 155-157, 179-181, 184-185
beneficiaries and	179-181
executors and	159
family provision and	70
intestacy and	51-55, 65-68, 92-98
pending	179-181
personal representatives and	172-173, 179-181, 185-188
trusts and	179-181
Divorce	
decrees *nisi* and	70-73
family provision and	70-73
revocation by	2, 35-40
Donatio mortis causa	1, 92-98
administration of estates and	136
capacity and	95
conditions for	117-119
construction of wills and	116-121
definition of	117
evidence and	117
gifts and	119, 121
inheritance tax and	119, 136
intention and	117, 118
proof and	95-96
reasonableness and	95-96, 117-118
suicide and	120

E

Evidence	
See also Proof	
affidavit	20-21
circumstantial	113
construction of wills and	99-101, 104-116, 122-123
donatio mortis causa and	117
family provision and	69
intention and	4, 6, 104
mental capacity and	12
survivorship and	64
Executors	132-134, 139-142, 158-160
See also Personal Representatives	
acceptance of office of	132, 139-140
acts of necessity and	140-141, 159

appointment of	132-133, 185	*locus standi* and	69, 71
renouncing	140, 141-142		74-76, 84-94
	143, 158-160	lump sum orders and	69, 76
revocation of	133	maintenance and	80-82, 83-84, 91
assent and	131	accommodation and	94-95, 97
chain of representation		standard and	75, 77, 78, 85-87
and	143, 160	reasonableness	
children and	131, 140, 141	provision and	88-93, 97
	160, 189-190	spouses and	69, 71-80, 85-93
de son tort	133, 139-141	standard of living and	81-82
	142, 159, 182	transfers of property and	69
death of	143, 144, 159-160	Forfeiture	124-126
debts and	155-157, 185-188	Formal validity	23-69

F

Family provision 69-98
  accommodation and 94-95, 97
  anti-avoidance and 69
  capacity and 92-98
  children and 71, 76-77
    adult 69, 80-81, 83
    illegitimate 82-84
    locus standi of 76-77
    step-children and 77
  cohabitees and 60, 71-72
    78-80, 85-87
  decree *nisi* and 70
  dependants and 60, 72, 73-80, 96
  distribution and 70-73, 92-98
  divorce and 70-73
  donatio mortis causa and 92-98
  evidence and 69
  gifts and 92-98
  Inheritance (Provision for Family and Dependants) Act 1975 and 73-93
  intention and 95
  intestacy and 70-73, 92-98
  judicial separation and 79

delay and	133, 143-144, 157
distribution and	159
duration of office of	143
inheritance tax and	141
intestacy of	144, 159
liability of	133-134, 139-141
nature of office of	132-134
oaths of	138
representation by	129, 131, 143
trustees and	131

See also Capacity, Signatures
  acknowledgments and 23
  Administration of Justice
    Act 1982 and 28-31
  insertions and 46-51
  intention and 23
  intestacy and 23-24, 51-63, 65-68
  personal chattels and 60-63
  revocation and 31-46
  signatures and 23-28
  survivorship and 63-65
  witnesses and 23
Fraud 1, 13-16

G

Gifts 2, 92-98
  assent and 177
  capacity and 92-98
  discretionary trusts and 135
  donatio mortis causa and 119, 121
  inheritance tax and 96, 135-136
  intention and 95
  proof and 95

I

Incorporation by reference 20-21
Inheritance tax
  administration of
    estates and 134-138
  Capital Taxes Office
    form and 138
  donatio mortis causa and 119, 136
  executors and 141
  gifts and 96, 135-136
  life assurance and 137
  spouse exemption and 96

Inheritance (Provision for Family and Dependants) Act 1975	73-93
children and	76-77
adult	80-81, 83
cohabitees and	78, 85-87
dependants and	75-80
judicial separation and	79
locus standi and	74, 76, 77
	85, 88-93
maintenance and	80-82, 83
	84, 85, 91
maintenance standard and	75, 77, 78
reasonableness provision and	88, 91, 94
spouses and	85-91
standard of living and	81-82
step-children and	77
Insolvent estates	160-162
actions on	182
debts and	160-162
expenses and	161
joint tenants and	161
mortgages and	161
trusts and	161
Intention	3-6
ademption and	102
alterations and	19
capacity and	14, 50
construction of wills and	101, 102
	104, 108
	111-114, 125-126
debts and	149-154, 156, 164-165
donatio mortis causa and	117, 118
evidence of	4, 6, 104
formalities and	23
gifts and	95
legacies and	102
maintenance and	178-179
mental capacity and	6, 11, 14
revocation and	34, 37-38, 46
signatures and	26, 27, 50
Intestacy	23-24, 51-63
	65-68, 92-98
administration on	127
advances and	58-59
children and	71-73
cohabitees and	71-72
construction of wills and	126
devastavit and	145
distribution and	51-55
	65-68, 92-98
executors of	144, 159
family provision and	70
formalities and	51-55
illegitimate children and	68
judicial separation and	51-55
locus standi and	94
partial	55-60, 70
personal chattels and	60-63
personal representatives and	145
priorities and	57
revocation and	35-40
spouses and	71-73
statutory legacies and	58, 67
survivorship and	52, 63-65, 97
trusts and	66
Insurance policies	136

J

Joint tenants	134-135, 137, 161
Judicial separation	51-55, 79

L

Lapse	122-126
Legacies	
account of	182
administration of estates and	163-169
assent and	174, 176
children and	178-179
codicils and	174
construction of wills and	99, 122-126
delays and	150-151, 163-169
demonstrative	123
general	102, 123, 150, 176-179
intention and	102, 179-180
interest on	177-179
specific	100, 101-102
	122-126, 153, 181
Life assurance	136
Locus standi	
children and	77
cohabitees and	71-72
dependants and	72
family provision and	69, 71, 74-76, 84-94

Inheritance (Provision for Family and Dependants) Act 1975 and	73, 75, 76, 85, 88-93
intestacy and	94
Lump sum orders	69

M

Maintenance	
accommodation and	94, 95, 97
children and	71, 80-82, 84, 178-179
dependants and	96
Inheritance (Provision for Family and Dependants) Act 1975 and	75, 77, 78, 80-82, 83, 85, 91
intention and	178-179
intestacy and	71
reasonable provision and	94-95, 96, 97, 98
standard	75, 77, 78
Manslaughter	124-126
Marriage	
expectation of	9, 39
revocation and	6-10, 32-34
void	39
voidable	39
Mental capacity	10-13
assent and	177
evidence and	12
intention and	6, 11, 14
knowledge and approval and	12
memory and	11
proof and	11
revocation and	41-42, 45-46
test for	6, 11
undue influence and	11
will-making process and	1
Mistake	1, 111-112
Moneys	107-116
Mortgages	149-150, 153, 156, 161

N

Nominations	135
Obliterations	2
Overreachable equities	129

P

Pensions	137
Personal chattels	60-63
Personal representatives	
See also Executors	
accounts by	182-183
actions against	181-185
administration of estates and	127-131, 140
appointment of	139-140
advertisements and	133, 145, 172
assent and	129-131, 174-177
barristers' opinions and	184
Benjamin orders and	133
breach of trust by	133
businesses and	185-188
chain of representation and	144
children and	128, 140, 177
illegitimate	173
contracts and	185-188
contribution and	170-171
courts and, applications to	183
creditors and	145, 147, 171-174
death and	191
debts of estate and	133, 163-164, 185-188
deed of release and	183-184
delay and	146
delegation by	134, 170-171
devastavit and	172, 183
distribution and	128, 145-147, 172, 173, 179-181, 184-188
duties of	185-188
expenses and	141, 145, 181, 182
failure to safeguard assets and	145-147
function of	128
gifts and	176-177
intestacy and	145
liability of	127-131, 144-147, 170-171, 172-173, 183, 185-188
limited appointment of	128
maladministration and	145-147, 172
mental capacity and	177
misappropriation of assets and	145-147, 172

Index

negligence of 134
overreaching and 129
powers of attorney and 171
protection of 171-173, 183
remuneration of 187
trustees and 128-131, 146-147
trusts and 133, 146-147, 179-181
valuations and 145
Potentially exempt transfers 135
Powers of attorney 1, 171
Privileged wills 183
Proof
   donatio mortis causa and 95-96
   gifts and 95
   mental capacity and 11

R

Receivers 182
Rectification
   alteration and 18, 19
   construction of wills and 112, 114
   will-making process and 1
Revocation 1, 2, 35-46
   acknowledgments and 32-34, 45
   alterations and 34
   attestation clauses and 32-34
   contracts and 6-10
   dependants and 35-40, 44-46
   destruction by 39, 40-43, 46
   divorce and 2, 35-40
   executors and
     appointment as 133
   formalities and 31-34
   intention and 34, 37-38, 40-43, 46
   intestacy and 35-40
   marriage by 6-10, 32-34
   mental capacity and 41-42, 45-46
   presumptions and 42
   signatures and 32-34, 44-45
   witnesses and 32-34, 44

S

Shares 99-106, 138, 142, 150-152
Signatures 23, 24-28, 50
   acknowledgments and 26-27
   Administration of Justice
     Act 1982 and 28, 29-30
   admissibility and 26
   alterations and 27
   initialling and 48, 50
   intention and 26, 27, 50
   revocation and 32-34, 44-45
   witnesses and 25
Statutory wills 1
Suicide 120
Survivorship 63-65
   administration of estates and 135
   construction of wills and 114
   evidence and 63
   intestacy and 63-65, 97

T

Tenancies in common 135
Tracing 102-103, 184-185
Trustees
   administration of
     estates and 127-131
   appointment of 130
   chain of representation and 144
   corporations and 131
   delegation by 170, 171
   executors and 131
   function of 128
   judicial 183
   liability of 127
   personal representatives
     and 128-131, 146
   title and 129-130
Trusts
   See also Trustees
   beneficiaries and 179-181
   breach of 133, 146-147, 171
   devastavit and 146-147
   discretionary 135
   insolvent estates and 161
   intestacy and 66
   life assurance of 136
   personal representatives
     and 133, 146-147, 170181
   sale for 165-166
   undue influence and 16

U

Undue influence
   capacity and 13-16
   coercion and 15
   conflicts of interest and 16
   mental capacity and 1

persuasion and	15
solicitors and	16
trusts and	16
Unlawful killing	124-126

W

Will-making process	1-21
alterations and	2
capacity and	1
contracts and	6-10
deeds and	1
divorce and	2
donatio mortis causa and	1
fraud and	1
gifts and	1
intention and	3-6
mental disability and	1
mistake and	1
obliterations and	2, 41
powers of attorney and	1
rectification and	1
revocation and	1, 2
statutory wills and	1
suspicions and	1
undue influence and	1
validity and	2

Wills. *See* Construction of wills
  Will-making Process

Witnesses	
acknowledgments and	29, 30, 32-34
Administration of Justice Act 1982 and	28-29
alterations and	27
attestations and	32-34
beneficiaries as	27
blind testators and	21
formalities and	23
revocation and	32-34, 44-46
signatures and	25